The political writings of Eva Gore-Booth

MANCHESTER 1824

Manchester University Press

The political writings of Eva Gore-Booth

Edited by
Sonja Tiernan

Manchester University Press

Published by Manchester University Press
Altrincham Street, Manchester M1 7JA
www.manchesteruniversitypress.co.uk

British Library Cataloguing-in-Publication Data
A catalogue record for this book is available from the British Library

Library of Congress Cataloging-in-Publication Data applied for

ISBN 978 0 7190 8874 2 *hardback*
ISBN 978 0 7190 9768 3 *paperback*

First published 2015

Typeset in Garamond by
Koinonia, Manchester
Printed and Bound in Great Britain by
Bell and Bain Ltd, Glasgow

In memory of a truly inspirational woman,
my grandmother Molly Harmon (1916–2014)

The New Woman is still with us and shows herself where least expected. In the far-away regions of County Sligo, among the wives and daughters of the farmers and fishermen, the three pretty daughters of Sir Henry Gore-Booth are creating a little excitement (not to say amusement) for the emancipation of their sex. Miss Gore-Booth and her sisters, supported by a few devoted yokels, have been holding a few meetings in connection with the Woman's Suffrage (or, shall I say, 'The Revolt of the Daughters?') movement. Their speeches are eloquent (un) conventional, and (non)convincing. They are given to striking out a line for themselves, in more senses than one; for Miss Gore Booth has already distinguished herself as a lady steeplechaser, and public oratory is their newest toy. The sisters make a pretty picture on the platform; but it is not women of their type who need to assert themselves over Man. & Co., However, it amuses them – and others and I doubt if the tyrant has much to fear from their little arrows.

Vanity Fair, December 1896, from the Lissadell Collection

Contents

Illustrations

Images 1, 2, 3 and 13 reproduced from the Lissadell papers at the Public Records Office Northern Ireland by permission of Sir Josslyn Gore-Booth. Image 5 reproduced with permission from the People's History Museum, Manchester. Images 6 and 9 reproduced with the permission of Rare Books and Manuscripts, Special Collections Library, the Pennsylvania State University Libraries. Images 7, 10, 11 and 12 are reproduced Courtesy of the Irish Capuchin Provincial Archives, Dublin.

Acknowledgements

This volume is the culmination of years of research during which time I have been supported, encouraged and assisted by many individuals. I am thankful to Sally Munt, Margaret Kelleher, Maryann Valiulis, Diarmaid Ferriter and to Catriona Crowe for their encouragement and enduring support of my work.

I consulted many archives during this research and I am grateful for the assistance of Brian Kirby of the Irish Capuchin Provincial Archives for taking the time and effort to source valuable images for this edition. Many thanks also to Pamela Cassidy of the Lissadell Estate who has taken a keen interest in this research from the onset. To Sir Josslyn Gore-Booth, for again generously providing full access to the Lissadell Papers held at the Public Records Office of Northern Ireland. I am grateful to Neil Watt and Sara Greer at PRONI for their help with sourcing images and arranging copyright reproductions. Thank you to Malachy Gillen of Sligo County Library for confirming ownership of the beautiful image reproduced on the cover of this book. To Aedin Clements for helping me to source material during my time at the University of Notre Dame and also to Sandra Stelts of Pennsylvania State University Libraries.

This volume is born out of my work on the biography of Eva Gore-Booth, and I would like to recognise the support of individuals who have helped ensure the success of that volume. Thanks to Brian Merriman, Director of the Dublin Gay Theatre Festival, for his dedication to the memory of Eva Gore-Booth and for establishing a festival award in her honour. I am indebted to President Michael D. Higgins for accepting a copy of the biography at *Áras an Uachtaráin* in 2012 and for his insightful references to Gore-Booth at public events since. I would also like to show my appreciation to Wally Young for facilitating what was a momentous occasion for me and my family at the *Áras*.

Finally, many thanks to Liverpool Hope University for financial research support for this book.

Chronology of Eva Gore-Booth's life

1870 Born at Lissadell House, County Sligo
1874 Birth of Mabel, Gore-Booth's sister
1876 Paternal grandfather, Robert 4th baronet, dies at Lissadell House
Cousin, Isabella Gore-Booth, dies at Lissadell House
Father, Sir Henry, succeeds to family title and estate
1878 Birth of Mordaunt, Gore-Booth's youngest brother
1879 Famine revisits Sligo area – Gore-Booth family distribute food and medical attention to their tenants
Eva's maternal grandmother, Lady Hill, dies at Lissadell House
Founding of the Irish Land League by Michael Davitt
Davitt and members of the Land League address tenant farmers on Gore-Booth land at Gurteen County Sligo
1880 The Ladies' Land League formed
Artist Sarah Purser paints portrait of Eva and her older sister, Constance
1882 Miss Noel employed as governess for the Gore-Booth daughters
1886 Prime Minister Gladstone introduces the first Irish Home Rule Bill– defeated in the House of Commons
1887 Eva and Constance presented at the court of Queen Victoria (see Figure 1 for a picture of Eva around this time)
1893 Second Home Rule Bill passes in House of Commons but fails in the House of Lords
Constance leaves Lissadell to attend art school in London
1894 Travels to the West Indies and America with her father
Meets W. B. Yeats for the first time
Older brother, Josslyn, joins the Irish Agricultural Organisation Society
1895 Travels throughout Italy and Germany with her mother
Manchester & Salford Women's Trade Union Council formed
Josslyn establishes the Drumcliff Creamery Co-operative in Sligo
University Settlement in Manchester founded

1896 Tours Europe with mother and sister
Recuperates from illness in Italy
Meets Esther Roper, her lifelong partner
Women's Poor Law Guardian (Ireland) Act introduced, enabling women with property qualifications to vote for and stand as Poor Law Guardians
Forms Sligo Irish Women's Suffrage and Local Government Association
1897 Moves to Manchester to live with Esther Roper
Attends House of Commons meeting for the first time
National Union of Women's Suffrage Societies formed
1898 Publishes first volume of poetry simply entitled *Poems*
Local Government (Ireland) Act extends the vote to qualifying women at local elections
1899 Becomes executive member National Union of Women's Suffrage Societies
Forms Elizabethan Society in University Settlement, Manchester
Attends suffrage conference in the House of Commons
Joins Manchester Women Student's Debating Society
Poem 'The Place of Peace' is published in *New Ireland Review*
1900 Appointed co-secretary Manchester Salford Women's Trade Union Council
Becomes representative on Manchester Education Committee
Launches suffrage petition including factory women
Labour Representation Committee formed
Adopts vegetarian diet
1901 Forms alliance with Labour Representation Committee
Petition of factory women presented to MPs in Westminster
Becomes active member of the Labour Church
1902 Labour candidate David Shackleton elected at Clitheroe by-election
Holidays in Venice with Roper and Christabel Pankhurst
1903 Forms Lancashire & Cheshire Women Textile & other Workers' Representation Committee
Women's Social & Political Union formed by Emmeline Pankhurst
George Russell includes her poems in *New Songs: A Lyric Selection*
1904 Resigns from Women's Trade Union Council
Establishes Manchester and Salford Women's Trade and Labour Council
Publishes poetry collection *The One and the Many*
Publishes first play, *Unseen Kings*
1905 Publishes *The Three Resurrections and the Triumph of Maeve*
WSPU members become militant

1905 Ends association with Christabel Pankhurst
Resigns from North of England Society for Women's Suffrage
Forms the National Industrial and Professional Women's Suffrage Society
Publishes article 'Fair Pay for Women' in *Women's Tribune*

1906 Puts forward a suffrage candidate at general election
Addresses Prime Minister, Henry Campbell-Bannerman, at suffrage deputation
Contests proposed update to the Dangerous Performances Bill
Campaigns on behalf of Labour candidate at Huddersfield by-election
LRC reforms as the Labour Party

1907 Launches journal *Women's Labour News*
Participates in the NUWSS march – becomes known as the 'mud march'
Organises suffrage demonstration to Trafalgar Square
Establishes the Barmaids' Political Defence League
Play *The Sorrowful Princess* published
Poetry collection, *The Egyptian Pillar*, published
Submits essay 'The Women's Suffrage Movement among Trade Unionists', to Brougham Villiers book, *The Case for Women's Suffrage*

1908 'Women and Suffrage' published in *Nineteenth Century and After*
Successfully campaigns against Winston Churchill at North West Manchester by-election
Raises issue of women's suffrage at Labour Party Conference
'Women and the Suffrage: A Reply to Lady Lovat and Mrs. Humphry Ward', published in *Nineteenth Century and After*
Irish Women's Franchise League founded by Hanna Sheehy-Skeffington and Margaret Cousins

1909 Irish Transport Workers' Union founded by James Larkin
Pamphlet *Women's Right to Work* published by William Morris Press
Article, 'Women and the Nation', published in *The Englishwoman*

1910 January general election results in a hung Parliament
The Parliamentary Franchise (Women) Bill is abandoned
Pamphlet *Is the Case Urgent?* published
Puts forward suffrage candidate at Rossendale in December general election

1911 Irish Women's Workers Union founded
The Women's Enfranchisement Bill abandoned
Spends time working in a coalmine with pit brow women
Joins the radical organisation the Aëthnic Union
In protest for women's suffrage many women, including Gore-Booth and Roper, boycott census return in Britain and Ireland

1912 Parliamentary Franchise (Women) Bill reintroduced in House of Commons – fails after second reading
Play, *Unseen Kings*, performed at the Abbey Theatre Dublin
Poetry collection, *The Agate Lamp*, published
Labour Party officially agrees to support women's suffrage
Third Home Rule Bill introduced to House of Commons
1913 Ulster Volunteers established (January)
Irish Citizen Army established (November)
Co-establishes and circulates *The Phœnix*, a newsletter of the Aëthnic Union
Dublin Lockout, major labour dispute begins
1914 Outbreak of First World War
Delivers her first anti-war speech, 'Whence come wars?' in London
Government of Ireland Act offers Irish Home Rule, suspended for the duration of the war
No Conscription Fellowship founded
1915 Attends Pacifist Philosophy of Life Conference – befriends Bertrand Russell and Fennor Brockway
Speech, 'Religious aspects of non-resistance', published as a pamphlet
Poetry collection, *The Perilous Light*, published
Joins the No-Conscription Fellowship and defends conscientious objectors
1916 Military conscription comes into effect in UK, excludes Ireland
Publishes *The Tribunal*, an illegal pamphlet denouncing conscription
An armed nationalist insurrection against British rule in Ireland is staged – the Easter Rising
Sister, Constance Markievicz, sentenced to death for her part in Rising – commuted to life imprisonment
Visits Dublin in the aftermath of the Easter Rising
Delivers a speech justifying the Rising to an English audience in London
Publishes the play *The Death of Fionavar* in memory of Easter week
Fifteen leaders of the Rising are executed and Roger Casement is sentenced to death at the Old Bailey
Launches high-profile campaign for reprieve of Roger Casement's death sentence – ultimately unsuccessful
Article 'The Sinn Fein Rebellion' published in the *Socialist Review*
Along with four others, establishes the journal *Urania*
1917 *Rhythms of Art* pamphlet published by the League of Peace and Freedom
Poem, 'For God and Kathleen Ni Houlihan' published in *Catholic Bulletin*

1918 Poetry collection *Broken Glory* published
Play *The Sword of Justice* published
Extension of Military Service Bill to enforce conscription in Ireland
Formation of Irish Anti-Conscription Committee
End of First World War
Representation of the People Act extends suffrage to women over 30, with certain qualifications
General election in December returns a majority for Irish Sinn Féin party
Constance Markievicz is first woman to be elected to the House of Commons – declines her seat on nationalist grounds
1919 First Dáil Éireann is formed
Irish War of Independence begins
Officially joins the Theosophical Society
1920 Attends Humanitarian Conference
An auxiliary force of the Royal Irish Constabulary, the Black and Tans, are sent to Ireland by Prime Minister David Lloyd George
Publishes poems in many theosophical and religious journals including: *Herald of the Star*; *The Flame*; *The Venturer*; *Occult Review*
1921 Along with Roper, moves to Hampstead in London, due to ill health
A pacifist article 'A Sketch in Florence' published in *The Flame*
War of Independence ends with signing of the Anglo-Irish agreement, creation of the Irish Free State excluding Northern Ireland
1922 Irish Civil War erupts between Treaty and Anti-Treaty sides
1923 Her large theological prose work, *A Psychological and Poetic Approach to the Study of Christ in the Fourth Gospel*, published
Irish Civil War effectively comes to an end in May
1925 Play *Sword of Justice* performed in Tokyo
Poetry collection *The Shepherd of Eternity* published
1926 Article 'Art and Peace' published in *Service*
Volume of religious poetry, *The House of Three Windows*, is published
Short prose volume, *The Inner Kingdom*, is published
Dies at home with partner Esther Roper by her side, at 56 years of age
1927 *The World's Pilgrim* published by Longmans
Constance Markievicz dies
1928 Stained-glass window in Gore-Booth's memory installed in Round House, Ancoats, Manchester
Equal Franchise Act grants women votes on the same terms as men
1929 Roper edits and oversees publication of *Complete Edition* of Gore-Booth's works

1930 Roper oversees publication of Gore-Booth's play *The Buried Life of Deirdre*
1934 Roper edits Markievicz's letters to Gore-Booth, *Prison Letters of Countess Markievicz* – Gore-Booth's letters to her sister remain missing
1938 Esther Roper dies
1951 Poem 'Easter Week' published in *Poetry Ireland*
1991 Frederick Lapisardi edits and republishes the plays of Gore-Booth
2010 *Fiametta*, a five-act play by Gore-Booth, is published for the first time

Figure 1 Eva Gore-Booth as a teenager at Lissadell House

Introducing the political writings of Eva Gore-Booth

The surprise announcement in May 2003 that Lissadell House, the historic home of the Gore-Booth family, was to be sold on the open market generated a great public debate. There ensued lengthy correspondence in the pages of the *Irish Times.* National and British news channels carried the story of the sale of the house. Lissadell was described by the BBC as one of the 'Republic of Ireland's most historic homes'.[1] Its then owner, Sir Josslyn Gore-Booth, was unable to finance the upkeep of the house, making a public announcement that 'few of the Big Houses of Ireland remain in the hands of their families and I regret that my decision will reduce their number'.[2] The Irish public responded by demanding that the government buy Lissadell House and establish it as a heritage property.

Irish cabinet ministers openly supported a State acquisition of the house. Minister for Community, Rural and Gaeltacht Affairs, Éamon Ó Cuív TD, proclaimed that he personally had 'a huge emotional attachment to Lissadell House'.[3] Minister for the Environment and Local Government, Martin Cullen TD, called for the government to appraise the situation. The subject was debated in Dáil Éireann on 28 May 2003. Deputy John Perry TD raised the issue stating, 'Lissadell House ... embodies much history of landlordism, good and bad. It was the family home of Countess Markievicz and William Butler Yeats was a regular visitor. Was there ever a better case for the State to intervene?'[4]

Months passed and after an appraisal of the costs of a State acquisition the government decided that it was not viable to advance with the purchase.[5] The national interest in the sale of Lissadell House demonstrates the importance of the Big House to Irish political, historical and cultural discourse.[6] The

1 'Mystery over mansion sale', BBC News/Europe, 12 August 2003.

2 Dermot James, *The Gore-Booths of Lissadell* (Dublin: Woodfield Press, 2004), p. 344.

3 *Ibid.*, pp. 344–5.

4 'Architectural Heritage', Dáil Éireann debate, vol. 567, no. 6 (28 May 2003.)

5 Constance Cassidy and Edward Walsh began a restoration project on the house shortly after purchasing it in August 2003.

6 For an overview of the importance of historic homes in contemporary Ireland, see:

house represented a vital era in Irish history and the Gore-Booth family had made a significant contribution towards the development of an Independent Ireland. However, it was the association of Countess Markievicz and the author W. B. Yeats with Lissadell that was continually cited as a central reason why the house should be established as a heritage property. Eva Gore-Booth was rarely mentioned in any of these public debates. See Figure 2, a picture of Eva outside her home, Lissadell House.

Markievicz is one of the few women to reach iconic status in Irish history. Prior to the sale of Lissadell House, Mary Condren observed that 'when the history of those times was written, she herself [Eva Gore-Booth] was relegated to being a mere afterthought to her more famous sibling. For Irish schoolchildren, her sister was their role model: Constance Markievicz – the sole woman to appear, complete with military weapons, in the iconography of Irish revolution.'[7] Eva Gore-Booth did not adopt anything as dramatic as a military uniform or carry arms; she was far more radical than that. For so long in the shadow of others, Eva Gore-Booth is finally receiving recognition for her many political and literary accomplishments both in Ireland and in Britain. In 2012, the first dedicated biography, *Eva Gore-Booth: An Image of Such Politics*, was published.[8] This publication has revealed the importance of this, to date, vastly overlooked figure.

In 2014, at the launch of the Theatre of Memory Symposium at the Abbey Theatre, Dublin, President of Ireland, Michael D. Higgins, lamented that 'there have been exclusions, [from Irish historical records] most notably of women, such as Eva Gore-Booth'.[9] Significantly during the first State visit of an Irish President to Britain, President Higgins, in his address to the Houses of Parliament, highlighted the importance of Irish immigrants to the development of modern Britain. Higgins noted how 'Eva Gore-Booth, who is buried in Hampstead, had been making, and would continue to make, her own distinctive contribution to history – not only in the Irish nationalist struggle, but as part of the suffragette and labour movements in Britain.'[10]

Hugh Maguire, 'An End to the Open House?', *Heritage Outlook* (Dublin: Heritage Council, 2004), pp. 28–9

7 Mary Condren, 'Theology and Ethics: The Twentieth Century', in Angela Bourke, Siobhan Kilfeather, Maria Luddy *et al.* (eds), *The Field Day Anthology of Irish Writing Volume IV: Irish Women's Writing and Traditions* (Cork: Cork University Press, 2002), p. 655.

8 For a fuller discussion on the topics in this volume, see: Sonja Tiernan, *Eva Gore-Booth: An Image of Such Politics* (Manchester: Manchester University Press, 2012).

9 Sophie Gorman, 'Higgins laments "exclusion" of women from history,' *Irish Independent* (17 January 2014).

10 Address by Michael D. Higgins, President of Ireland to the Houses of Parliament, Westminster (8 April 2014), Áras an Uachtaráin speeches.

Figure 2 Eva Gore-Booth and a friend outside Lissadell House, *c.*1894

It is remarkable that such a woman was excluded from the records of history. Born in 1870 into Anglo-Irish aristocracy in the West of Ireland, Gore-Booth chose an exceptional path in life. She left her privileged heritage and the beauty of county Sligo to live with her female partner, Esther Roper, in a working-class district of Manchester. Gore-Booth became a celebrated author of her day publishing volumes of poetry, revival dramas and philosophical prose. However, she also became a significant and a revolutionary political activist. Gore-Booth played an intrinsic role in the formation of women's trade unions in the North of England and was one of the first to take suffrage out of the preserve of middle-class concerns. After the outbreak of the First World War she worked tirelessly on behalf of conscientious objectors and her outspoken declarations against the war were radical during a pro-militant age. Although a forthright advocate of pacifism, Gore-Booth was quick to support militancy when her sister was condemned to death for her part in the Irish nationalist Rising of Easter 1916.

While researching for the biography of Eva Gore-Booth a vast body of original sources were discovered scattered across archives and personal collections throughout Ireland, Britain and America. These papers included political pamphlets, letters, newspaper and journal articles written by Gore-Booth. The vast majority of these writings are out of print and are difficult to source. Many of the writings were published by independent sources or by uncompromising political organisations as penny pamphlets, and copies are therefore rare. Some of the writings are previously unpublished or, due to strict codes of wartime censorship, were never widely circulated. This is the first published collection of Gore-Booth's political writings. Publication of these writings will provide a greater understanding of Gore-Booth's work but perhaps even more importantly, it is hoped that this collection will add to the body of research available on issues which are in the main under-researched. These are topics which were viewed as controversial in the early twentieth century such as conscientious objectors during the First World War, the death penalty in Ireland and England and the development of women's trade unions. These topics have often suffered from a lack of available source material. Lack of available sources has meant that the history of constitutional suffrage activities has been dramatically overshadowed by the history of militant suffragettes whose activities were regularly reported in newspapers and other media.

Eva Gore-Booth's writings have been divided into three sections: women's suffrage and women's trade unionism; pacifism and conscientious objection during the First World War; and Irish nationalism before independence. These sections are broadly chronological, highlighting Gore-Booth's developing political focus. The majority of the pamphlets and journal articles were written solely by Gore-Booth. Many of the letters to newspapers are signed on behalf of members of relevant organisations. Gore-Booth's most popular co-author was her partner, Esther Roper. Roper was a noteworthy suffrage campaigner in her own right and was the most significant influence over Gore-Booth's political, literary and personal life.

The papers in this volume have been reproduced as originally published or written by Gore-Booth, including the use of what would now be termed as standard American English spelling. In transcribing and editing these texts, detailed explanatory footnotes have been inserted by the present author throughout. The few notes that were supplied by Gore-Booth herself have been placed at the end of the relevant documents and not in the run of footnotes.

Figure 3 shows Eva Gore-Booth shortly before she left Ireland to live in Manchester.

Figure 3 Eva Gore-Booth, *c.*1896

PART I

Women's suffrage and women's trade unionism

Eva Gore-Booth began her political career campaigning for women's suffrage. In 1896 she met a young suffragist from Manchester, Esther Roper, while convalescing in Italy. Inspired by Roper and her tales of the vibrant suffrage campaign in Manchester, Gore-Booth established the first such organisation in her home county. She founded a Sligo branch of the Irish Women's Suffrage and Local Government Association and was duly elected as Secretary. Earlier that year the suffrage movement in Ireland was shaken back into action by the introduction of the Women's Poor Law Guardian (Ireland) Act. The Act extended the vote to women, who adhered to certain property qualifications, in elections for Poor Law Guardians.[1] The establishment of the Sligo suffrage society was timely. Within fewer than two years a further law, the Local Government (Ireland) Act, extended even more rights to women. This Act granted women, again with certain qualifications, the right to vote in local elections.

The improvements to women's voting rights were slight and may well have been motivated by the introduction of a series of Reform Acts which dominated the political landscape of nineteenth-century Britain. The Reform Acts of 1832, 1867 and 1884 extended votes to various categories of men, but only to men who adhered to certain property qualifications. Enfranchisement was a class as well as a gender issue at the beginning of the twentieth century in Britain, and this caused clashes between organisations representing the interests of these groups.

Suffragist organisations campaigned through constitutional means to secure votes for women on the same terms as they were granted to men. The number of local groups spread across Britain at a constant rate and by 1897 it was deemed necessary to establish an umbrella organisation, the National Union of Women's Suffrage Societies, to coordinate the work of five hundred groups nationwide. This was the same year that Gore-Booth moved to live in the industrial and mainly working-class city of Manchester. Extending the vote to women on these terms would not impact on the lives of these working-class women, few of whom owned or rented property in their own right. The suffrage movement was predominately controlled by middle-class and aristocratic women who sought equal terms with their male folk and often overlooked the needs of working women.

The cause of universal male suffrage was taken up by a group of liberal politicians and trade unionists who joined together to establish the Labour

1 Maria Luddy (ed.), *Women in Ireland, 1800–1918: A Documentary History* (Cork: Cork University Press, 1995), p. 242.

Representation Committee (LRC) in 1900. The aim of the Committee was to represent the needs of working-class men in the House of Commons; it was effectively a precursor to the British Labour Party. The LRC did not support the cause of women's suffrage, fearing that if women were granted the vote on the same terms as men there would simply be an increase in middle-class voters. In the first general election after the LRC's formation, out of fifteen candidates put forward only two, Keir Hardie and Richard Bell, were elected.[2] The fact that the LRC found progress slow only compounded its opposition to women's suffrage.

The issue of gender equality in labour caused further complications. Male-dominated trade unions did not openly welcome female membership, concerned that women undercut male wages and therefore threatened general rates of pay. It was necessary to form separate women's trade unions which often viewed the campaign for female suffrage as a separate political agenda, outside of their remit. Gore-Booth attempted to resolve the divide: she was adamant that industrial and political reforms were intrinsically linked. In her many writings on this subject, she argued that it was not enough to grant women the vote with property qualifications, as so few women owned or rented property it would make little difference. Furthermore, Gore-Booth argued that it was working women who suffered the most in the industrial world. Women received less pay than their male counterparts, had few opportunities to progress within their employment and had no legal protection against sexual harassment in the workplace. Women, Gore-Booth maintained, would only become equal in the workplace when they received a political franchise through voting at general elections. In this way she was one of the first people to take suffrage beyond the domain of middle-class concerns and make it a working woman's issue. Gore-Booth refused to separate the issues of women's suffrage and trade unionism and, therefore, her writings on these areas are grouped here in Part I. Gore-Booth's was a radical campaign, a new direction which was not readily embraced by mainstream trade unions, suffrage groups or political parties.

The writings in Part I often represent the interests of organisations which Gore-Booth was involved with or founded. Her first official trade union role was as co-secretary, along with Sarah Dickenson, of the Manchester and Salford Women's Trade Union's Council (WTUC). The Council was established in 1895 by a group of local radicals who recognised the importance of encouraging and establishing trade unions for women workers.[3] Gore-Booth

2 Paul Alderman, *The Rise of the Labour Party 1880–1945* (London: Longman, 1996), p. 30.

3 The WTUC was established by a number of people including the Bishop of Manchester; Mrs H. Arnold and her husband Matthew Arnold of the Manchester and Salford Trades Council; G. D. Kelly, secretary of the Trades Council; Reverend Steinthal, an active suffrage campaigner; and C. P. Scott MP, editor of the *Manchester Guardian* newspaper.

and Dickenson were appointed to the joint role in 1900. Dickenson had worked in a cotton mill in Salford from the age of 11 and was conscious of the harsh working conditions women endured in factories. Together Gore-Booth and Dickenson helped establish many trade unions for women workers, mainly cotton operatives and weavers.

Along with Sarah Reddish, Selina Cooper and Esther Roper, Gore-Booth and Dickenson went on to establish the Lancashire and Cheshire Women Textile and other Workers' Representation Committee in 1903.[4] The title reflects that this was a local female equivalent to the Labour Representation Committee. The female group focused on securing a Member of Parliament who would advocate for women's suffrage. Gore-Booth and the executive members wrote pamphlets on behalf of the committee assessing women's position in the labour force. Their writings highlight how women were disempowered in the workplace due to their lack of a political franchise. Similar to Dickenson, Cooper and Reddish also began working in the cotton mills at 11 years of age. In their research, historians Jill Norris and Jill Liddington stress that these women differed from their middle-class counterparts, possessing a political radicalism which has now earned them the apt title of radical suffragists.[5] A number of female members of the Independent Labour Party did not support Gore-Booth's new committee. Emmeline Pankhurst was inspired to form her own organisation devoted to achieving votes for women, she established the Women's Social and Political Union (WSPU) that same year.

As the work and writings of the radical suffragists began to intensify, politicians and philanthropists appeared to react, with many calling for the protection of women in the workplace. Protection came mainly in the form of proposed legislation which would control the basis of female employment. Gore-Booth viewed such legislative proposals not as protection but as a restriction for women workers. She retaliated, fighting against government moves to curtail employment. The vibrant work of the Representation Committee on this issue drew the attention of the chair of the Women's Trade Union Council, Amy Bulley. Bulley protested that as secretaries of the Council, Gore-Booth and Dickenson should concentrate their attention on women's trade unionism and not on the issue of votes for women. In 1904, Gore-Booth and Dickenson felt compelled to resign from their positions on the Council. They established their own trade union council, the Manchester and Salford Women's Trade and Labour Council.

The next year, the face of the suffrage movement would be changed by the

4 Jill Liddington, *The Life and Times of a Respectable Rebel: Selina Cooper 1864–1946* (London: Virago, 1984).

5 Jill Liddington and Jill Norris, *One Hand Tied behind Us: The Rise of the Women's Suffrage Movement* (London: Virago, 1984).

actions of the Women's Social and Political Union members. In October 1905, founder member Christabel Pankhurst, who had until then worked closely with Gore-Booth, turned militant. Pankhurst and another member of the WSPU, Annie Kenney, were arrested and later imprisoned for disrupting a Liberal Party meeting and for spitting at a police officer. Pankhurst was an executive committee member of the North of England Society for Women's Suffrage (NESWS). At their annual general meeting in 1905 the NESWS condemned her behaviour. She instantly resigned from the society and was supported in this action by Gore-Booth, Dickenson and Reddish. A group, led by Gore-Booth, refused to condemn Pankhurst's actions and formally resigned from their positions on the committee. This was the last time that Gore-Booth would support Pankhurst in any way. Many of the following writings identify the deep split in the suffrage movement which saw the increasingly militant actions of the suffragettes, actions which Gore-Booth abhorred. The militancy of the suffragettes was often reported by journalists, leaving behind accessible records for historians. The writings in this section provide a valuable source of information regarding the many activities of constitutional suffragists.[6]

Gore-Booth and the group of dissenters established yet another organisation, a replacement society for anyone who did not wish to remain aligned with the North of England Society for Women's Suffrage. Before the end of 1905 they formed the National Industrial and Professional Women's Suffrage Society. The society was the ideal organisation for middle-class radical suffragists, who were not directly related with trade unionists or factory workers and who remained non-militant.[7] Figure 4 shows the offices at 5 John Dalton Street, near Albert Square in Manchester, where the Women's Trade and Labour Council, the Lancashire and Cheshire Women Textile and other Workers' Representation Committee and the National Industrial and Professional Women's Suffrage Society were all based.

The regulation of women's employment was quickly becoming a contentious issue in the political arena. From the beginning of the twentieth century numerous legislative controls were introduced through the Factory Acts which regulated health and safety in the workplace and under this guise structured the employment of women. As regulation increased, so too did attempts to ban women from working in certain occupations thought to be harmful to their feminine sensitivities. The occupation of barmaids became a contentious issue. Under the direction of the Chancellor of the Exchequer, Henry Asquith,

6 For more discussion on this aspect, see: Sonja Tiernan, 'Tabloid Sensationalism or Revolutionary Feminism? The First-Wave Feminist Movement in an Irish Women's Periodical', *Irish Communications Review*, 12 (2010), 74–87.

7 Elizabeth Crawford, *The Women's Suffrage Movement: A Reference Guide 1866–1928* (London: Routledge, 1999), p. 435.

Figure 4 Office building at 5 John Dalton Street, Manchester, where Gore-Booth's main organisations were based

the government proposed to include a section in the 1908 Licensing Bill, effectively banning women from working on licensed premises across Britain. The legislation was seen by many as a measure to protect women from the path to moral ruin. Gore-Booth established the Barmaids' Political Defence League and lobbied MPs to resist this legislation.[8] This was to become one of Gore-Booth's most vibrant campaigns and perhaps her most successful.

Gore-Booth's writings on suffrage and labour issues were published in a number of formats. Her letters were printed in numerous esteemed newspapers including *The Times* but appeared most often in the *Manchester Guardian*. The frequency of her letters in the *Guardian* is testament to her relationship with its editor, C. P. Scott. Scott was instrumental in establishing the Manchester and Salford Women's Trade Union's Council and was a fervent supporter of women's suffrage and Irish nationalism.[9] Gore-Booth's letters to newspapers are often in response to other commentators and provide an interesting snapshot of how individuals openly debated such contentious issues as regulation of women's work and female suffrage. In certain cases Scott provides an editor's opinion about Gore-Booth's letters and she in turn responds. This aspect provides for a lively and interesting read.

Gore-Booth also offered open debates on the subject of trade and suffrage in *Nineteenth Century and After* and *The Academy*, leading intellectual journals of the time. Her longer prose works on these topics appeared in suffrage journals such as the *Women's Tribune*, the organ of the Women's Declaration Committee, the *Common Cause*, the journal of the National Union of Women's Suffrage Societies and in the *Englishwoman*.[10] Throughout her political activities Gore-Booth continued to write poetry which often reflected her personal feelings regarding her many campaigns.

The final piece in Part I was originally published in January 1919 and relates to the first general election in which women were entitled to vote. The introduction of the Representation of the People Act 1918, after the First World War, vastly reformed the British electoral system. In recognition of women's service to the war effort the act granted women over 30 years of age, who adhered to some qualifications, a vote at general elections. After this groundbreaking advance in women's rights, Gore-Booth concentrated her efforts on campaigning for peace and Irish independence.

8 Sonja Tiernan, 'Countess Markievicz and Eva Gore-Booth: In Defence of Barmaids', *History Ireland*, 20(3) (May/Jun. 2012).

9 See J. L. Hammond, *C. P. Scott of the Manchester Guardian* (London: G. Bell & Sons, 1934).

10 The *Englishwoman* was not directly associated with a suffrage organisation. It was edited by Elisina Grant Richards with an editorial committee including Lady Strachey and Lady Frances Balfour. Crawford, *Women's Suffrage Movement*, p. 459.

Views of the Manchester Women's Trade Union Secretary

The Times, 12 February 1903

May I make a few comments on Mrs. MacDonald's letter in your issue of February 7, which I have only just seen?[11] Mrs. MacDonald says that the work of a barmaid is not suitable for women 'on the grounds of long hours, close atmosphere, and general condition incapable of radical improvement.' Without desiring to impugn the motives of the joint committee of ladies who have undertaken to investigate this matter, I must protest against such a sweeping and wholesale treatment of a complicated problem in which clashing interests and much-confused issues are involved, and which is surely worthy of most careful consideration. These ladies, actuated by what is, no doubt, a very genuine philanthropic sentiment, seem to be unaware of the present stress of competition in the labour market and the sex restrictions and 'lines of demarcation' which make it so hard for a woman to earn her living, else they would surely pause before they tried to turn the barmaids out of their employment.

From the standpoint of a leisured class, no doubt, it is not an ideal one, but, judged by this standard, there are a few alternative women's trades that would not be found wanting. The average barmaid may be underpaid and overworked, but anyone familiar with the trades now open to women must realise that for them bad conditions, low wages, and long hours are the rule and not the exception in the industrial world. In these matters the 'abolition of the barmaid' cannot possibly affect the smallest reform. In fact the sudden invasion of a crowd of unemployed and unskilled workers must inevitably tend to depress wages in other trades where women are employed. Anyone interested in the improvement of the wages and conditions of working women must view with grave anxiety the tendency that has been growing steadily during the past few years to turn women out of their work for their own good, especially as there is no corresponding movement to open any of the more skilled and 'nicer' processes to them, so that the very cutting of women's coats and skirts is still considered exclusively 'man's work.'

It will not be denied that trade competition is a very strong factor in all

11 Margaret MacDonald, wife of then Chairman of the Labour Party, Ramsay MacDonald, pictured in Figure 5. The couple actively campaigned to abolish the employment of barmaids. Suffragist campaigner Dora Montefiore described how 'the National Union of Women Workers resolved itself into a Society for the Abolition of Barmaids. It has appointed a joint committee, with a Mrs. Macdonald as its secretary, and the work that this committee has set itself to do is, according to that lady, to stamp out within the next five years the genus "barmaid"' (Dora B. Montefiore, 'Women's interests', *New Age* (19 Feb. 1903), p. 123).

Figure 5 Mrs Margaret Gladstone MacDonald (1870–1911), photographed by Elliott & Fry, 1906

these matters, and it is a somewhat illuminating fact that a certain waiters' union actually passed a resolution of thanks to the Glasgow magistrates for their action in turning out the barmaids.[12] While it is the avowed aim of members of men's trade union to 'check the encroachments of female labour,' surely the committee of the National Union of Women Workers will hesitate

12 In 1902, Glasgow implemented a ban on employing barmaids. The only females then permitted to work in Glaswegian licensed premises were relatives of the publican.

before they ally themselves with these societies in their efforts to turn women out of any honest employment.

Yours, &c., Eva Gore-Booth.

The employment of barmaids

Manchester Guardian, 23 December 1903

Sir,

May we say a few words re Mrs. MacDonald and Mrs. Gooch's letter on the employment of barmaids?[13] To anyone acquainted with the present state of the labour market and the difficulty of obtaining employment it seems a policy dictated by the most short-sighted philanthropy to close up any avenue of honest work to those engaged in the incessant and very rough struggle for existence which, whatever those whose lines are cast in pleasanter places may think, is the commonplace average lot of workaday womankind. As to the temptations which are evidently supposed by some optimists to be peculiar to bars, every working woman knows that she has to hold her own in a world full of snares, not least of which are (1) the difficulty of finding honourable employment and (2) the pressure of those low wages which are too often caused by an excessive and disproportionate supply of labour in those few trades that are at present open to women. Already the influx of barmaids thrown out of employment in Glasgow has caused complaints among the London barmaids, who have found in them competitors in their work. It seems hard that labouring women should have their difficulties increased by the interference of people of leisure, who do not feel the pressure of want but are able to pick and choose their own employments. Anyone who is interested in the industrial future of women must view with alarm the possibility that is so cheerfully suggested that 'if this course were adopted (that the licensing magistrates should accompany the granting of licenses with the condition that no new barmaids should be engaged), within a few years no women, unless members of the licence-holder's family, would be found in an occupation which offers peculiar temptation.' Translated into the language of the labour world this means that in a few years' time 27,000 unemployed and unskilled women will be trying to find employment in an already much over-stocked market, and by their competition bringing yet lower the rate of wages among a body of already inadequately

13 The wife of George Gooch, a temperance advocate and MP for Bath. Gooch went on to introduce a bill in October 1906 proposing the abolition of barmaids. Gooch argued that this measure would protect young women from the attentions of inebriated customers and ensure that men would not be lured into drinking by attractive servers.

paid workers.[14] As far as economic conditions and the fluctuating nature of the work are concerned, the arguments for the abolition of barmaids could, every one of them, be applied with exactly the same amount of truth to the employment of waitresses, shop assistants, and, indeed, to the workers in most other trades – that is to say, of course, among the lesser skilled occupations.

Yours, &c.,
Eva Gore-Booth.
Sarah Dickenson.

The employment of barmaids

Manchester Guardian, 27 January 1904

Sir,
In answer to Mrs. MacDonald's letter, may we say that she has totally misunderstood our position in the matter?[15] We venture to protest against the following deductions: – (1) That because we disapprove of women being excluded from this employment we object to any regulation of the trade; (2) that because we disapprove of one method of political interference, we disapprove of all political interference in industrial matters, and that therefore 'laissez-faire must resign supreme'; (3) that because we say the world is full of snares we shrug our shoulders and pass by, and do not attempt to improve the conditions of women's work. Any defence of our action is wide of the matter, but these are not our views nor our motives.

We fail to see any parallel between the action of the Factory Laws as observed by us in Lancashire and the results that must follow the carrying out of Mrs. MacDonald's proposal. Regulation which has for its aim the amehoration of the hours and conditions of work, sanitary and other, is not to be confused with a totally different issue, the proposal by a gradual process of weeding out to supplant one set of workers with another, and the distress that will result among those deprived of employment.

Any attempt to improve the condition of the workers will be heartily welcomed by us as by every sincere trade unionist. But we must again state that the proposal to turn women out of their employment, attended as it must be by grave economic consequences, is a very different matter. Mrs. MacDonald in her very natural impatience with present economic conditions seems to

14 Gore-Booth quoted these figures from the 1901 census return, showing that England and Wales employed 27,707 barmaids. However, in her later writings this number was increased to 100,000; see her letter to *Manchester Guardian* on 28 November 1907.

15 Margaret MacDonald replied to Gore-Booth and Dickenson's previous letter on 16 January 1904.

have lost sight of the fact that to keep people forcibly out of one trade is not necessarily to put them into another and a better one. It is hardly the experience of the industrial worlds that a restriction of the field of labour and the consequent increased competition involved create an upward pressure among the excluded workers. To use a homely illustration, it is doubtless a more ideal condition to be able to walk unassisted down the road but if you take his crutch from a cripple he is more likely to fall than to run.

The present shortage of work and the acute distress that has followed in its train makes us in Lancashire most unwilling to increase the number of the unemployed. We are indeed glad to hear that efforts are being made in London to open the technical classes to women and to encourage them to attend, and are pleased to be able to endorse strongly Mrs. MacDonald's opinion of the importance of increasing the facilities for women in skilled trades and the efficiency of technical education.

One authority for the statement we made with regard to London barmaids was taken from interviews with the disaffected barmaids reported to us.

Lastly, we would venture to appeal to Mrs. MacDonald to consider the prospects and the often difficult circumstances of the workers themselves. One whom we know here in Manchester told us that she lay awake at night thinking what would happen if the trade were closed to women. Employment is not easy to get, and there must be many in the same case. The Manchester Labour Bureau, dealing only with men has over 1,100 applications for work, and has only been able to find places for fifty applicants. When one thinks, how much harder it is, as we know from every day experience, to find work for women, one cannot escape the feeling that those who seek to lessen their opportunities of honest employment from however good a motive, are taking upon themselves a very grave responsibility.

We are, &c., Eva Gore-Booth. Sarah Dickenson.

Manchester, January 18.

Women workers and parliamentary representation

Textile tracts – no 1: A pamphlet on behalf of the Lancashire & Cheshire Women Textile and other Workers' Representation Committee

Amongst those who have for their present ideal, in industrial matters, a fair day's wages for a fair day's work, the low payment of women remains one of the great problems of our modern civilization. In considering the importance of this subject of wages, it must be remembered that the lives of the poor are inevitably regulated in every detail, and their standard of comfort ultimately fixed by the amount of the weekly return they receive for their labour. Whilst making due allowance for the mental and moral influences that affect the lives of all classes alike, it will easily be seen that the distinctive difficulties and trials of the extremely poor are the difficulties and trials peculiar to extreme poverty. The wretched houses, insanitary and overcrowded, that disfigure our great towns, the children going hungry to school, the old people left penniless and uncared for, the numbers that sleep out every night of the year, these and many other evils are the direct result of poverty. They cannot be attributed to that want of virtue which is common to all classes, but which one class is apt to see very clearly in another. We do not find these things among the dwellings of the rich, however wicked. And when we think what the wage-earning power of more than half the race has fallen to, we cease to be surprised at the conditions under which so large a proportion are forced to exist.

Whilst engaged in organising a Trade Union among the Cradley Heath chain-makers, the writer of this paper was horrified to find that multitudes of these women receive, after a hard week's labour, wages varying between 2/6 and 5/-.[16] The work they are doing is heavy, requiring a good deal of physical strength and some skill. How can anyone hope to keep up their strength on such a starvation pittance?

Again, the wages of women in the Potteries average from 8/- to 12/-. The women who work in the warehouse get 9/- for work which, when done by men, is paid at the rate of 25/- to 30/- per week. Millions of women employed in the endless number of small and lesser skilled trades, such as machining, folding and sewing, cigar making, cap making, fancy-box making, &c., can never hope to bring home more than 7/- to 12/- a week all their lives.

In spite of the fact that the Cotton trade is universally allowed to be the best paid women's route, trade in the country, Miss Clara Collet gives the average of women's wages in the mills at 14/- a week.[17]

What wonder, then, that there is no poverty so crushing as the poverty of a family, where, through force of circumstances – as indeed often happens a

16 Cradley Heath is a small town in the West Midlands which was a central location for chain making during the industrial revolution. The large factories in the town employed male workers to produce large chains. Smaller chains were produced by women using a procedure known as hand-hammering in outbuildings near their houses. The work was dangerous and conditions would later be described as sweated labour. Gore-Booth established the women workers into a trade union around 1905. The women would later stage a ten-week strike over wages in 1910. From Modern Records Centre, University Library, University of Warwick.

17 Clara Collet, an English civil servant, who became an influential commentator on women and employment. She authored a number of significant books on the issue including *The Economic Position of Educated Working Women* (1890), *Educated Working Women* (1902) and *Women in Industry* (1911). David Doughan, 'Collet, Clara Elizabeth (1860–1948)', *Oxford Dictionary of National Biography* (Oxford: Oxford University Press, 2004).

woman is the principal bread-winner! The theory that working men keep their families, and that the earning of women are merely an extra help to the family finances, may in the past have had some force, and has often been quoted as a justification for the low wages of women, but it has grown to be wholly untrue to the facts of life. The struggle for life has in the world's history gone through many phases. It has been a national struggle against invading nations, a tribe struggle, a struggle of class against class, of families, or clans against the world; but it has in this generation tended to become more and more an individual struggle for existence. This is specially true of the labour world. Directly a girl is grown up, or, indeed, long before the age that is considered full grown amongst people who have leisure to grow up comfortably, she is expected to earn her keep. Young children and old people are, of course, dependent, and many married women. But in the Cotton trade alone there are 74,000 married women among the workers, – and, indeed, there is not a working woman in the country, married or single, who does not know that, probably, for one reason or another before the end she will be thrown on her own resources, and that there comes a time in most people's lives when only their capacity for wage-earning stands between them and the workhouse.

Apart from the suffering involved to the individual, and her immediate surroundings, all Trade-Unionists must agree that there is something radically wrong with the present position of women in the labour market. The low wages, which are a misfortune to the individual, are, in the eyes of the community, a crime and a danger. Undercutting, the inevitable result of low wages, gives rise to much natural bitterness among the more fortunate workers, who are apt to mistake what is, after all, an economic necessity, the mechanical revenge of the industrially oppressed on society, for proof of the innate inferiority of a politically defenceless body of workers.

The work of English women is classed as cheap labour, and the working men have grown to believe that their own wives and mothers and sisters and daughters, whose wages, after all, go to make their families more comfortable, are as much their enemies and rivals as the Chinese in South Africa are the enemies of white labour.

Many reasons have been given to account for this deplorable state of things. Some people say that women have no power of organisation, and, therefore, they cannot hope to receive an adequate return for their labour. This reason was given seriously to the writer by an official of a local Lancashire Union, in which there were 8,900 women and a very small proportion of men. There are 20,000 members of the National Union of Teachers, yet the women teachers are paid, roughly speaking, about half what the men get for the same work. In the Cotton Unions alone there are 96,000 women members as against 69,000 men. It has been said, and is in the main true, that working women as a body are not so skilled as working men. This is, of course, the direct result of their exclusion from apprenticeship in the skilled trades, it exists co-extensively with that exclusion, and it brings us face to face with wider issues, illustrating, as it does, the interdependence of the industrial and political worlds, and showing that there are other factors of more importance even than Trade Unionism that go to determine the scale of reward people receive for their labour. A Government clerk may be a very valuable member of society, but it will hardly be contended that the disproportion between his salary of, say £300 a year, and the wages of an engineer paid at the rate of 30/- a week, represents the true proportion of the value of their respective services to their country. It must be at the same time remembered that the engineer has in all probability a strong Union at his back, while the clerk has been able to wrest his pay single-handed out of the community. This fact is a very significant one; we have only to follow it up into other fields of inquiry to find out the real secret of the industrial world, the source alike of its weakness and its strength, its absolute unconditional dependence on the social and political forces of the time. It has often been said 'Money is Power,' it is equally true that Power is Money. With social traditions at his back, or real political influence to support him, the individual finds it easy enough to make good his claim to a fair share of the wealth, intellectual or material, owned by the community. Taking this fact into account, it will be seen that the working woman's position is, indeed, a forlorn and a difficult one. She has no social or political influence to back her. Her Trade Union stands or falls by its power of negotiating; it cannot hope to have the weight with employers that the men's Unions have, for instead of being a strong Association of Voters, bound together by common interests in trade and politics, and able by numbers to change the issue of elections, and force its policy on the House of Commons, it is merely a band of workers carrying on an almost hopeless struggle to improve conditions of work and wages forced on them by arbitrary authority. A vote in itself is a small thing, but the aggregate vote of a great Union is a very different matter. The Cotton Unions of Lancashire – some of the largest Trade Unions in the country have a majority of women members – 96,000 women against 69,000 men. It will be seen then that this great industry is to a very large extent disfranchised. What wonder that the trade, except in the mule spinning department, where women are rarely employed, is considered a poor one for men? The rate of wages, although supposed to be good as far as women are concerned, is not high enough for men with the superior standard of comfort that Society has allowed them.

Trade Unionism is a step in the right direction it is all very well as far as it goes, but it does not go far enough, and it is not an exaggeration to say that all the more thoughtful Trade Unionists in the country are gradually coming to the conclusion that political power is an absolute necessity for the protection of the workers' interests. This generation has suffered too much from the devastating results of industrial warfare to wish to continue a method that is so dangerous to the interests of all concerned. The strike that jeopardises the daily bread of the worker brings embarrassment and difficulty to the employer, and more and more the tendency has begun to assert itself on both sides to shift the ground of the struggle, and settle industrial difficulties by political methods. As this tendency grows, the position of the women workers becomes more and more intolerable. The matters that concern her daily bread, and the amount of money she takes home at the week-end, are rapidly passing into a sphere she is not allowed to enter.

With the formation of the Labour Representation Committee, and the affiliation to it of the more important, Trade Unions, the nationalising of trade questions from the men workers' point of view has taken tangible and practical form. Few and foolish are the human beings who are ultimately content to have no say in the management of their own affairs, and among the working women a feeling of dissatisfaction is steadily and rapidly growing, especially among the hardy cotton operatives of the North. This feeling has led to the formation of the Lancashire and Cheshire Women Textile and other Workers' Representation Committee. The Committee consists mainly of women cotton operatives from the different Lancashire and Cheshire towns. They are conscious that their trade is too important a one to be thus permanently crippled. They appeal confidently to their fellow-workers in other trades to help them, that they may gain those political rights absolutely necessary to all wage-earners if they wish to improve their condition and receive a just reward for their labour.

Lancashire & Cheshire Women Textile and other Workers'
Representation Committee.
5, John Dalton Street, Manchester.

Fair pay for women

Women's Tribune, 1906

A friend of mine, who is a shirt maker of many years standing, was taking a turn the other night at the sewing machine, whereby the more adventurous spirits of our Trade Union office make beautiful garments to be sold in a cause in which we are interested. I said to her, 'I should have thought you must have been about tired of machining by now.' 'Oh,' she said, 'I've made a lot of shirts in my time.' 'What did you get for them?' said the Folders and Sewers secretary, looking up from a terrific array of accounts. 'Well,' said my friend, 'you'd be surprised at the amount I've made in my time for 7d. per dozen. You get very quick at it after a bit.' 'How long does it take you to make one?' I asked. 'Oh, about ten minutes,' was the answer.

I meditated. She would take then two hours to make a dozen shirts. How can anyone make a dozen shirts in two hours? Surely there are giants on the earth in these days. And by this Herculean labour she would be able to earn 7d.

And ten hours a day at high pressure all the time would bring her in exactly 16s. 0½d. at the end of the week. And surely this woman of the clever fingers who could make a dozen shirts in two hours, in the curious productiveness of her labour, was worth as much to the State as a young man of my acquaintance who sticks bills on hoardings for 23s. a week. So I said laughing, 'If I were you I'd go and stick bills on hoardings, it's much easier than making shirts even I can do that, and it's much better paid.' 'Fancy if a woman tried to do that, what a row there would be, they'd say it was bad for her health,' said the weaver. 'Or her morals,' put in the secretary of the Trades Council. 'They'd think she might catch cold,' suggested a young member anxiously.

Women's position in industry

A visitor told us how she had heard a famous woman doctor get up at a meeting and say 'I think the Suffragette movement and the Territorial movement are both excellent, they both take people out into the open air,' and we all agreed about the absurdity of the prejudice that makes people think that a woman should always work indoors in a hot room, and that the fresh air, and the wind, and the sun and the rain are God's gifts to men only. There is another curious English prejudice that women's work should never be seen, thus the vast army of women workers are hidden away in factories and workshops whilst most of the showy outside work is done by men, so that as we go about from place to place in omnibuses and trams and trains and tube, everything seems managed by men, and people get totally false ideas of women's position in industry.

This prejudice and others akin to it are responsible for forcing the labour of women into a few overcrowded channels and thereby through over-pressure and competitions bringing down the rates in those poor trades that are reserved for them. The fact of the matter is there are no workers in England so poorly paid as those women who carry on the smaller less skilled industries, huddled away in those obscure workshops, that crowd in their multitudinous littleness the narrow streets and dingy quarters of our great town.

Women who work in the big cotton factories are as a rule under healthier conditions, and are able to earn fairly good wages, though even here it must not be forgotten that by that strange English law of sex payment what is poor money for a man is considered the very best pay for a woman, and the one trade in England where piece work rates are equal for men and women (the weaving trade) is considered a poor one for men whilst the weavers are the aristocracy of women's labour. The weaver's 25s. would no doubt seem very low wages to the male spinners, whose work, which is kept rigidly in the hands of men, brings them in £2 a week. Still the weaver's 25s. would seem riches to the women who, working all their lives in the trade, cannot hope in the end to earn more than 15s. a week at folding and sewing. The men working beside them are able to earn 36s. at book-binding. This is because women are ruthlessly excluded from all the more skilled and highly paid processes in the trade.

Not incapacity

Oddly enough, they are not excluded because of their incapacity. A friend of mine who has worked many years in the trade has shown me books she has bound for her own amusement. She tells me the bookbinders laugh, and are forced to admit that the women can do the work well provided they do not do it for money. For in the book-binding trade the old 'line of demarcation' is only just beginning to give way, and until it is gone women cannot hope to earn good wages. For by this strange and rather naïve law all the good work is kept for men, and all the inferior (less paid) processes are given to women. And this evil custom, absolutely irrespective of the skill of the workers, or indeed of ordinary fairness, is of course part of a much bigger question. For it seems as if whilst women are unenfranchised, and the claims of their labour to a sharing of national life are not recognised by the State, the past traditions of inferiority must still dog their path, and act as a barrier in the way of their industrial advancement. Exclusions founded entirely on sex bar the progress and depress the wages of women in every industry. Yet they are in the main good trade unionists. In the cotton trade unions there are 96,000 women and 30,000 in the National Union of Teachers. But anyone with experience knows that in the smaller and lesser skilled trades both sexes are hard to organise. And beyond a certain point trades unionism cannot do much. In spite of the huge female membership of the National Union of Teachers under every Education Committee there is a scale by which women are paid steadily all the way through from head mistresses down to pupil teachers at a far lower rate than men. Skill, training, hours are all equal, but a woman is fined even to the half of her salary for being a woman, which is after all more of a misfortune than a crime.

In those small trades that by their conditions seem to be outside the power of trade unionism to help, wages sink to their lowest level, and it is an indisputable fact there are many thousands of women who not only earn but have to live on 5s., 6s. or 7s. a week.

An individual struggle

People have some strange kind of idea that women do not really want money as much as men do. In old days when the man was the family bread winner this may have been true. But in these times the struggle for life has become to a great extent an individual struggle. Girls are brought up to bear their own burdens, and to fight their own way in the world in the same way as boys are. True it is there are people who seem incapable of earning, who for one reason or another, depend on others for support. But these are quite as often men as women. When men claim more money than women on account of the wife they have to keep, it must always be remembered that even in the most orthodox cases where the man keeps his wife and children on good wages, say £2 a week, his sister is most probably keeping her mother on 12s. a week. And in a few years' time the children will be earning and supplementing the married man's income, so that in the end the £2 will be spent entirely on himself and his wife, while the unmarried sister must go on keeping the old mother on the same 12s. till the time comes when her care is no more needed.

One of the greatest tragedies of our modern civilisation is the slowness with which economic conditions adapt themselves to changing social needs. While the modern development of industry has forced women into independence and positions of responsibility towards others, the old traditions of dependence and inferiority still bring down their industrial value and hamper them in their efforts to maintain themselves and those who depend on them.

Government rates

Go far to crystalize the evils of the past, and we have the President of the Board of Education calmly and unblushingly allowing.[18] 'He could not, however, hold out any hope of raising the salary of women inspectors to that of men. In all other Government departments and in every business or profession – except the medical profession – women were paid less than men.' At the end of last session the Government took to itself credit for initiating a minimum wage for women in post office and other Government contracts. In the following clause is embodied the conditions on which they are prepared to insist.

Clause 15. The Postmaster General will not consider that Clause 14 is being properly complied with unless –

(a) Piece work rates are so fixed that the wages which an average female worker can earn shall be not less than thirteen shillings and sixpence per week of 54 hours, free of all deductions.

18 President of the Board of Education, Augustine Birrell, opposed women's suffrage and equal pay.

(b) The average wages actually earned in any four consecutive weeks, by any person working on the contract, are at a rate not less than three pence per hour.

Thus the Government crystalizes and holds up for imitation a regular sweating rate of wages for women. Three pence per hour in London and 2¼d. outside is what they recommend as fitting pay for skilled women's labour. The importance of their action in this connection cannot be overestimated.
The Government is the largest employer of labour in the country, and therefore, also because of its independent position, the scale of Government wages are a power in the labour market, and so act on the rates given by private employers, who cannot afford to undercut, and public boards that are bound to keep down their expenses. Three pence an hour is the answer of the nations' representatives to women's demand for a living wage. But even that is the bright side of the picture. Last March at Woolwich, among those who applied for out relief were 14 bag workers in the Arsenal, employees of the Government.[19] They were earning 2s. 7½d. a week. So were ten shirt-makers. Three pence an hour is certainly an improvement on this. Fifteen shillings a week earned by skilled women workers in the Pimlico Clothing Factory is better still. But anyone who feels satisfied with such payment should remember that in the very same factory no man, be he ever so unskilled, receives less than 23s. a week.

Undercutting the result

Mr. Runciman seems to see no wrong or injustice in this state of things.[20] He does not defend it, he merely states it as a fact and appeals tacitly to the strange lethargic English standard of whatever is, is right. Everywhere in England women are paid less than men, and if everybody does it, it must be the best thing to do. Government must follow, it cannot lead, it is an inert force, if you want it to move you must push it, and women have not got the only pushing power, the Franchise. Private employers on the other hand cannot afford to be pioneers. No individual employer can afford to give more than the market rate. Nor can municipal boards. And so the evil works on and spreads in a vicious circle, and the sweating employers go on undercutting one another and having it all their own way. Whilst all the time more and more women keep

19 The Royal Arsenal at Woolwich manufactured armaments and employed women for various roles even before the First World War broke out.

20 Walter Runciman, Liberal politician and parliamentary secretary to the Local Government Board. Martin Pugh, 'Runciman, Walter, first Viscount Runciman of Doxford', *Oxford Dictionary of National Biography*.

flooding into the labour market and the competition among them gets fiercer and fiercer – and all the better processes and work are still kept rigidly for men and the Government and the nation and the trade unions and the world at large still keep thinking and saying practically to every man, 'Ye are of more value than many women.' But a state of society founded on such mischievous falsehood is doomed. For the natural forces of the world make for righteousness, and they always assert themselves in the end. It may well be through such tribulation, but the time will come when the industrially strong will have to learn the terribly dangerous power of the industrially weak. Men can no more keep women from crowding into the labour market than Canute could stop the tide coming in, and surely as their labour is hindered and penalised by exclusions and restrictions so large a body of workers are bound in their difficult struggle for existence to take less wages than men. And directly one sex systematically undercuts the other the wages of both must automatically go down. No man will go on paying 36s. a week to a book-binder when he can get the same work done for a woman for 15s.

Emerson says 'no god dare wrong a worm.' And this is particularly true, for in industry at all events the most crushed worm has in itself the power, nay the inevitable necessity of vengeance. Reactions are swift and merciless. There are 5,000,000 women workers. Every industrial or political handicap that tends to reduce their wages or penalise their labour is a wrong that must automatically revenge itself by undercutting on the whole community of working people. For indeed the chain is no stronger than its very weakest link.

The Dangerous Performances Bill

Manchester Guardian, 4 July 1906

Sir,

May I draw attention to the Dangerous Performances Bill, which is at present before the House of Commons?[21] This bill provides that any person causing any woman of any age to take part in a public performance dangerous to life or limb should be fined £10. (This when there is no accident.) It is left entirely to the discretion of the local magistrates to decide what performances are

21 The Dangerous Performances Acts comprised the Children's Dangerous Performances Act of 1879, which regulated the 'employment of children in places of public amusement' and the Dangerous Performances Act of 1897 which extended the age limit to include boys under the age of 16 and girls under the age of 18. The acts made it illegal to employ children to partake in a public performance which would endanger their life or limbs. Herbert Samuel, under-secretary at the Home Office, presented a proposed bill to the House of Commons on 25 June 1906, which if introduced, would alter the basis of these acts to include women.

dangerous, and to enforce the fine.

This means practically that every performance where women are employed will be at the mercy of the local magistrates. Now in feats of skill it is a very hard thing for any outsider to know what is dangerous and what is not. A performance that would be very dangerous to an amateur can be easily and safely done by a trained athlete; feats that look both alarming and dangerous are often really safer than much quieter-looking performances. It is quite impossible that the magistrates can have any real or technical knowledge of these matters. It will easily be seen that the prosecutions and fines will be terribly unfair and harassing to managers and performers. Surely only the fact that these performances were productive of great loss of life could justify such an amazing interference on the part of the Government. When questioned on this subject Dr. Albrecht, whose practice is almost exclusively among music-hall artists at the different theatres and halls in Manchester; expressed his surprise at such a measure being brought forward. From his personal experience during the last ten years, he said, there had only been one serious accident in any theatre or music-hall in this neighbourhood. This accident had happened to a man, and was therefore no proof that the profession was especially dangerous to women. Mr. Broadhead, the 'manager' of nine variety theatres in the neighbourhood of Manchester, Preston, Ashton, and Bury, remembers in the course of twenty years' experience only one serious accident, where the sufferer was again a man. The unfairness of the law would easily be seen if it was applied to engineering, and the employer was forced to give the workman compensation, although there was no accident, because the magistrates thought that some technical process was unsafe. Of course no industry could be carried on under such circumstances.

It cannot be too deeply regretted that one woman should have fallen from a parachute, from no want of skill on her part, but through a fault in the mechanism of the parachute.[22] Yet it is surely an absurd and panic-stricken view that because of this all women should be prevented from engaging in any performance which a magistrate might happen to consider dangerous to life or limb. Thousands of men are unfortunately killed every year in mines, railways, and engineering works. According to statistics these trades are a thousand times more dangerous than the performances of skilled gymnasts. Yet no one proposes to penalise these employments.

The managers are quite awake to the necessity of taking all precautions

22 On 11 June 1906, a 21-year-old woman, Lily Cove, died in a parachuting accident. Miss Cove engaged in a parachute display at Haworth near Keighley in aid of the Haworth Oxenhope District Nurses' Association. Her parachute failed to open and she fell to her death in front of an audience of thousands. 'Terrible accident at Keighley', *Hull Daily Mail* (12 June 1906).

possible for the safety of the artists, and as a consequence of this the accidents are comparatively few. No detail is overlooked – even a loose plank is pointed out to a performer, – and these are tested before every performance.

It must be remembered that if the Public Performances Act passes it will not save human life, it will only substitute the injury or death of a man for the injury or death of a woman; on the other hand, it will take the bread out of the mouths of hundreds of women. To quote Dr. Albrecht again, it would mean 'ruination to hundreds of people.' For when such a penalty is attached to the employment of women, and the manager knows that he may be fined any moment on any trivial pretext, there are very few who will be able to afford the risk and worry that will result from their employment.

There are six societies of artists, and over 1,200 women in one of them alone; it is roughly estimated that 10,000 will be turned out of their work if this bill passes into law. A large displacement of labour will mean sharper competition in other callings, and increased poverty. All thoughtful people must know that if the aim of this bill was to save life and limb it would be absolutely necessary that it should apply to men and women alike, as from the recorded cases it seems more men than women are hurt.

The Government need not be surprised at the growing bitterness of women who see irresponsible legislation of this kind proposed and have no vote to protect their trade and secure a continuance of their incomes. One would have thought that the Home Secretary had enough with the unemployed working people, without causing, on such narrow grounds, the same difficulty among the professional classes.

Yours, &c., Eva Gore-Booth. Women's Trade Council,
5, John Dalton Street, Manchester.

Women's suffrage in the Transvaal

Manchester Guardian, 3 August 1906

Sir,

Surely all moderately minded English people must be deeply shocked at the levity with which Mr. Winston Churchill treats the political claims of the Transvaal women. It seems to some of us a very short time ago that Mr. Churchill's colleagues were sympathising with the terrible sufferings and admiring the desperate courage of these very women, who were no passive politicians in time of war. It is true that this courage was shown in resistance to British arms.[23] But it seems strange that a Government which claims to be

23 Transvaal is a former province of South Africa. War broke out between Britain and the two Boer republics after the Transvaal demanded the withdrawal of British troop reinforcements.

generous to our enemies should treat the question of their political enfranchisement as a subject for refined pleasantry.

Yours & co.,

Eva Gore-Booth.

Women's wages and the franchise and certain legislative proposals

Manchester, 1906

It will be allowed by political economists that the chief factors in determining rates of wages are the laws of supply and demand. Just as any article that is scarce and much sought after for gains money value, so when the demand for any particular labour is greater than the supply the price of that labour rises.

And it is thus assumed that

1. The demand for labour depends on the demand of the public for the goods that the labour is able to produce. Thus it is inferred that *the demand for commodities comes to nearly though not quite the same things as the demand for labour, and that, apart from the consideration of the profit of the capitalist, the rates of wages are governed by the same laws of supply and demand as the price of goods.*

Other considerations that are generally allowed to affect wages are

2. The easiness and cheapness or difficulty and expense of learning the occupation.
3. Skill or want of skill on the workers' part.
4. Personal attributes of the worker, such as stability, honesty.

In considering the case of the five million women working in mills and workshops, it will at once be observed that there is some universal cause in operation that depresses their wages wherever they are employed. So that, broadly speaking, in every trade, however skilled (with certain small local exceptions) women's labour is paid at about the third, or at most a half, of the price given to men.

At the same time it is remarkable that the cause or causes that cheapen women's labour in the industrial world are also effective in the professional

In September 1900 Britain annexed the Transvaal. The area became a British colony in 1902 and they restored self-government in 1906. Winston Churchill, then Under-Secretary of State for the Colonies, was questioned in the House of Commons regarding the issue of female enfranchisement of women under the new Transvaal constitution. He denied the request. 'House of Commons Debate', vol. 153 col. 1093 (13 March 1906).

world. The mass of professional women, with few exceptions, are paid less than men for the same work. Where they are highly paid it is because of some very individual intellectual capacity, such as that of a novelist, or a supreme and special work, as in the case of women instead of men doctors for many women's illnesses and actresses for women's parts. But journalists, teachers, secretaries, clerks, and all allied professions get a very low rate particularly unknown amongst men in the same work.

In searching for the cause of this depression it is necessary to make some examination of the laws that affect wages as they work themselves out under the present condition of women's labour.

The laws of supply and demand

According to this law, anything that affects the numbers of men able and willing to do a particular kind of work, affects the wages of such men. Under present circumstances this law is very much restricted in its operation on the work of women by artificial causes, dependent to a large extent on their political disability. All economists must allow that there is not such a disproportionately large supply of women's labour that it could account for low wages by exceeding the demand. This result, the excess of the supply over the demand and the consequent reduction of prices, has been obtained by strictly artificial methods. The people who go into trades and professions are, for the most part, people who, for one case or another, must earn their living. If they cannot enter one industry, they must enter another. Now, in the professional and labour world alike, from the top to the bottom, it will not be disputed that a very great many of the better paid industries are openly and avowedly, or less quietly and practically, shut to women. This exclusion has two results: it artificially protects the labour of men from women's competition, and the supply of women's labour which would naturally flow into all trades and professions according to individual capacity, is forced into a few channels where the unnatural size of the supply greatly exceeds the demand, and is one of the chief causes of the very low rate earned. Thus, educated Women High School Teachers often enough cannot earn more than £100 a year, a little less than the ordinary standard rate (£2 a week) of a male spinner in the Manchester district. Thus the earning power of training, skill, and qualifications are easily overbalanced in the industrial market by the disadvantage of a restricted field for the product of your energies.

But where restrictions on women's labour are merely industrial, and have been enforced by men's unions, they have for the most part failed in displacing the women, and the only result has been (as in the case of Bookbinders) that the women have been forced to take a low rate of wages to make it worth the master's while to go on employing them. Trade unionist opposition is a great difficulty to women in the industrial struggle, but that must right itself in the natural course of evolution by the aid of the laws of supply and demand and the other forces that govern the labour market. The women are taking their part in the industrial struggle in such numbers with such force and determination that there can be no possible doubt of the final result. It is only when the action of natural forces is interfered with by special Parliamentary legislation that the exclusion of women from well-paid trades can be kept up.

The Trade Unions have found they cannot fight what they call the 'evil of female labour' in the industrial world, because the women are too many and too strong for them, and in the end ability and determination will always hold their own where competition is allowed. But a new method has begun to be put in force. They are appealing to parliament to protect their labour artificially from the competition of women, and this appeal, made in many direct and indirect ways, has already borne fruits, and we have been given to understand by semi-official and authoritative statements that in the immediate future measures will be brought forward, here and there, in one trade or another, on various pretexts, to further restrict their energies and force their labour back into a few already hopelessly crowded channels.

And here it is as well to say that much confusion has been caused in people's minds by the speciousness of the arguments used to persuade Parliament to give the rigidity and finality of law to certain measures for the exclusion and repression of women's labour. The working women's point of view and sense of the danger of such legislation has never been put forward. And this has been so because it has never been the plain and simple duty of any Member of Parliament to study and represent the interests of the women worker apart from the men even in the great textile centres of women's labour. Their case is being tried without their being allowed to employ a lawyer in their own defence. Therefore we think it is necessary to our purpose, although it is somewhat outside the plan of this statement, to go into the reasons assigned by those who are anxious to justify such an interference with the laws of supply and demand, as must lead to the preponderance of the supply over the demand with the inevitable result of a depression of wages.

There are roughly speaking three classes of work in which constant efforts are being made to displace the labour of women and substitute men.

(1) Married women and work.
(2) Work in which women undercut men.
(3) Work supposed to be injurious to health or morals.

(1) On the question of married women's work as yet we have but little actual Parliamentary legislation. But when questioned on the subject,

the Home Secretary announced his intention of considering it in his next Factory Act.[24] 74,000 married women are working in the Lancashire Cotton Trade alone, and in view of its economic and moral results this suggestion of Parliamentary interference is looked upon by Lancashire Women Trade Unionists as disastrous. Loss of employment is regarded as the greatest misfortune in the industrial world, and the attachment of this penalty to marriage or motherhood cannot of necessity mean anything but an increase in the one case of irregular relations, and in the other of all evils attendant on the wish not to have children – a reduced birth rate, increased infant mortality, &c. Economically it would depress the wages of women by forcibly, in a wholesale and final manner, taking the valuable quality of stability from the work of all women. The reasons given for this legislation are for the most part reasons of health founded on an assertion that the homes of the working class are healthier than mills. Anyone with personal experience of the narrow streets and airlessness and dirt and bad smells of quarters in our great towns when the rest is within the wage earner's capacity, will be surprised at this argument, especially as the mills have to conform to a fairly high standard of cleanliness and space and airiness, and are protected from those terrible odours that working people in towns cannot keep out of their thinly-walled houses. And it is noticeable that it is also constantly urged that the work of married women at home should be abolished for similar reasons, which would then mean that a married woman whose husband, as often happens, for some reason could not earn, would not be allowed by law to help herself or her family. A law such as that suggested by Mr. John Burns[25] the other day that women should not be allowed to work for three months before and five after their confinement is equal to displacing their labour altogether, as no employer will find it worthwhile to employ a worker who is going to be 'off ill' eight months out of twelve.*

(2) Of work in which women undercut men, the Bookbinders' Trade might be taken as a very good example. The Bookbinders' Union from the first moment it was strong enough (see History of Trades Unionism, Sidney Webb), laid down a rule that no woman should be allowed to be apprentice.[26] The power of the Union was able to prevent

24 Herbert Gladstone, then Home Secretary.

25 John Burns, Labour politician and president of the Local Government Board in 1906. Burns was the first working-class man to become a government minister.

26 Sidney and Beatrice Webb, *The History of Trade Unionism* (London: Longmans, Green and Company, 1894). John R. Commons highlights this publication as a leading economic resource stating that it 'is preeminent among works in economic history. Its

the woman from being apprenticed and learning the trade thoroughly, and getting the ordinary journeyman's rate. But it was not enough to prevent the employers from taking the women on to do the less skilled work at a much lower rate. The women who had been debarred by the Union from getting the normal rate, were forced to take a lower price for this labour by the force of economic pressure; they were intelligent and quick, and soon picked up some regular technical instruction, the men found themselves confronted with competitors whose work was satisfactory to the employers. Every method, even strikes were resorted to by the Bookbinders, and after a strike in Manchester Mr. Richard Bell brought the matter up for discussion in parliament.[27] The same process has gone on in many other trades, notably the Tailoring Trade. We know that the House of Commons will not make a law to turn women out of their work simply on the grounds that men want it, but there are no other Parliamentary methods of lessening their employment such as legal disqualifications for technical training. When a regulation was made by the House of Commons, on grounds of general philanthropy, that women could not work at night in factories and workshops, the industrial result was that women compositors were thrown out of employment, and their places taken by men. Here a displacement of women's labour was the direct result of a regulation of the House of Commons, and according to the law of supply and demand every displacement of labour that increases the supply and lessens the demand involves the reduction of wages. At the present time, now that the Men's Trade Union element is so strong in parliament, and the women have no representation, the position has become very serious.

(3) These proposals are usually made on the grounds that the work is injurious either to health or morals.

The Miners' Federation, horrified at the increase of female labour at the Pit Brow, does not appeal to parliament to protect the men's work, but they appeal on sentimental grounds that the women should be protected against the moral deterioration of the miners' conversation and the strain of hard work. The self-condemnation in the miners' first protest surely needs no comment. And there is something absurd in making the law to protect the women from the society of their own relations and friends. Anyone who has been at the Pit Brow and

first edition, in 1894, set a model of interpretation and exhaustive research in economic documents. In its special field it has guided government bureaus and individual investigators' 'Review', *American Economic Review*, 10(4) (Dec. 1920), 834.

27 Richard Bell, a trade union leader and a Labour MP. Bell had a troubled relationship with the Labour Party and eventually split from it.

knows the work the women are doing, at Wigan for instance, will realise the absurdity of the second contention. The work is done in a fresh, breezy place and half under shelter, half in the open air. The women are, for the most part, fine, healthy, and good looking. A great part of their time on the 'Belt' is spent in picking small pieces of dross or 'dirt' out of a never-ending stream of coal that passes them by along a kind of gangway.[28]

It will be remembered the chain makers of Cradley Heath have undergone the same kind of harassing which renders their employment a kind of reproach to the employer, so that unless they sell him their labour very cheap he does not care to employ it.

Mr. Gladstone proposed to legislate against the employment of women in dangerous performances. Are then all the women circus performers, high divers, gymnasts, bicycle performers, and acrobats to be turned out of their work because one woman is killed by an accident with a parachute, an accident caused by a fault in the machine, not the performer? Accidents are less common amongst female performers than amongst men. It is idle to deny that there are those of both sexes whose instinct it is to seek distinction in feats of skill, dexterity, and danger. This is no sex question. If Mr. Gladstone's purpose is to protect the woman's life against her will, surely the man's life is of some account too. The laws of gravity apply to men and women alike. Again, it is a very difficult matter to decide exactly where danger to life and limb begins. It largely depends on the skill of the performers. The individual cases will be decided by magistrates probably ignorant of the laws of physical training and development, especially in their application to women. The obvious result of this will be that theatres and music halls will cease as much as possible to employ women sooner than risk the inconvenience and expense of a prosecution and fine, and thus numbers of workers will be turned out of the employment that they have spent their life being trained for. They will have to earn their living, and the labour of the 10,000 involved will go to swell the ranks of the unskilled workers in one of the already crowded trades open to women, thus bringing down the rate of wages in these trades by increasing the supply of labour. It seems now that this law is going to slip through without any discussion of its industrial significance for women.

Again, it is alarming to those interested in the women workers to hear the no doubt well-meant proposals that are so common now-a-days, to turn 27,000 barmaids out of their employment, on the ground of its immoral tendency. This would mean 27,000 women absolutely unskilled, out of work and struggling for a living in the least skilled and worst paid processes, bringing down

28 For further discussion of the work of pit-brow women, see Alan Davies, *The Pit Brow Women of the Wigan Coalfield* (London: The History Press, 2002).

the already low rate by sharp competition.

On the whole, it may be said that among all the trades in which, for any of the above-mentioned reasons, it is proposed to displace female labour, there is not one displacement that will not result in the over-crowding of other labour markets, and the subsequent reduction of wages through increased competition.

But it must be remembered that besides the law of supply and demand, there are other considerations that affect wages. One of the most obvious of these is the easiness and cheapness, or difficulty and expense of learning the occupation. Naturally the more skill people have, the higher rate of wages they are able to command. In most trades it is very hard for women to get technical instruction. The case of the Bookbinders will illustrate this. It has been seen that the Bookbinders' Union will not allow women to become apprentices. Under the Act creating technical Education, every trade class is shut to any student who is not working in that particular trade. Now, although there are practically many thousands of women working in the Bookbinders Trade,[†] the Union will not allow them to be apprentices, therefore they are not theoretically and technically in the trade; therefore they are debarred by Act of Parliament from attending bookbinding classes. Thus their facilities for obtaining skill are decreased, and their wages consequently depressed. Thus, in this and other trades, such as tailoring and silversmith work, and even in some parts of the cotton trade, it is very difficult for women to obtain technical knowledge, indeed, often it seems impossible. This legal hindrance, of course, affects the question of skill, and makes it well-nigh impossible for a working woman to obtain sufficient knowledge of her trade to command a very high rate of wages.

Questions of individual honesty and stability are said by political economists to have their share in fixing wages. It is impossible that anyone should contend that honesty is not characteristic of working women as of working men; but the equally valuable asset of steadiness and certainty would be interfered with by the law, because no woman would be exempt from the possibility of marriage and the subsequent industrial disqualification.

It seems hardly necessary to argue that the wages of the thirty thousand women working directly under Government are affected by their unenfranchised position. The advantages of choosing your own employers by popular election are very obvious. The working men, through their representatives, have been able to get a Resolution passed securing a Trade Union rate of wages to all men in Government employ. The women, who have no representatives to defend their interests in parliament, are excluded from the benefits of this regulation. So that their wages are very low indeed (as may be easily verified) – for instance, the average wage for women at Pimlico clothing factory is 15s.

a week, whilst for men the lowest rate is 23s.

This fact is more important than it seems at first sight because it affects indirectly the wages of a great many more workers. The natural tendency of all employers, individuals or public bodies, is of course to buy labour as cheaply as they can. The weak position of the women with regard to the Government low rates have given reason and justification to all local bodies, because they are bound to keep down their expenses in every possible way, for adjusting their wages to the Government standard; and directly one private employer, seeking naturally to buy labour at the cheapest rate, begins to follow the public example, other employers are at once bound by the laws of competition, if they do not wish to be ruined, to reduce the expenses of production in the same way.

Thus, Mr. Sidney Buxton admitted a short time ago that the action of the Post office, as largest employers of labour in the country, must have a considerable influence on the general position of the labour market.[29] It will be seen from the following table what influence is likely to be as far as the payment of women is concerned:

SALARIES OF CLERKS

Men – Second Division, Lower Grade	£70 to 250
Women – Second Class	£65 to 80
Men – Second Division – Higher Grade	£250 to 350
Women – First Class	£85 to 110

The industrial portion of these men and women is precisely the same.

In the District Offices and Provinces the Scale is –

	MEN	WOMEN
First Class Sorting Clerks	40/- to 56/-	18/- to 40/-
Second Class Sorting Clerks	28/- to 35/-	15/- to 28/-

In spite of the strong organisation of women teachers, and the fact that there is no complaint of their want of skill as compared to the men, it is noteworthy in this connection that there is no education Committee in England under which they are paid the same price for their work as their equals among the men. The exact rate varies in different localities, but the proportion of half to two-thirds is steadily kept up all through the scale from boy and girl pupil to fully qualified men and women.

To sum up, then; it seems clear –

(1) That as the rate of wages is to a great extent dependent on the proportion of the supply of labour to the demand, all Government interfer-

29 Sidney Buxton, Liberal Party member who held the position of postmaster-general in 1906.

ence that excludes women's labour, or leads to its displacement in any trade, and its consequent over supply in another, must lead to a depression of wages in the over supplied trade.

(2) That as the rate of wages also depends on the amount of skill exercised by the workers, and by their facilities or difficulties in gaining technical instruction, all denial of the usual technical training through the action of Parliament must depress wages.

(3) That as stability and honesty of the worker are recognised factors in determining wages, and as legislation forcing married women not to go out to work must rob all women's labour of that stability which has given the Lancashire weavers so good an industrial position, so legislation of this kind must depress the wages of women.

(4) That the standard rate of men, Government employees, has been deliberately forced up by Act of Parliament through the exertions of working men's representatives, while the House of Commons has not concerned itself with the women's rate. So that the Government, which is a model employer for men, is keeping down the rate for women by taking advantage of their political weakness in its industrial dealings with them, and by that action converting a political disability into an industrial disadvantage. This is not the fault of any individuals, but the mechanical and inevitable result of the law by which Governments follow the line of least resistance, and it must be remembered that the franchise is the nation's only constitutional method of resistance to unwelcome or partial legislation.

As women's wages are depressed in these ways by the action of the House of Commons, and as every action of the House of Commons in England depends admittedly and absolutely on the results of the franchise, therefore it follows that women's wages are depressed, and their low rate accounted for by their entire want of the most elementary political rights. Further, as legislation that will interfere with the working of the law of supply and demand in a very marked degree is threatened in the immediate future, the position has become very dangerous to all working women who are threatened, through their want of the protection of the franchise, with a further reduction of already low wages which, all persons of experience must know, will inevitably lead to widespread and extreme poverty.

Eva Gore-Booth,
Co-Sec. Manchester, Salford, and District Women's Trade a
nd Labour Council,
5 John Dalton Street,
Manchester,

July, 1906.

NOTE – The subject is a very large one, and we have only attempted to touch on certain aspects of it. Much more could be said on certain of the problems used as illustrations, especially the employment of married women in mills, women's work on the pit brow, chain making, barmaids, dangerous performances, &c.; exhaustive discussion of these points is outside our present scope. No attempt is made in this statement to discuss the general utility of factory laws framed on a wide and impartial basis. Any mischievous result of their working on women's wages pointed out here can be directly traced to the partial and sex character of these laws, as at present, or embodied in immediate future proposals.

* The question of the children has to be considered, and here many practical methods of reform could be suggested, such as crèches with trained attendants, all real projects for street and house sanitation, and a better food supply. The present individual arrangements by which the children are looked after by the old people are sometimes good and sometimes bad (as is also the case when the mothers stay at home), and the substitution of skilled and trained attendance ought and probably would be beneficial to health.

† According to the last Census papers there are 10,404 Women Bookbinders in London.

Mr. Asquith and women's suffrage

Manchester Guardian, 19 October 1906

Sir,

Mr. Asquith's statement with regard to the number of women who desire women's suffrage has caused surprise amongst those interested in the movement.[30] As the Chancellor of the Exchequer must know, there is no possible means by which the opinion of the majority of the population, male or female, ever is obtained on any subject whatever except by the referendum, which is not a political institution in England. It will be allowed that even the present Government does not represent the opinion of a majority of the male population of the country taken on any one subject only.

A manifesto was signed by 437,000 trade unionists and members of the co-operative and political societies whose representatives were present at the deputation to the Prime Minister in May, demanding the franchise for working women of all class. Several years ago a special appeal to Parliament was signed by over a quarter of a million women.[31] It will be seen that the

30 Herbert Henry Asquith was an opponent of women's suffrage and became a target of suffragette militancy, especially after he became Prime Minister in 1908.

31 Esther Roper oversaw the special appeal which was completed in March 1894. Roper ensured that over 3,500 people across the country collected nearly a quarter of a million signatures demanding suffrage for women. The volumes of signatures were displayed in the library of the House of Commons.

latter figure represents twelve times the numbers of the Independent Labour party, one of the most powerful political societies in the country, with many representatives in the House of Commons. Judging by what we know of the membership of all political parties, we do not think a quarter of a million is a negligible body of supporters. Added to this, many special petitions have been sent from different trades, such as the potteries, chain-makers, slipper-makers, and 68,000 women in the textile trades in the North of England.

As to Mr. Asquith's second point that the franchise would only serve to ventilate and remedy special grievances of special classes of women, we presume he must mean that the franchise can remedy only industrial grievances. But surely industrial grievances are, after all, the most important, because the industrial classes are the majority of the nation. Why should anyone despise the special grievance of special classes. The Trade Disputes Bill is being passed absolutely and entirely to remedy the grievances of the trade unions. The special interests of the Chinese in South Africa are dear to the hearts of the Liberals. It is only when it comes to English working women that the class is too small and insignificant to matter. For the rest, this is a practical generation, and to know that there are ladies in London of undoubted influence and unique status will not comfort in the least the mass of women who have to earn their own living in all classes from the journalists and teachers down to those who earn six or seven shillings a week in many and many a trade, and who are suffering from that depression of wages which always accompanies absence of all political rights.

Further, we would appeal to these ladies, how is it possible that to give votes to these 500,000 women to enable them to better their industrial position could injure the unique status and influence of the select few? It is, after all, only the select few who may not find themselves forced into the competition of the labour market through no fault or fancy of their own.

Finally, it must be remembered that the special class whose grievances would be remedied is not a small and insignificant section, but a body of workers eight times as large as the number of voters in Scotland at the last general election, and seven times as large as the Irish electorate, acknowledged by all to be a potent factor in politics.

It is the grievances of this 'special class' that we would urge on the attention of the Government.

The fact that the Government persistently turns its blind eye to the telescope of public opinion and refused to see any agitation, however large, carried on on [*sic*] the usual lines of constant meetings and demonstrations in all industrial districts, trade union protests, and petitions, has brought us face to face with the one constitutional means left to us. The time has come when women must appeal from the Government to the good sense of the men they represent. We took the first step in the general election, when a women's franchise candidate stood in Wigan under the auspices of our Committee.[32] In a three-cornered election he gained 2,205 votes. This is our first experience, made under very difficult circumstances, and it has determined large bodies of women to continue this policy.

Yours, &c.,
Eva Gore-Booth and Esther Roper.
Secretaries Lancashire and Cheshire Women Textile
and other Workers' Representation Committee.

A correction

Manchester Guardian, 20 October 1906

Sir,

In our letter which you published this morning the number of women wage-earners should have been given as 5,000,000, not 500,000 a number seven times as large as the Irish electorate, who are represented in the House of Commons by 102 members.

Yours, &c.,
Eva Gore-Booth.
Esther Roper.

The suffragist demonstration in Trafalgar Square

Manchester Guardian, 6 November 1906

Sir,

Will you allow me to explain the position of the Lancashire and Cheshire Women Textile and other Workers' Representation Committee, and the Manchester, Salford, and District Women's Trade and Labour Council, who principally organised the Trafalgar Square demonstration on Saturday, and who are in no way connected with the Women's Social and Political Union.[33] The

32 The Committee chose to contest the jurisdiction of Wigan as it had a large number of cotton workers and the Labour Representation committee was not contesting a seat there. Gore-Booth initially chose a local teacher, Hubert Sweeney, to stand for election. Sweeney later withdrew and Thorley Smith stepped in as a suffrage candidate. The Conservative candidate, Sir Francis Powell, won the 1906 general election for the Wigan constituency. Although Smith was not elected he did defeat the Liberal candidate.

33 Gore-Booth was opposed to militant suffragette activities and ensured that the public were aware that there was no connection between her non-militant organisations and the WSPU.

representatives of these societies have been on deputations to the Chancellor of the Exchequer, the Secretary of State for India, the Postmaster General, the President of the Board of Trade, the President of the Local Government Board, the Under Secretary of State for the Colonies, and the Chief Commissioner of Works. The meeting on Saturday, at which over 5,000 people were present, was called that the working women's representatives might bring the facts of the industrial condition of women before the London public.

May I also correct the statement that the speakers were subject to interruptions. In spite of its large size, the meeting was extraordinarily orderly; the speakers were listened to with sympathy and the resolutions passed with acclamation.

Yours & c.,
Eva Gore-Booth, Esther Roper (Secretaries)
5 John Dalton Street, Manchester.

'The Repentance of Eve'

Poems of Eva Gore-Booth: Complete Edition (1929)

This is our Mother Eve, who shall not win
Respite or peace, in vain she makes lament
She ate but half the fruit, sinned half the sin
Eternal hunger is her punishment.

She weeps and mourns for that sweet apple's sake
Whilst high above her in the sacred tree,
Coiled round its withered boughs, the wily snake
Smiles over her lost opportunity.

'Joan of Arc'

Poems of Eva Gore-Booth

The treasure of age and the hope of youth
And the hidden light of the dreamer's heart,
A treacherous word in the ear of Truth,
The breath of fools on the mirror of Art;
Honour and glory and slander and shame,
These are the golden gifts of Fame.

And the soul that fought for a laurel crown
Shall flaunt it aloft in the victor's car,
But his golden fancies must dwindle down

Like the flames that kindled a burnt out star;
Indolence, safety, a glorious name,
These are the golden gifts of Fame.

But she whose spirit was strong in the strife
Has gained the guerdon that was her due –
The torture of death and the height of life,
The blackness of Hell and the Heaven's blue,
Strength and rapture and sword and flame
These are the golden gifts of Fame.

The Belfast conference

Manchester Courier and Lancashire General Advertiser, 31 January 1907

Sir,
With regard to the women's franchise controversy at the Belfast conference, may we point out that precisely the same adult suffrage amendment was passed at the same conference a year ago in London.[34] In spite of this in November last, the Textile Workers' Committee approached the Labour Party in the House of Commons, asking them to take immediate action with regard to women's suffrage. In reply the Labour whip said the Labour Party were very anxious to take immediate action in the matter, and promised to give the question a prominent place in the first ballots of next session.

The Press has given currency to the idea that the Labour Party in the House of Commons are in a peculiar position that they are obliged to take their orders from an annual conference. This would be a very unusual course in politics. If such a rule applied to the Liberal party, our enfranchisement would be secured, because shortly before the Liberal Government came into office, the National Liberal Federation passed a very definite and practical women's franchise resolution.

At the Belfast conference there was not one vote given or speech made against the enfranchisement of women, the whole discussion was one of methods and qualifications. Surely it is absurd to suppose that a conference of over three hundred people discussing this question for an hour, could possibly settle the final mode of attack and wording of a Bill to be brought forward in the House of Commons. We, as an organisation representing the expressed opinions of tens of thousands of working women, have confidence that the Labour Party will be true to their pledge given to us. We recognise that they

34 At the Labour Party Conference in Belfast in 1907, Labour Party leader Keir Hardie proposed that the party place women's suffrage as a central focus of their programme. There was an overwhelming vote against this proposal.

are suffering from a very natural annoyance at an election programme carried out by one women's organisation at Cockermouth and Huddersfield, but strongly disapproved by the Lancashire and Cheshire industrial women's franchise societies and trade unions, and actively opposed by them at Huddersfield.[35] Surely the Labour men will not allow the action of the irresponsible minority to outweigh the solid work and reasoned policy of the majority of a very great movement. Signed on behalf of the committees, Manchester and Salford Women's Trade and Labour Council; Lancashire and Cheshire Women's Suffrage Society; and Lancashire and Cheshire Women Textile and Other Workers' Representation committee.

Yours &c.,
Eva Gore-Booth,
Esther Roper,
Sarah Dickenson,
Sarah Reddish.
5, John Dalton Street, Manchester, Jan 30.

Women's suffrage

Manchester Guardian, 18 February 1907

Sir,
In answer to Miss Pankhurst's letter in your issue of to-day, will you allow me to explain some of the reasons why the women's industrial organisations here are in such strong disagreement with the policy of the Women's Political and Social Union in the by-elections?[36] The policy of the Union as carried out in Huddersfield and elsewhere is entirely negative. They are against the Liberals and for nobody. The comment of the elector is obvious: 'Those women don't seem to know what they want; anyway they don't know the difference between a Conservative and a Socialist.' We do not think that a negative policy can influence votes to any extent; it is simply a source of mingled amusement and exasperation to the electors.

Miss Pankhurst appeals to the example of the Irish party in defence of

35 In 1906 Christabel Pankhurst adopted a new WSPU election policy. Rather than supporting election candidates advocating suffrage for women, the WSPU actively campaigned against any government candidates. At the 1906 Cockermouth by-election the WSPU refused to pledge their support for the Labour candidate, Robert Smillie. A similar occurrence happened at the Huddersfield by-election months later. See Harold Smith, *The British Women's Suffrage Campaign 1866–1928* (2nd edn, London: Longman, 2009), p. 41.

36 In response to Christabel Pankhurst's letter; 'The enfranchisement of women', *Manchester Guardian* (15 Feb. 1907).

what she calls the policy of political independence. The Irish party showed their independence by running their own candidates and building up an independent party. In no case, even in England, do they pursue a negative policy; they have always thrown in their weight with one side or the other. This is the precise position taken up by the working women's organisations. At Wigan in the general election we put forward our own candidate on the women's franchise question alone, entirely independent of party. No subject but women's franchise was mentioned in Mr. Thorley Smith's election address, and the appeal to the working men was very strong, so that he came out second in a three cornered election with 2,205 votes on that one clear issue, placed before the electors by a band of women trade unionists and other women workers.

At Huddersfield, according to our principle of adopting an active policy, we had two courses before us (1) to run our own candidate; (2) to choose between the Liberal, the Conservative, or the Labour party. We decided for various reasons against running our own candidate. We could not support the Liberal party, because they are refusing to enfranchise us. Neither could we support the Conservatives, because they have been twenty years in power and have steadily refused to enfranchise us. We went and worked for the Labour party, because we had in our possession a letter from the Labour Whip saying that the 'party had already decided to give a Women's Suffrage Bill a prominent place in the earliest ballots of next session.'

Miss Pankhurst expresses herself as entirely satisfied with the results of the negative election policy. On the other hand, it is idle for us to blind our eyes to facts, and the repeated assurances of prominent Labour leaders that the bitterness caused by this policy was largely responsible for the Belfast defeat and the subsequent refusal of the Labour party to carry out their written pledge of October 25. We are not party women; we strongly condemn the action of the Labour party in thus going back on their word, but we also deeply deplore the irresponsibility of a few who have definitely decided to adopt a wholly wrecking and unconstructive policy, which, however showy it may be, never did, and never can, benefit any cause.

Yours, &c.,
Eva Gore-Booth.
Sarah Dickenson.
Manchester and Salford Women's Trades and Labour Council.

Women's suffrage

Manchester Guardian, 23 February 1907

Sir,

May I say in answer to Miss Sharp that I am not a party woman, and that, unlike herself, I have never belonged to any party in my life, because no party has ever made women's enfranchisement a party question.[37] Anybody who knows the organizations with which I am connected must be aware that their only object is the political and industrial emancipation of women. We worked for a Labour party candidate at Huddersfield for the first and only time because the Labour party had promised to ballot as a party for a Women's Suffrage Bill.

On the other hand, it must not be forgotten that while we were running an independent women's suffrage candidate at Wigan in the general election, at least two of the best-known officials of the Women's Social and Political Union were working for a party candidate.

But the real reason why working women in the North of England will never support Miss Sharp's policy in any numbers is because if they enter into an election they must have something to work for, not only someone to work against. 'Vote against Sherwell' was not an inspiring election cry.[38] I quite understand that those who have been strong partisans must feel that they have made a great step when they have decided to go against their own party. But the consciousness of independence and freedom from party trammels, and also the holding of large and enthusiastic meetings are experiences common to all women's suffrage enthusiasts for many years. From an election we want more definite results. That is why the Women's Textile Workers' Representation Committee have determined to bring into the elections not only an independent women's suffrage policy but an independent women's suffrage candidate.

In conclusion, may I point out that it was not I who accused Miss Sharp's colleagues of alienating the Labour party? I merely quoted the written and printed words of Mr. Keir Hardie, the leader of that party.

Yours, & c.,

Eva Gore-Booth.

37 Evelyn Sharp, member of the WSPU and a columnist for the *Manchester Guardian*. Sharp took exception to Gore-Booth's attack on the 'entirely negative' electioneering policy of the WSPU and responded with a letter; 'Women's suffrage', *Manchester Guardian* (22 Feb. 1907), p. 12.

38 Arthur Sherwell, Liberal candidate.

Woman suffrage

The Times, 12 March 1907

Sir,

In Mrs. Humphry Ward's letter in your Friday's issue she says that 'the argument that wages can be raised by the possession and use of the vote, however keenly it may appeal to the sympathies of those who realize something of the stress and strain of women's industrial life, can hardly convince anybody who had any knowledge at all of economic history and speculation.'[39] No facts are brought forward in proof of this somewhat sweeping assertion which it is hard to reconcile with our ordinary practical industrial experience.

Mrs. Ward's position is very much the same as the position of the great trade unions 50 years ago, when they were so determined that the use of the vote could not improve the industrial position of men. People learn by what they suffer, and those very trade unions whose members cried out 'No politics' at their meetings are now running their own candidates for Parliament and devoting large sums of money to secure special representation in the House of Commons. The Labour party in the present Parliament is the outward and visible sign of the working men's belief in the connexion between the franchise and their own industrial welfare; and the Labour party already claim to have repaid in various ways to the working men the large sums of money spent on the general election.

'The place to fight this out is at the ballot-box,' said the president of the Engineers' Union, to the society, after the failure of one of the last great strikes.

'Trade unionism is not enough to protect the interests of the workers, you must have Labour represented in Parliament,' is one of the commonplaces of modern Labour politics.

Indeed the idea which Mrs. Humphry Ward rejects so contemptuously is at all events the corner stone of the men's Labour movement.

The 'economic history' we would appeal to in support of our view of the franchise as an industrial force is the history of the gradual development of political activity in the Labour world, and the 'speculation' is the industrial faith of the majority of organized working people.

As to the undoubted fact that working women hold strong opinions as to the advisability of certain factory laws and restrictions based on sex, surely this is an argument for, not against, their enfranchisement. Industrial issues are very much involved, and it is often hard for the most intellectual person

39 Mrs Humphry Ward, a novelist and political activist who opposed enfranchisement for women. Ward announced the formation of the National Women's Anti-Suffrage League on 21 July 1908. In support of Lady Lovat she published 'The Anti-Suffragist', *Nineteenth Century and After* (Aug. 1908), pp. 343–52.

to frame a law that will be fair in all its dealings with the intricate and often confused issues involved. We do not undervalue general intelligence and kindly intentions. But surely all such legislation should be subjected to the practical technical criticisms of those who have to work under it. Lord Brassey, in speaking of the cotton trade lately in Manchester, praised the Lancashire textile workers, and said they were all excelled by none in the world in skill and intelligence. Mrs. Humphry Ward attributes a wonderful effect to our code of factory laws, but many of us who live in the north think that the reason why 'Lancashire and Yorkshire have grown to greatness and prosperity' is not to be found in any law or code of laws at all, but in the industry, skill, self-reliance, and courage of that great army of women workers who produce so large a proportion of the wealth of those countries.

Eva Gore-Booth

Manchester and Salford Women's Trade and Labour Council.

Women and politics; a reply

Nineteenth Century and After, March 1907

The writer of the article on 'Women and Politics,' in the February number of this Review, claims to speak for a 'great though silent multitude of women,' who shrink from their own enfranchisement because their already burdened strength would not be equal to the duties and responsibilities of voting at parliamentary elections.[40] She claims exemption as the special privilege of weakness, and a concession to what she conceives to be the retiring, unworldly nature of a large number of women. And if it is argued that, if women were enfranchised, no woman could possibly be forced to vote against her will, we are met with the unanswerable assertion that 'any woman could, of course, abstain from voting, but would this shelter her from being canvassed for her vote?' Alas, that no one tries to shelter us from canvassing other people, a far more unpleasant task!

As a simple matter of justice, it does not seem fair, or even reasonable, that the height of one personal intellectual ambition should be enforced as the legal limit of another person's activity. It may be that 'nuns fret not at their convent's narrow room;' but surely that is no reason why we should all be shut up in cells. I do not say there are not many who would prefer to have

40 The article to which Gore-Booth refers is Caroline E. Stephen, 'Women and Politics', *Nineteenth Century and After* (Feb. 1907). Stephen was a vocal anti-suffragist. In her article she claimed that it was unfair to campaign for female enfranchisement: if achieved, this would inflict 'a grave injustice' onto many women who did not want the responsibility of voting in general elections.

'protecting barriers between them and the rough outer world,' and who are only troubled and alienated by any appeal to their sympathies from the wider life of the nation, and the monotonous and involved issues of our present industrial struggle. The controversy is a very ancient one. There have been contemplative orders, and hermits, and enthusiasts, in all ages, who have consciously limited their sphere of action and shut out the business of the world, that they may the better pursue their own ideal of holiness and right living. I do not wish to undervalue the beauty of Miss Stephen's ideal of gentleness, piety, and devotion. But there is still a place in the world and a need for the sterner virtues, the more adventurous spirits. Honor, anger, valor, fire, 'were the qualities that Stevenson exulted over in his wife. She was, he says, steel-true and blade-straight.' And surely, even in this domesticated generation there are some whose hearts will respond to the ring of those brave words.

Patient Grizzel may have her admirers, but who would not prefer to *meet* Christina of Sweden, or even Catherine de Medicis, or *Maria* Theresa, or Queen Elizabeth, or any other of the great stateswomen of the past. Indeed, there are many people who would go so far *as* to feel more interest in Catherine of Russia, in spite of her indefensible moral attitude. Sir Walter Scott, with all his enchantments, could not make a heroine of the fair but passive Rowena. Who does not remember how, in their first youthful reading of *Ivanhoe*, they wept over the sorrows of the fierce Rebecca, and skipped the parts about the mild and amiable Saxon lady. And while there are lovers of romance and poetry still left among us, there will be many who find their ideal of a woman's character in the heroic soul and indomitable will of the *Antigone* of Sophocles. 'Yet remember in women, too, dwells the spirit of battle,' says Orestes in the play, and some of us are unregeneratedly [*sic*] proud that this is still one of the profound facts of human nature.

But there is another side to this question. However unpleasant or wearisome the idea of political activity may be, and probably is, to some women, as it is to some men, this distaste, founded on a peculiarity of temperament, must not blind our eyes to the wide and deep fines involved. In this work-a-day world, when women, as women, are in no way sheltered from the severity of the industrial struggle, it is idle to hold up to them as women an ideal of intellectual aloofness and seclusion. Miss Stephen speaks for those who 'dread the suffrage,' retiring, well-to-do people who fear change and exertion, and on whom the present industrial condition does not press heavily in practical life. Without answering her arguments in detail, I would appeal to her and others on behalf of those women who have something more serious to dread than the intellectual effort of voting at an election. Against the fastidious shrinking of the women who would feel their own enfranchisement too great a strain on their nerves, I would set the really urgent and practical suffering of another 'very great and very silent multitude,' the multitude of the women workers. The five millions of women who depend on their own exertions for their daily bread cannot afford the luxury of nun-like seclusion.

There is no possibility of shelter or protection for them. They are, whether they like it or no, in the thick of the world's battle, and the very disqualification that Miss Stephen welcomes as a kind of privilege is a source of disablement and extreme weakness in industrial warfare. It is a fact of common observation among people interested in economic questions, that in every trade where women are employed (with one or two local exceptions such as the weavers in Lancashire) they are paid at a much lower rate than men can earn for doing the same work, or work of a slightly different nature requiring the same amount of skill. This is no question of men doing more work than women, because this rule holds good of trades where piecework rates are given. Nowadays this question assumes a very serious aspect, because the old industrial conditions have changed, and it is a fact that, from one cause or another – the illness, drunkenness, or desertion, so lamentably common in our great towns – many and many a woman is forced into the – position of breadwinner for others besides herself. Now it is no easy matter to keep several people on what is considered a quite good wage for a woman, 15s. or 20s. a week; but when we come to the multitude of smaller and lesser skilled trades that swarm in all industrial centers, such as tailoring, fancy-box-making, shirt-making, folding and sewing, clay-pipe finishing, machining, and dozens of others, the rates in most cases are so low that the workers are never far removed from the starvation level, wages of 6s. or 7s. a week being the limit of the earnings of hundreds and thousands of women.

In the Potteries from 7s. to 10s. is a very usual wage for women, and the Cradley Heath chain makers earn as little as 5s. or 6s. a week. The condition of things that has brought such a large body of workers to the extremes of poverty has also had its effect upon the professional world. Roughly speaking, it may be said that the present position of women works out in the industrial market in this way. Educated and qualified women are able to earn as much as skilled working men. The salary of many high-school teachers is no larger than the male spinner's wage of 21s. a week, and often less than the wages of tailors' cutters. The wages of skilled working women at their best are about the same as those of unskilled working men, and at their worst a good deal lower; whilst the wages of the unskilled working women, varying as they do between 5s. and 10s. a week, have no parallel in the ranks of the inner workers. The only exception to this category are cases of special demands or special individual successes, as the special demand among sonic classes of women has enabled women doctors to keep up their fees, in face of the fact that public recognition and honor is almost exclusively a masculine monopoly.

The power of amusing and entertaining the public is so rare, and in such demand, that it is paid for irrespective of sex. Thus popular novelists, actresses, dancers, opera-singers, and music-hall artistes are able to command wholly exceptional industrial and economic conditions. But these are the small minority, the few who succeed.

The universal low rate of wages is not traceable to any lack of organising power amongst women. As elementary school teachers, men and women do the same work, their hours are the same, they have to go through the same training and pass the same examinations. Nobody even suggests that women are not as good teachers as men. And yet under every education committee in England there is a carefully calculated scale of salaries by which teachers of every grade are provided for; and in all cases, from pupil teachers up to headmasters and headmistresses, men are paid so much extra for being men, and women so much less for being women. And this in spite of the fact that there are 30,000 women members on the books of the National Union of Teachers. Again there are 96,000 women in the cotton trade unions, and yet Miss Collet (Board of Trade) gives the average of women's wages at 14s. a week, a rate practically unknown amongst skilled men workers. With unskilled men or women, owing to the comparative lack of value of the individual to the employer, Trade Unionism is never a great success, because people always know that, however large may be the number of the dissatisfied, the employer can easily fill their places at a moment's notice.

The laws of supply and demand go far to regulate, in normal cases, the rate of wages. But in the case of women's labour these natural economic forces have not had fair play. Artificial restrictions, that have narrowed down the sphere of women's activity, have resulted in the overcrowding of the few professions and trades open to them. Thus the natural supply of women's labour, arbitrarily forced into a few channels, has, in every case, largely exceeded the demand, with the inevitable consequence of a reduction of wages. When it is proposed to 'shelter' women from some sphere of paid activity, as, for instance, in the case of the barmaids, it should always be remembered that every protection of this kind increases the competition, and thereby lowers the rate of wages in the other trades where they are employed. But it is in those industries carried on under Government supervision that the direct industrial need of women for the franchise is perhaps most apparent. In the evidence before the Royal Commission to inquire into the wages of postal servants, it was very clearly shown how rigidly the principle of a sex basis for wages is adhered to, and how severely the able but unlucky women clerks in the Post Office are fined for not being men.

The post of woman clerk is the highest in the service open to women by public competition. Candidates for these appointments are examined in

English composition, geography, Latin, French, and German (two of these three); English, history, algebra, shorthand (two of these three). The minimum salary for this work is 55*l*. a year, the maximum 100*l*. The maximum salary of the second division of male clerks (lower grade) is 250*l*. whilst the higher grade of the second division of men are able to earn up to 350*l*. The disparity of salary holds good though men and women may be doing very similar, and in some cases identical, work.

Again, in the Pimlico Clothing Factory, 15s. per week is considered a good wage for a skilled woman worker, whilst, in answer to a question in the House of Commons last session, it was ascertained that 23s. per week is the lowest sum given to the most unskilled man labourer.

It is an undoubted advantage to choose your employers by popular election, and it is easy to see how the men are able to bring pressure through the House of Commons to secure a fair rate of wages for themselves in the Government factories; whilst the whole weight and prestige of the Government as the largest employer of labour in the country goes to set an example of underpayment and sub-contracting amongst women. The effects of this evil extend far beyond the 30,000 women actually employed by Government, and react on the whole of the labour market. All local bodies are bound to keep down their expenses as much as they can. Government low rates have given them reason and justification for adjusting their wages to the Government standard; and directly one private employer, seeking naturally to buy labour at the cheapest rate, begins to follow the public example, other employers are at once bound by the laws of competition, if they do not wish to be ruined, to reduce the expenses of production in the same way.

The whole question of the relation of industry and politics is too involved to enter into here. But it is nevertheless true that, whether we like it or not, since the days of Lord Shaftesbury's Factory Act we have seen a great change, and a gradual shifting of the ground on which industrial questions are fought out.[41] Technical difficulties relating to obscure processes in different trades are now national difficulties decided in Parliament. Working men have realised this, and the great sums of Trade Union money that in old days were kept exclusively for industrial objects, are now devoted unhesitatingly to parliamentary purposes. The employers also have their political organisations and methods of attack and defence. It is not to be wondered at if, in the clash of powerful conflicting interests, the grievances and claims of those millions of workers who are not allowed to make their voices heard should be ignored.

41 Anthony Ashley Cooper, 7th Earl of Shaftesbury, a Tory MP and leader of the Factory Reform Movement in the House of Commons. Shaftesbury supported the introduction of the Factory Act of 1847 which restricted women and children working in factories to a maximum working day of ten hours.

The late Lord Salisbury said that the condition of the working women of England was a 'blot and a menace to our civilisation.' Miss Stephen, on the other hand, congratulates women on possessing the key to men's reverence. It may be that she is right, that men reverence 'sheltered' women; but this I do know, that there are many hundreds of thousands of half-starved wage-earning women who are seeking yet in vain the key to men's justice.

The women's suffrage movement among trade unionists[42]

Lancashire and Cheshire Women Textile and other Workers Representation Committee, July, 1904

Fellow Workers. During the last few years the need of political power for the defence of the workers has been felt by every section of the labour world. Among the men the growing sense of the importance of this question has resulted in the formation of the Labour Representation Committee with the object of gaining direct Parliamentary Representation for the already enfranchised working men. Meanwhile the position of the unenfranchised working women, who are by their voteless condition shut out from all political influence, is becoming daily more precarious. They cannot hope to hold their own in industrial matters, where their interests may clash with those of their enfranchised fellow-workers or employers.

The one all-absorbing and vital political question for labouring women is to force an entrance into the ranks of responsible citizens, in whose hands lie the solution of the problems which are at present convulsing the industrial world.

In view of the complicated state of modern politics, and the mass of conflicting interests, the conclusion has been forced on those of the textile workers who have been working unceasingly in past years to secure the votes for women, that what is urgently needed is that they should send their own nominee to the House of Commons, pledged to work in season and out of season to secure the enfranchisement of the women workers of the country. A committee has been formed of women in the trade from various Lancashire and Cheshire towns, whose duties are (i) to select a suitable and zealous candidate, and (ii) to collect and be responsible for the spending of £500, which is the amount absolutely necessary for one candidate's election expenses. A balance sheet will be submitted to each town subscribing.

Anyone who wishes to better the position of her fellow-workers, and

42 Originally published in Brougham Villiers (ed.), *The Case for Women's Suffrage* (London: T. Fisher Unwin, 1907). The volume includes contributions by Keir Hardie, Millicent Garrett Fawcett, Christabel Pankhurst, Emmeline Pankhurst, Charlotte Despard and Mabel Atkinson.

the thousands of women outside the ranks of the skilled cotton operatives, who are being overworked and underpaid, should remember that political enfranchisement must precede industrial emancipation, and that the political disabilities of women have done incalculable harm, by cheapening their labour and lowering their position in the industrial world.

What Lancashire and Cheshire Women think to-day England will do to-morrow.

Yours fraternally,
The Committee: Sarah Dickinson, Selina Cooper, Sarah Reddish,
Esther Roper,
Eva Gore-Booth.

So ran the manifesto of the Lancashire Textile Workers in 1904, when, after years of patient work on the old lines, they came to the conclusion it was time to adopt newer and more forcible methods. In 1901 and 1902, petitions signed by 67,000 textile workers had been taken to the House of Commons by deputations of women employed in the trade, deputations of enthusiastic workers who could not believe in the indifference of the well-to-do world to the claims of unenfranchised wage-earners, and came back to Lancashire sadder and wiser women. A good deal of stir had begun inside the Cotton Unions, and, in various towns, votes were taken as to whether Women's Suffrage was to be a Trade Union question. It was felt by the women that the Cotton Unions should make a practical effort to secure the benefits of political enfranchisement for their 96,000 women members. It is noteworthy that, wherever this vote was taken (Bolton, Clitheroe, Colne, Nelson, Hyde, Haslingden), majorities of over 1,000 decided in favour of immediate action, and there were but few dissentients. The Burnley Weavers' Union specially instructed their Committee to bring the matter before the Trade Congress.

For many years, enthusiastic meetings and demonstrations had been held in all the great Northern towns and centers of industry. The matter was one very familiar to the working people. For it will easily be understood that a grievance that is hardly felt by women of money, and position, and influence, may become well-nigh intolerable in its practical bearing on the lives of those who are industrially an independent force, and politically the helpless competitive system. As time went on, and as the political power to which they were admitted in 1868 assumed more and more importance in the minds of working men, the question of the women's enfranchisement became more and more prominent amongst working people.

The climate of thought in England is not tropical. We are not subject to sudden cataclysms and earthquakes and cyclones. We pride ourselves on the absence of sudden and violent Revolutions, and on the slow growth and gradual fruition of our political ideas. During the last fifty years a great change has taken place in the minds of the more progressive working people, a change that was observed in the making by some of our more long-sighted politicians, notably Lord Randolph Churchill. 'The Labour community is carrying on at the present day a very significant and instructive struggle ... It realises that it now possesses political power to such an extent as to make it independent of either party in the State; the struggle it is carrying on is one ... for the practical utilisation in its own interest of the great political power it has acquired. The Labour interest is now seeking to do for itself what the landed interest and the manufacturing interest did for themselves.... We are now come, or are coming fast, to a time when Labour Laws will be made by the Labour interest for the advantage of Labour. The regulation of all the conditions of Labour by the State controlled and guided by the Labour vote appears to be the ideal aimed at.'[43]

Strangely enough, when the Labour Representation movement began to make itself felt in Lancashire, it was by the votes of women that it stood or fell. For there is one thing that women are usually allowed to vote, and that is their money (unless, of course, it is taken from them by the autocratic will of Parliament). Those progressive people who would deny votes to women for the statesman-like reason that they were supposed to vote Conservative in the London County Council election, would do well to place beside this hypothesis the incontestable fact that before the Cotton Unions could subscribe £900 a year to the Labour Representation Committee, and before a candidate could be run and his salary paid as Labour candidate for Clitheroe, a ballot had to be taken of the women who far outnumbered the men in the Unions. The women did not grudge their money for Labour Representation, and at the time Mr. Shackleton himself pointed out how large a part of the burden fell on the shoulders of these unrepresented workers. When Mr. Shackleton was returned unopposed for Parliament in 1902, 5,500 women trade unionists in the Clitheroe division petitioned him to bring forward and press on the Women's Franchise question so that they too might share in the benefits of Parliamentary Representation. Then came a period of apathy on the men's part to the women's claims, a period during which the unpleasant truth gradually soaked into these women's minds that those who had been their equals and comrades in industry, had passed wholly out of their sphere of influence, and were as deaf to the appeals of the politically helpless as were the 'princes' in whom the working men of old time 'put their trust.' Among the Lancashire working women there is a strong inherent sense of commercial honesty and personal independence, and it is no exaggeration to say that among the more

43 *Lord Randolph Churchill*, by Winston S. Churchill.

progressive workers there has grown up a deep feeling of bitterness and disappointment, a feeling which culminated this year when the Labour Party, led away by a theoretic inclination for the very stale red-herring of immediate complete and entire adult suffrage, refused to fulfill their written pledge and press forward a measure for the enfranchisement of women. It is apparently a very easy matter for men to muddle the issues with high-sounding protests against the terms of their own enfranchisement, a measure by which they do not themselves refuse to profit. Their position is absolutely indefensible. They have built up the whole of the Labour Party on what they are pleased to call a property qualification, a qualification that gives votes to houses and lodgings, not to flesh and blood, a qualification that, according to their own often repeated statements, no democratic person could accept, or even compromise with as a temporary installment of justice. If what these Labour men say is true, then it follows that the Labour Party is built in sin and founded on unrighteousness. If, on the other hand, what they say is not true, comment is surely superfluous. So far we have not observed amongst them any disinclination to use their own votes; nor do they even shrink from representing in Parliament thousands of arrogant enfranchised houses and politically emancipated lodgings without an effort to enfranchise poor enslaved flesh and blood. In fact, they have eaten their cake, and enjoyed and digested it; it is only when a hungry beggar asks for a slice that they find out that it is poisonous.

The working women had answered to the Labour appeal; they had supported with their votes and money the new movement for what they had fondly dreamt was the representation of working people, and now they understand that those workers who are most in need of the protection of the franchise are still to be outside the pale. They do not undervalue the kind offices of individual friends, but it is a Party they supported in the time of need generously, and on a large scale, and it is to that Party that they appeal. 'Be just before you are generous,' is the simplest appeal in the world, and surely it is the fundamental basis of all right doing and political honesty.

It is easy to blame the Lancashire women for their reckless confidence. Certainly they scattered their bread on the waters with a princely disregard of consequences. There is a curious power in this world, the working of which we all of us feel instinctively, the force that Emerson called 'The Law of Compensation.' As much as you give out you draw in; what you pay the price for you earn.

Again, according to the philosopher, 'There is no god dare wrong a worm'; 'Power to him who power exerts.' The justice inherent in things always in the end asserts itself. If you cast your bread upon the waters, you shall most certainly find it again. But alas! that all these good hopes are only fulfilled 'after many days.' Surely the working women of England have paid the price of political emancipation over and over again! It is no mere insignificant statistical fact that these millions of workers live laborious days of poverty-stricken and upright independence, and produce by their labour so large a proportion of the material wealth of the country. Here is a force that must in the end be reckoned with. 'Power to him who power exerts.' We know of course that it is only a question of time; that there is no government in the world, however autocratic, that can in the end keep five million of its responsible workers out of all political rights whatsoever. 'Great is the truth and shall prevail,' says Coventry Patmore; 'when no man care if it prevail or no.' This, at all events, does not seem likely, for the working women's representatives get more and more urgent in their appeal. Every month and every year that this measure of justice is denied to us, the condition of the working women becomes more and more desperately difficult. In fact, we are bound to care more, not less; and this for a very simple reason: Every year that goes by sees the slow development of the tendency to nationalise all industrial questions. Political and industrial issues can be no longer disentangled. The very trade unions that forty years ago shouted down their more progressive members with cries of 'No politics,' are now running candidates of their own at elections. Industrial questions are gradually shifting their ground and becoming political questions, and, as this happens, the working women are more and more beginning to feel the disadvantage of not being able to enter the sphere where questions connected with their bread and butter and hours of labour and weekly income are fought out.

Anybody who studies with an impartial mind the industrial position of women in England must surely come to the conclusion that there is something radically wrong and unfair in that position. To begin with, wherever they are employed, with few exceptions, they are paid at lower rates than could be offered to men, and their work is restricted to the poorer and lesser paid parts of those trades. In fact, they get all the kicks and none of the halfpence. And when they have gone home with the wretched 7s. or 10s. which they are forced by hunger to accept for wages, they are bitterly reproached by men for undercutting, and for 'having a lower standard of comfort than men.' This low rate of wages among women is, of course, not due to original sin, or to some strange sex aberration which makes them unable to understand the usefulness of money. Neither is it due to want of organisation. There are thirty thousand women members of the National Union of Teachers, and yet, under every Education Committee in England, there is a reasoned-out scale by which every girl pupil-teacher is paid less than every boy pupil-teacher. And this principle is carried through right up to the head-masters and head-mistresses, irrespective of qualifications or training. Even in the cotton trade, which is, I suppose, the best trade for women in England, and where there are ninety-six thousand women in the Unions, the average is quoted by Miss

Collet (Board of Trade) as 14s. a week, a sum far below the wage of even an unskilled labouring man. In this connection the experiences of the men are somewhat illuminating. During the last sixty years, Mr. Sidney Webb points out, the wages of working men have increased by 50 to 100 per cent., whilst the wages of working women have remained stationary or grown less.[44] Since their enfranchisement the agricultural labourers have been able to increase their wages largely, in spite of the fact of their Union falling to pieces.

The present tendency of Government to involve itself more and more in direct industrial enterprise has caused great enthusiasm among progressive politicians, who welcome it as a way of securing good industrial conditions for thousands of working men. Beyond this again, as Mr. Sidney Buxton pointed out last year, the Government, as the biggest employer of labour in the country, exerts a very great, if indirect, influence on the whole labour market. Thus the men workers are in the position, not only of having their biggest employers elected by public election, but one of the great forces that react on the male labour market is also at the mercy of public election. The Trade Unionist politicians were right to congratulate themselves. They are able to keep up the rate by unceasing vigilance and application of political pressure in the House of Commons, with the result that Government is a model employer for men. But not for women.

In the evidence before the Royal Commission on the Wages of Postal Servants, it is very clearly shown how the Government wages for clerks are lower than those given by other employers. Lancashire employers are able to give weavers the same rate whether they are men or women, but everywhere in Government employment wages are carefully calculated according to sex and not work. So that, in the Pimlico Clothing Factory, the skilled woman worker gets an average of 15s. a week, while no man labourer gets less than 23s. The Government mechanically gets its female labour as cheap as it can, unchecked by political considerations. The example spreads to public boards and private employers, who cannot afford to be undercut by one another, and thus their political weakness first depresses the wages of thirty thousand women, and then, through them, depresses the standard of women's remuneration all over the country.

I once heard a learned Professor assert with beautiful simplicity to a crowd of tailoresses [*sic*] earning about 7s. a week each, 'your low wages are due to yourselves. Perhaps, someday, if you work very well, you may be worth 14s. a week.' This was, no doubt, a comforting doctrine for the Professor, whose

44 Sidney James Webb, Baron Passfield (1859–1947), social reformer and politician. Along with his wife, Beatrice, they 'were among the most prominent and productive pioneers of social science in Britain'. John Davis, 'Webb (Martha) Beatrice', *Oxford Dictionary of National Biography* (Oxford: Oxford University Press, 2008).

salary could not have been less than £400 a year. But I think most people must realise nowadays that your payment is not so much for what you do, and its value to the world, but for what you are. The parlor-maid may be a better worker and a more valuable servant than the footman, but he gets higher wages for being a man.

Social barriers are growing less and less amongst men, since the working men have become the ruling political force in the nation, but still, you will find that a Foreign Office clerk, without any Trade Union at all, is able to get a higher rate of pay for his work than an engine-driver or skilled engineer, however valuable his services may be to the community, and in spite of the fact that he belongs to one of the strongest Trade Unions in England. A Government clerk may be a very valuable member of society, but the proportion of his salary to the wages of the engineer is hardly accounted for by a correspondingly lower rate of utility in the engineer's highly skilled work. If you want to increase a person's industrial value, you must increase his importance, you must make it worth somebody's while to please him. A hundred years ago the working men had no political importance, and they suffered from fining and low wages exactly in the same way that women do now. It is not one party or the other party that has improved their position, it is the pressure of the working men's votes on all parties. In practical life, these things are not doubted by working men. 'My opinion should have some weight,' said the Weavers' Secretary at a Lancashire Trade Council meeting, 'for I represent by far the biggest Union in the town.' 'What's the good of your Union?' said the Engineers' Secretary, 'why, it's all women; mine mayn't be large, but, at all events, they're voters.' One vote more or less may be a matter of small importance, but an organised industrial Union of voters is a weapon of real political force, and the possession of this weapon makes society very sensitive to the grievances and claims of the band of workers who are so well equipped. There are some people nowadays who still see the world in water-tight compartments. They will tell you that industrial results are due to economic causes, political results to political causes, social results to social causes. But we have seen a war a great political event that was undoubtedly the result of economic causes; we have watched every Factory Act that passes the House of Commons become more and more fraught with consequences to the industrial lives of women; we have seen indeed the gradual widening of the social chasm between the men who have emerged into political power and position, and their women comrades who are still washing dishes and cooking dinners. And we realise that all the arbitrary limits between the political and industrial world are only limits of the imagination. They do not, in fact, exist. Few people will deny that money is power; the discovery of this generation of English people, the discovery which is gradually working its way into the minds of the poor, is that power is money. Industry, society, politics, there is one magic key that opens the doors of prosperity in all the worlds, and that key is power. In the case of the working women, they have to break through a vicious circle of political disability working itself out in industrial weakness and social impotence. There are many causes given for the low rates earned by women, and doubtless many factors go to decide the vexed question of wages; but I venture to assert that there is not one of them that you can impartially examine and not find that it is but a new form behind which masquerades the ancient and ubiquitous fact of the political subjection of women. It is unjust of people to reproach us with the fact that we are people of one idea. Because it is not we who follow the idea, but the idea that follows us. It dogs our footsteps wherever we go. In the mills and workshops, it regulates our lives and depresses our wages. It holds the constant threat of abolition and starvation over the heads of those who work in their own homes. It follows us on to the pit brow, and waits for us vindictively on all licensed premises, even showing its face in the harmless railway restaurants, and scaring the poor manageress who has attained a position of responsibility through hard work. It walks abroad among the variety artistes, and thinks nothing of proposing that ten thousand people should be turned out of their work because, contrary to human experience in that profession, they might break their legs. It arranges the education of children, and the hours of labour the poor woman can never escape from the harassing experiences of her subjection.

As regards the more educated classes, it stands as a lion in the path between them and the higher branches of the professions, or the recognition of their abilities.

But it must never be forgotten that the sufferings of the poor are the most urgent sufferings because, though the opportunities of educated women may be stunted, and their careers spoilt and their ambitions thwarted, they can at least possess their own souls' light, and, like Wordsworth's 'forgotten taper,' to the last 'drive from themselves all frightful gloom,' whilst the very life itself of the poor is stunted by that terrible struggle with poverty that leaves them, too often, neither leisure nor energy nor physical strength enough for self-development or education or the joy of life.

This is what the Trade Union women realized when, in 1904, the Women's Textile Committee and the Manchester and Salford Women's Trade and Labour Council laid their plans for the General Election. The need of strong and effective action had been brought home to them by recent events. They decided on a wholly new policy. They were not Party women; they would take up and use the only real political weapon that it is in the power of women to use at present. They would lead the way in a new warfare; they would choose a constituency and fight an election in the interests of the working women's franchise against all comers. They would appeal from party feeling to the industrial knowledge and sympathy of working women. People said they would not get five votes. They said then they would do with four, and always they hoped that this election would be the beginning of a new movement. They would try again and again, no matter how few votes they got, and then other women would join in the fray, and by degrees the idea would spread and Women's Suffrage candidates would be brought forward in all the by-elections.

When they went to Wigan the expected happened, and they were repudiated by all parties and sections.

They appealed from the parties and organisations to the men at the mills and factories and workshops and mines and football fields. After a fortnight's work of twenty women and three men, unsupported by parties or organisations, a vote of 2,200 was gained by Mr. Thorley Smith, the women's candidate, and he was second at the poll in a three-cornered fight. Thus our appeal is from the Government to the nation, from the House of Commons to the electors, from the rich to the poor.

The rich may say that 'women should stay at home and cook the dinner'; the poor know that if women did stay at home there would often be no dinner to cook. The Government says, 'We have nothing to do with you, you can bring no pressure to bear on us'; but the nation says, 'We feel the pressure of your poverty.' In spite of the deafness and blindness of the political parties to human needs, working men everywhere are beginning to realise that the exclusion from all political rights of a body of 5,000,000 workers is not only a source of industrial weakness and poverty to themselves, but a danger to the whole of the world of labouring people.

Women's suffrage and the French Revolution

The Academy, 14 September 1907

Sir,

In vindication of Madame Roland's memory, may I point out that her deeds were better than her words.[45] In words she may have advocated the subjection of women, but it is amusing to find that a woman who said her sex should have no power save that of passive 'inspiration' – whatever 'passive' inspiration may be – should have herself gone twice to the National Assembly and each time accepted their invitation to share the honours of the sitting. (See Sergent

45 Marie-Jeanne Phlippon Roland was an influential writer and political activist during the era of the French Revolution. She directed her husband's political activities after he was appointed as minister of the interior. She was arrested and guillotined during the Reign of Terror in 1793.

Marceau's Memoirs.) Indeed, her personal active interference in public affairs is notorious. Her stormy, showy, ambitious career gave in every possible way the lie to the adulatory and servile words quoted by Mr. Rivers, which no doubt served their purpose in her intercourse with the vainest of all people, political leaders. You might just as well take them seriously as you would take seriously the flowery and even groveling dedications to noble lords and patrons which you will find signed by very proud names in the literature of the past. These people did not really think themselves inferior. They were practical writers, and wanted to please the powerful.

Madame Roland did not really think herself inferior, but she was a practical politician, and understood that, as Blaker says, 'sneaking submission knows how to live.' But even if, in the exigencies of political diplomacy, she may have swerved for once from the narrow road of noble independence and pride, is there any politician in the world who has not done so? If so, let him cast the first stone at her.

The record of a life can surely not be cancelled by the writing of one unworthy letter. And women Suffragists may be forgiven for thinking that the deeds and sufferings of her adventurous political career speak louder and are more impressive than the cringing tone and manifestly insincere attitude of self-depreciation which she once adopted, no doubt to disarm jealousy, or for what she considered a sound reason of expediency. In that supreme moment, when she met her death on the scaffold (mainly as the result of the political action of another woman – Charlotte Corday), the thought uppermost in, her mind seems to have been the thought of Liberty.[46] It remains for this generation to say that it was 'for men only.'

Eva Gore-Booth.

Women's suffrage and the French Revolution

The Academy, 28 September 1907

Sir,

May I explain to Mr. Rivers that when I connected the execution of the Girondists with Charlotte Corday's action I did not the least mean to imply that anyone ever dreamt of accusing Mme. Roland of complicity with Charlotte Corday.[47] I had in mind the famous exclamation attributed to Vergniaud

46 Charlotte Corday assassinated the Jacobin leader, Jean-Paul Marat, for which she was guillotined in July 1793.

47 A man named John Rivers wrote to *The Academy* responding to Gore-Booth's letter of the previous week. In it he disagreed that Madame Roland met her death due to the

when he heard of her execution, 'She has killed us, but she has taught us how to die.' Popular feeling was inflamed against the Girondists by the death of Marat, not because of any suspected complicity with Charlotte Corday, but because Charlotte Corday was one of their followers, and, coming straight from Barbaroux and the other deputies at Caen, was undeniably inspired by hatred of their great enemy, Marat, who had determined on their destruction.

As for the formal accusation of plotting against the unity and indivisibility of the Republic, and the liberty and safety of the nation, one would not have thought that anyone in these days disputed the fact that these accusations were a mere formula used by people of any party or creed to cover their real motives when they wanted to denounce their own particular enemies. As to Mme. Roland herself, I said the servile words quoted by Mr. Rivers were obviously insincere, because they do not stand the only real test of sincerity, the test of life and action. I cordially agree with Mr. Rivers that Mme. Roland made a pleasant picture sitting in silence at her desk or doing embroidery and listening to other people talking. But such occupations and realisations are surely common to everybody, whether they are politically ambitious or not. Even Mr. Balfour plays golf. But I admit that Mme. Roland's power of silence is indeed a rare gift among politicians. And at that very desk in, what she says, Mont was pleased to call her 'boudoir,' important political documents were written, one of which is described as a letter 'to the Pope,' in the name of the Executive Council of France, 'drawn up' by the hand of a woman.

That Mme. Roland was a shrinking, feminine woman, keeping out of politics unless she was thrust into them, I do not think is at all an accurate description of her, who was a Republican before the Revolution, and a political enthusiast who believed that 'everything becomes a noble spirit.' Nor can one imagine that she would have sat in the National Assembly even for one day and made eloquent speeches if she really and truly considered 'any public rôle idle, however insignificant as unbecoming to her sex.'

What she said in her defence – 'I never passed the limits imposed on me by my sex.' –needs no comment, as it was manifestly in answer to the repeated criticisms of her enemies, who did not share Mr. Rivers's view of her retiring nature, but were much irritated by her interference in public affairs. Danton, asking the Assembly from the Tribune whether it would not be well to find out the opinion of Mme. Roland, would no doubt have been surprised at such an estimate of her character.

Mme. Roland's real opinion of herself and her abilities was not at all a humble one. In her memoirs she describes herself quite simply as being of a gentle disposition, a strong mind, a solid understanding, an extremely affectionate

---

actions of Charlotte Corday. John Rivers, 'Women's Suffrage and the French Revolution, *The Academy* (12 Sept. 1908), pp. 932–3.

heart and an exterior which announced these qualities. She explains how she was engrossed with public affairs, how she considered women who were everlastingly preoccupied with their households, were insupportable. Her reasons for her own political activity were very simple and beautiful 'I loved my country, I was an enthusiast in the cause of liberty.' She was very candid in her memoirs and she lets us see the pettier side of her nature in sentences like this: 'Never did I feel the slightest temptation to become one day an author. I perceived very early that a woman who gains this title loses far more than she wins. The men do not love her, the women criticise her.'

In face of such sentences it is not decrying Mme. Roland's character to say she was not free from the last infirmity of noble minds, and loved personal success so that she would sometimes sacrifice absolute sincerity to the practical necessity of pleasing men. And here and there in Mme. Roland's otherwise noble character we find traces of a weakness common enough in all times and lands among the successful members of an oppressed class, nation or sex. Moses was a great hero because, although he was adopted by an Egyptian Princess, he was true to his own people. I fear that most people who receive honour at Pharaoh's Court are quite ready to fight on the side of the Egyptians. Thus one would not be the least surprised to hear to-morrow that Catharine of Russia, Queen Elizabeth, Maria Theresa, Joan of Arc, Christina of Sweden, or Queen Victoria had said that 'Women's sphere is the home,' and they should never 'meddle in politics' just as I was not the least surprised to hear a working man, who had become a Cabinet Minister, gravely tell a deputation of weavers that politics were no use to working people. This chasm between personal practice and precept, applied to other people of your own sex or class, you may call hard names if you like, or else you may simply say it is one of the tendencies of that dreadful thing called human nature which you 'always get down to in the end.'

Eva Gore-Booth.[48]

The employment of barmaids

Manchester Guardian, 28 November and *The Times*, 29 November 1907

Sir,

As there has been some misunderstanding with regard to the scope and effect of the proposals that have been made for the abolition of barmaids, will you allow us to make the following statements?

48 Rivers responded to this letter in the following edition of the periodical, noting 'I regret that my view of the French Revolution in general, and of the life and character of Mme. Roland in particular, does not meet with Miss Gore-Booth's approval.' John Rivers, 'Women's Suffrage and the French Revolution', *The Academy* (5 Oct. 1907), p. 996.

It has been repeatedly said that there are only 27,000 barmaids. These figures are wholly inadequate. It must be remembered that 'barmaid' is taken to include all women employed wholly or in part in the sale or supply of intoxicating liquor in or about a bar, bar parlour, or compartment on licensed premises. The publicans' wives and daughters are provided for by a separate clause, which puts their employment at the discretion of the licensing justices. There are over 122,000 licensed houses in Great Britain. Omitting 22,000 beerhouses as not employing women, of the remaining 100,000 houses some do not employ any barmaid; on the other hand, there are a very large proportion of licensed premises, such as restaurants, hotels, railway restaurants, and so on, that employ from four to ten women, or even up to twenty, in the sale of alcoholic liquor. Taking the lowest average possible to common-sense, one barmaid to each house, there are at least 100,000 barmaids.

The proposals as formulated in the Employment of Barmaids, 1906, are twofold: – (1) To prevent women in future entering the career of barmaid: (2) to force all present barmaids to register themselves and to give power to the licensing justices to forbid the employment of the publican's wife or daughter.

It has been asserted that this second proposal would not interfere with the present employment of barmaids. The action of the Glasgow magistrates in 1891 and 1903, when they mistakenly thought they had the power which this Act would confer, leaves no doubt as to what the barmaids would have to expect in many parts of the country. It is unthinkable that the livelihood of 100,000 people should depend on the fluctuating opinions and theories of men who are not infallible, but, like the rest of us, sometimes fair and reasonable, and who in no other case are allowed this supreme power over the lives and incomes of those employees who have not in any way broken this law.

But even if this second proposal is, because of its entirely obvious cruelty, for the moment not insisted on, there remains the chief proposal – to prevent women in future entering the barmaid's trade. This proposal, with its apparent consideration for the workers' interest, is founded on an extraordinary misunderstanding of the daily lives and difficulties of working women and the fierceness of competition among them. Any experienced person knows that being out of work is the worst industrial misfortune and the most severe temptation to evil known amongst these millions of women whose daily bread depends on their daily labour. Those who know the endless struggle and difficulty to get work and the lowness of wages in those very restricted fields of industry into which women have made their way must view with something very like terror the abolition of a trade that has hitherto absorbed female labour on such a large scale, for they realise that it must lead to sharper competition, lower wages, less work, and more poverty for the already overburdened mass of less skilled women workers. People say that the barmaid's trade is not an ideal one.

Is any working women's trade ideal from the standard of the leisured class? Everyone would like the conditions to be as good as possible for barmaids, but in this world, where it is so very hard to make your living, to remove a possible source of honest income from 100,000 people and throw them back into an already overcrowded labour market to cut one another's throats in the industrial struggle is surely an action indefensible on the grounds of reason or expediency.

We appeal to those who condemn the barmaid's work to pause and consider the alternatives, the crushing competition in the more skilled trades, the terrible conditions in the unskilled and sweated trades, and the worst industrial and moral misfortune of all – the calamity of unemployment.

Yours &c.,

Eva Gore-Booth, Women's Trade and Labour Council.

Esther Roper.

Sarah Dickenson, Machine and Electric Workers' Union.

Barmaids' Political Defence League,

19 Buckingham Street, Strand, London.

Woman's vote; from Hull to House of Commons

Daily News, 25 January 1908

Sir,

As a mover of the Women's Franchise amendment at the Labour Party's conference at Hull, may I explain the circumstances under which this amendment was defeated.[49]

By a singularly unfortunate arrangement on the part of the authorities, the Women's Suffrage and Adult Suffrage motions, instead of being complementary to one another were all pitted against one another, so that one could not vote for the working women's franchise without voting against adult suffrage. Considering that the conference professed themselves by large votes in favour of the complete political, economic, and social equality of the sexes, it can hardly be said that the conference 'shelved' the women's suffrage question.

Mr. Quelch's annual protest against the cunning devices of his enemies of the upper classes (who pay 4s. a week rent for their houses) affects in no way the present situation.[50] The Women Textile Workers' Representation Committee

49 The Labour Party Conference in Hull in January 1908 was attended by four hundred delegates. The Women's Labour League was admitted to the conference. A motion was put forward to extend suffrage to women on the same terms as it was granted to men; the motion was rejected. An amendment was carried in favour of full adult suffrage.

50 Henry Quelch, socialist and writer.

and the Manchester and Salford Women's Trade Council last October requested the Labour Party to move an amendment to the Address 'regretting the omission of the claims of women to the franchise from the King's Speech' and we have been supported in this policy by Women's Cooperative Guild and many trade unions and Labour societies.

We are pressing and urging the Labour Party to move an amendment to the Address, and we fail to see how any resolution passed against any Bill 'limited' or 'unlimited' could in any way affect the matter. We expect that all honest Adult Suffragists, as well as Women's Suffragists, in the House of Commons, will welcome this solution of the difficulty and support a policy which should be acceptable to both sides.

Yours, etc.,
Eva Gore-Booth.
Women's Trade and Labour Council,
5, John Dalton Street,
Manchester.

Barmaids' Political Defence League

Letter to Members of Parliament

Women's Trade and Labour Council Office.
5, John Dalton Street,
Manchester.
March 12, 1908.

Sir,
May we draw your attention to Clause 20 (1) in the Licensing Bill.

'Licensing Justices may attach to the renewal of an on-licence any condition which they think fit to attach in respect of any of the following matters:

(a) The employment of women ... on the licensed premises';

It will be seen that should this Clause pass into law every one of the 100,000 Barmaids and women assistants at present employed on licensed premises will find her employment suddenly placed in an entirely precarious and insecure position, irrespective of any good conduct or misconduct on her part. The magistrates are in fact to be given absolute irresponsible power to do what 'they think fit' with regard to the means of livelihood of 100,000 people; they will judge, condemn, and punish without the necessity for a shred of evidence, a prosecution, or even so much as an accusation against the person whose livelihood is in question. We are not bringing any accusation against magistrates as a body, but we protest it is against the most simple and elementary principles of justice, and the legal spirit that has hitherto inspired the British Constitution to give any set of men power to deprive another set of their employment without any question of crime or even misconduct. As to the practical result of this Clause we quote from a pamphlet published by the Society working for the Abolition of Barmaids: 'A movement was carried through early in 1904 for bringing the subject of barmaids' employment before the magistrates' benches throughout the country with a view to its abolition. As a result of this movement, twenty-one benches of justices expressed their official disapproval of the practice of employing barmaids, while none approved it.'

The Abolitionists are in fact quite sure of the practical support of the magistrates. And we have experience to go upon. In 1903, the Glasgow magistrates through a misconception of the law exceeded their powers, and prohibited the employment of Barmaids. Those who believe that if the magistrates had these powers they would use them in a discriminating and impartial manner, making a difference between the good and bad licensed houses, should consider the action of the Glasgow Licensing Justices on this occasion. They did not try to distinguish between good and bad. What they did was to abolish the employment of every Barmaid in every public-house in the area under their jurisdiction in an absolutely sweeping and wholesale way.

Those who study these facts will realise that this Clause in the Licensing Bill means in plain practical English the Abolition of all Barmaids. In view of the undoubted industrial calamity and the distress that must be caused by the loss of the means of subsistence of 100,000 people, and of the wretched alternatives to which everybody knows they must be reduced, may we urge upon you to oppose this Clause of the Licensing Bill by every means in your power at the very earliest possible opportunity in the House of Commons.

We remain,
Yours faithfully,
Eva Gore-Booth, Sarah Dickenson, Esther Roper. (Hon. Secs.)

The Licensing Bill and barmaids

Manchester Guardian, 4 April 1908

Sir,
In your leading article of April 1 the members of the barmaids' deputation to the Home Secretary are accused of 'wild speaking' because they said (1) That the Licensing Bill (clause 20) interfered with the employment of women; (2) that the clause meant the abolition of the barmaids' calling; (3) that the barmaids were to be got rid of without any trial. Will you allow us to explain our reasons for these statements?

1. Under clause 20 of the Licensing Bill the magistrates will have power to attach any conditions they think fit to the employment of barmaids. If this clause is not meant to interfere with the employment of barmaids, what is it meant for?
2. It may be said that, technically speaking, this clause turns nobody out of work. It only gives somebody else the power to do so. In the same sense you might say that Joan of Arc was not burnt by the Church. The Church was only responsible for her imprisonment and for handing her over to the secular arm for punishment. The State took the hint and did the rest, and the Church was not guilty of innocent blood. But such hair-splitting does not save the Bishop of Blauvais from the blame of posterity. The State does not directly turn out the barmaids, but it shifts the responsibility on to the shoulders of a body of men whom it can trust to carry out its desire. Members of the Government have openly said that they wanted to abolish barmaids; why pretend that they do not? As to the magistrates we have experience to go upon. In 1904 an inquiry was made by abolitionists among the magistrates' benches on the subject of the employment of barmaids 'with a view to its abolition.' As the result of this movement, 21 benches of justices expressed their official disapproval of the practice of employing barmaids, while none approved it (official report). When the Glasgow magistrates thought they had the power that would be conferred on them by this clause they turned out all the barmaids from public houses without any distinction or humane consideration. Now it would take a very extreme fanatic to think there was not one respectable public house or one respectable barmaid in the whole of Glasgow.
3. What we said was that the barmaids would find themselves judged, condemned, and punished without a shred of evidence, a hearing, or even an accusation against their character. This was what happened in Glasgow, and everyone knows that many magistrates are pledged to the abolition of the barmaids as a matter of abstract principle without any reference to the claims of individuals. We have no accusation against the magistrates; they are doubtless worthy and honourable people, but we protest that being an excellent citizen is not in itself a qualification for the exercise of absolute authority over other people's livelihoods and financial interests.

The Home Secretary at any rate did not suggest the rather futile argument that there was no danger in giving these powers to the magistrates, because if they had them they would not use them. As to their 'not regarding it as an encouragement to licensing justices to limit the employment of barmaids,' one would think the magistrates would be puzzled to find another meaning for the action of the Home Secretary, which is the direct outcome of his promise to the deputation which waited on him last year to ask him to shut the trade to women.

We want to say a few words about barmaids themselves. Let no one imagine they do not feel something more than the loss of income with which they are threatened. The bitter insult of the assumption on which such legislation rests, the insidious attack on their prestige among fellow-workers have been most deeply felt and resented by a great many respectable and hard-working women. The very fact that their characters form a common topic for public discussion and argument is a very real grievance to those who have done nothing to deserve the slur that is being cast on them as people who are either too weak to insist on proper behaviour among their customers or too easy to wish for it.

Yours, &c.,
Eva Gore-Booth.
Esther Roper.

[We must confess an inclination to extend the charge of 'wild speaking' to part of our respondents' present restatement of their case: 'The State does not directly turn out the barmaids, but it shifts the responsibility on to the shoulders of a body of men whom it can trust to carry out its desire.' We should rather conjecture that the Government, as a whole, desires not to turn out the barmaids, and that it trusts the average licensing bench not to want to turn out either. When our correspondents say that 'members of the Government have openly said that they wanted to abolish barmaids,' is it suggested that this has been declared by any responsible member of the Government to be the Government's real intention? If not, it is a pity that a loose and equivocal phrase, from which many readers are likely to derive an incorrect impression, should have been used. Ed. 'Guard.']

The Licensing Bill and barmaids

Manchester Guardian, 6 April 1908

Sir,

So long as the Government succeed in abolishing barmaids, it does not seem to us a very important matter whether they proclaim their intention before carrying it out. However, in the 'Times' of February 27, 1907, will be found an open declaration of the Government's policy. It will be seen that the present clause of the Licensing Bill is even stronger and more drastic than the measure asked for by the Society for the Abolition of Barmaids. The following is the extract from the 'Times' and the justification of our 'wild speaking.'

'A deputation organised by the Joint Committee on the Employment of Barmaids waited upon the Home Secretary yesterday to urge upon him the desirability of including in the Government Licensing Bill some provisions for dealing with the employment of women and girls in bars of licensed premises. The deputation having been introduced by the Bishop of Southwark, Mrs. Ramsay MacDonald, Miss M.E. Docuers, Lady MacDougal, Miss Turner (Salvation Army), and Mr. Gooch, M.P., advocated legislation on the lines of the bill introduced by Mr. Gooch last session. The object of this bill is to prohibit the entrance of girls and women into the calling after a given date, whilst licensing those already employed to continue their work, allowing the wives and daughters of publicans to serve, and giving power to the licensing justices to forbid the employment of barmaids on any particular licensed premises. Mr. Gladstone, in reply, expressed himself in general agreement with the object and arguments of the deputation. He was convinced that the employment of girls and women in bars was open to all the objections and condemnations raised, on grounds of health, economic disadvantages, temperance, and morals, and promised to deal with the matter in the forthcoming Licensing Bill.' The 'Times,' February 27, 1907.

We fear there is not much room for conjecture as to the Government's intentions. Yours, &c.,

Eva Gore-Booth.

Esther Roper.

Cringlebrook, Victoria Park, Manchester.

[Have not our correspondents forgotten a more recent piece of evidence as to the Government's intentions – the declaration of the Home Secretary on November 28, 1907, to a deputation of which both our correspondents were reported as members, that 'any Government and any parliament should think twice and thrice before they did anything which materially interfered with the employment of women'; that the Government 'had no intention of putting an end to the occupation of women on licensed premises'; and that the Government 'realised that any drastic provisions to check, or diminish, or put an end to the employment of women on licensed premises might have a result far more immediately disastrous than any mischiefs which can be shown under the present system'? Our report of the interview went on to say that 'Miss Gore-Booth thanked Mr. Gladstone for his kind reassuring words.' Ed. 'Guard.']

Barmaids' Defence League

Manchester Courier and Lancashire General Advertiser, 1 May 1908

Sir,

With the present threat of the abolition of their employment hanging over the heads of women employed on licensed premises, may we appeal to the public for help for the Barmaids' Political Defence League? Besides holding meetings and taking two deputations of barmaids to the Home Secretary to protest against the calamity that loss of work would mean to any or all these hundred thousand women, the league took an active role in the North-West Manchester election. A coach was hired and driven all day and half the night by a lady who volunteered her services. Crowds were collected and speeches were made constantly from the top of the coach by the honorary officials and members of the league, who explained the position of the barmaids to enormous and sympathetic crowds. Literature was sent into every house in the constituency, and the matter was thoroughly well ventilated and put before the electors, with a result of sympathy and support from electors which was almost startling. It will be allowed that the work of the league in spreading information and rousing public sympathy was efficiently carried out.

But, before the fight is over, much more of the same kind of work must be done. Those who wish to abolish barmaids are trying to work quietly, and get the clause passed while no one realises what is happening. We, on the other hand, are sure that the public are sorry for the barmaids, and think it a shame that they should be turned out. Therefore we want the fullest publicity; we want to drag the whole question out into the light, and rouse the public in time to save the barmaids from being abolished quietly and secretly in a subclause of a clause of the Licensing Bill.

The barmaids are poor, wage-earning, hard-working women. They have not the leisure to conduct the fight themselves; people who are working all day long cannot enter into the struggle of a contested election. The agitation is, therefore, mainly carried on by volunteers, women who are ready to fight for other women. And the barmaids are poor; they cannot afford to pay for the expenses involved in a political campaign.

The league is entirely supported by contributions from barmaids and a few donations sent in response to a public appeal. In the North-West Manchester election it was found simple enough to gain the sympathy and votes of the electors on the barmaid question for the only candidate who was in favour of complete freedom, political and industrial, for women.[51] But the danger

51 In 1908 Winston Churchill was appointed to cabinet for the first time as President of the Board of Trade. Under the law of the time, a newly appointed cabinet minister had to resign his seat and stand for re-election. On his appointment, Churchill was forced

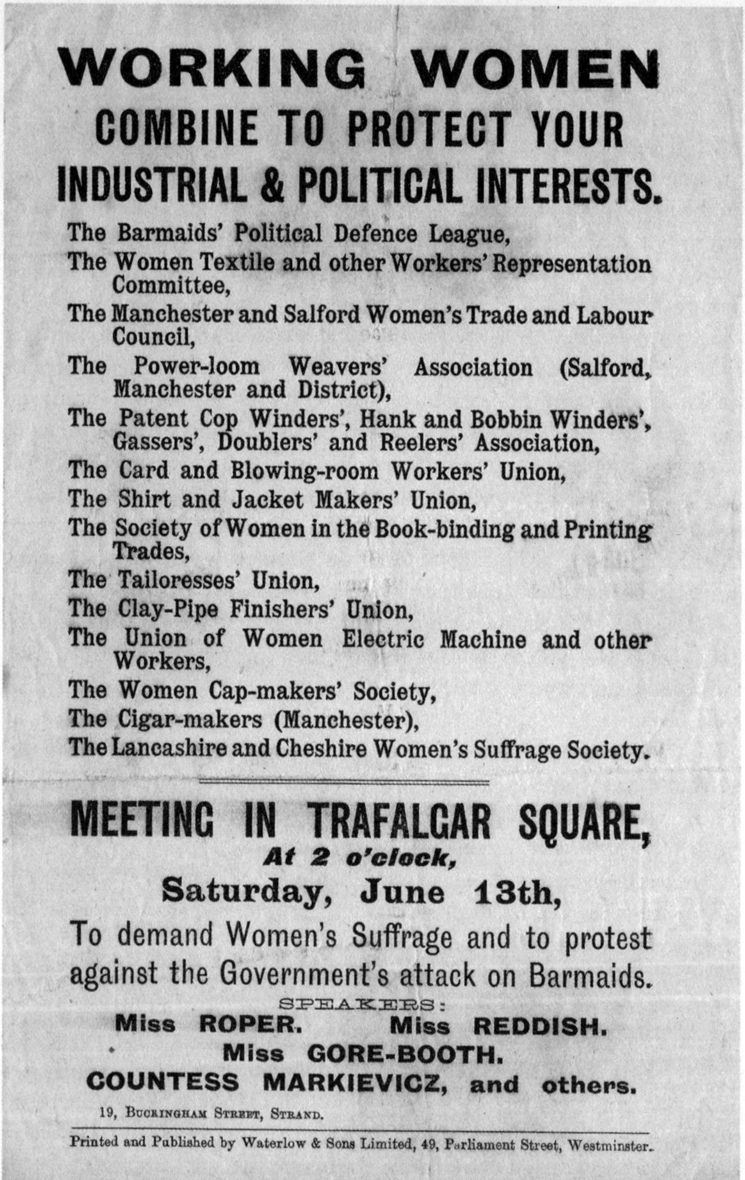

WORKING WOMEN

COMBINE TO PROTECT YOUR INDUSTRIAL & POLITICAL INTERESTS.

The Barmaids' Political Defence League,
The Women Textile and other Workers' Representation Committee,
The Manchester and Salford Women's Trade and Labour Council,
The Power-loom Weavers' Association (Salford, Manchester and District),
The Patent Cop Winders', Hank and Bobbin Winders', Gassers', Doublers' and Reelers' Association,
The Card and Blowing-room Workers' Union,
The Shirt and Jacket Makers' Union,
The Society of Women in the Book-binding and Printing Trades,
The Tailoresses' Union,
The Clay-Pipe Finishers' Union,
The Union of Women Electric Machine and other Workers,
The Women Cap-makers' Society,
The Cigar-makers (Manchester),
The Lancashire and Cheshire Women's Suffrage Society.

MEETING IN TRAFALGAR SQUARE,

At 2 o'clock,

Saturday, June 13th,

To demand Women's Suffrage and to protest against the Government's attack on Barmaids.

SPEAKERS:

Miss ROPER. Miss REDDISH.
Miss GORE-BOOTH.
COUNTESS MARKIEVICZ, and others.

19, Buckingham Street, Strand.

Printed and Published by Waterlow & Sons Limited, 49, Parliament Street, Westminster.

Figure 6 Poster announcing a mass demonstration on 13 June 1908 in support of barmaids

still menaces us, and to carry on this campaign at bye-elections and London meetings funds are urgently needed. Will anybody who is interested in the barmaids' fate send a contribution to the funds of the league?

Yours &c.,

Eva Gore-Booth, Esther Roper, Hon. Secs.

Women's Trade and Labour Council office,

5, John Dalton Street, Manchester, April 30.

Barmaids' Defence League

Manchester Courier and Lancashire General Advertiser, 21 July 1908

Sir,

May we draw attention to the allocation of time to be given to the discussion on the remaining stages of the Licensing Bill? Two days are to be given to the debate of the Clauses 18, 19, and 20. This includes such important subjects as Sunday closing, the exclusion of children from licensed premises, and the giving of Licensing Justices the power to attach any conditions they think fit in respect of seven matters embodied in various sub-clauses.

The first of one of these sub-clauses deals with the employment of barmaids, and thus it follows that the fate of the hundreds of thousands of women employed in any capacity on licensed premises will be decided by the House of Commons as an insignificant and minor detail unworthy of prolonged discussion, or even of being mentioned by the Prime Minister in his enumeration of the different points to be discussed. Anyone who thinks the industrial ruin of so large a class of workers a matter not lightly and carelessly to be decided on will sympathise with working women's demand for the defence of the franchise, the possession of which would make such treatment as impossible for them to receive as it would be now in the case of working men. To be turned out of their work is the worst industrial calamity that can happen to anyone. To be turned out in multitudes through no industrial cause, but through the direct, hurried, and contemptuous action of the Government as what no man has to bear, but is obviously the direct result of the political exclusion of women.

Yours, &c.,

Eva Gore-Booth, Esther Roper.

---

to resign as MP for Manchester North-West and stand for re-election in the same constituency. Churchill had become a central figure in the barmaid issue. The only candidate to support the cause of the barmaids was the Conservative candidate William Joynson-Hicks and he was backed by the Barmaids' Defence League. Gore-Booth launched an intense campaign in support of Joynson-Hicks; against all odds he won the election and Churchill was ousted from his Manchester constituency and temporarily out of politics. See Figure 6 which announced a further demonstration on 13 June 1908.

Women and the suffrage; a reply to Lady Lovat and Mrs. Humphry Ward

Nineteenth Century and After, September 1908

In the July number of this Review, Lady Lovat quotes various writers, ancient and modern, in support of her skillful defence of what she calls the old-fashioned side of the Women's Suffrage question.[52] And indeed she has a wide range of choice, for probably there have been more theories advanced on this and kindred subjects than on any other in the world. To judge from folklore sayings and proverbs alone, women seem to have been the victims from the earliest times of the first crude efforts of the savage intelligence to make a large generalisation out of a small and very narrow experience, and of the fatal facility that first enabled people to conceive of a great multitude of various human beings as one simple abstract personality, governed by easily attainable mechanical laws and called Woman. 'Woman' in the abstract has indeed been the 'Aunt Sally' of the world's childhood, pelted by many missiles.

And age does not seem to stale the infinite variety of this exercise of the imagination. Since the days of Solomon's Proverbs to those of Ruskin's *Sesame and Lilies* these generalisations have been and still are the stock in trade of imaginative writers. Time has brought one change, however. In old days the subject was considered a simple one, and certain well-worn maxims were thought sufficient to meet all needs. Now everybody who is anybody is bound to have a different interpretation of 'Woman' and her place in the scheme of things. Thus to those who take such speculation and theorising seriously, the world is full of confusion and contradiction on this subject. But to anyone who is interested in the growth of thought and understanding among individuals or nations, the interest is mainly a psychological one, for it may be safely presumed that these theories reveal more of the mental caliber and nature of the theorist than of the unfortunate human beings who, since the world began, have been ceaselessly vivisected, with varying degrees of success, by everybody who is trying to be intellectual. Thus, when Solomon says that women's value is above rubies, whilst the Kaffirs decree a wife is worth ten cows, we are not so much struck with the truth or wisdom of either pronouncement as with the difference of the point of view between Solomon and the Kaffirs. And when we hear that some Eastern nations believe women to have no souls, whilst a council of the Church decided by a small majority that they may really hope for a humble share of man's privilege of immortality, a woman may perhaps

52 The article in question is: A. M. Lovat, 'Women and Suffrage', *Nineteenth Century and After* (Jul. 1908), pp. 64–73. In it Lady Lovat asserts that 'women would lose infinitely more than they gain by parliamentary enfranchisement'.

be pardoned if she thinks less of her own no doubt remote chances of salvation, than of that precious and enlightening sense of humor that seems to have been denied to so many learned and law-making assemblies of men. Souls are not thought so important in this generation, and we are allowed to possess them in peace; but when some men say women have inferior brain capacity, we can always comfort ourselves with the thought that so little do they believe this that they find it necessary to protect themselves legally and artificially from women's competition. As Mill said long ago, you do not have to make laws to prevent people without muscles being blacksmiths. The people who want to restrict women because they are inferior mentally are really those who believe no such comfortable doctrine, but are, in simple English, afraid of their competition. Just in the same way the men Trade Unionists who say women can never be as skilled as men, say it because they do not want them to be employed, whilst the masters who say they are neater and quicker are those who want to employ them. Schopenhauer, no doubt, had some good spiteful human reason for proclaiming that women were an 'undersized, broad-hipped, narrow-shouldered, short-legged race.' Lady Lovat may argue as the result of her experience that women's souls abhor the abstract. Against that dictum we must set the undoubted fact that some university professors affirm that women excel in mathematics and logic. But all these are simply matters of personal opinion and belief. It is certainly amusing to see that Solomon was more progressive in his views about women than Ruskin, and that his ideal lady could at all events speak with her enemy in the gate, while Ruskin's could only sit at home and arrange things, 'entering into no contest.' But these theories are too vague and random to be of any value except as they throw light on the character of the theorist. Ruskin's ideal of women was, of course, sentimental and impossible. 'What woman is there in the world, be she never so old-fashioned, who enters into no contest? And may Heaven defend us from people, men or women, who spend their lives in 'sweet ordering, arrangement, decision.' Indeed, it is that sort of thing that makes a great many of the world's worst fights, because, however ideal and womanly it may be, other people will not always stand being 'sweetly ordered and arranged.' Lady Lovat quotes Ruskin's saying that women should rule and not fight, and one is tempted to think how strange it was that Ruskin did not seem to know that, everywhere and in every sphere, physical, mental and spiritual, it is the hardest fighters who, in the end, rule, and must rule. Because the hardest fighters are simply those who are most in touch with the Divine Force.

As a refutation of the claims of women to political life, Lady Lovat quotes a very romantic speech of Portia's in the *Merchant of Venice*; but it is difficult to see that it has any bearing on the case, as even men have belittled themselves and called women their 'ladies and queens,' and other extravagant things, on similar occasions, when they were in love (especially in plays), and the rhapsodies of these ecstatic moments cannot be seriously debated as a basis for legislation.

In discussing the question of Women's Suffrage, it is not with Ruskin's Early Victorian ladies we have to deal, 'women who enter into no contest,' 'who are protected from all danger and temptation,' 'whose great function is praise.' Nor is it with the heroines of history or fiction. Portia would have been most certainly just as blatantly in love with Bassanio if she had been a plural voter or a member of the Council of Ten. The serious charge brought by Lady Lovat against modern women is that they are, like Shylock, insisting on their pound of flesh (the suffrage) and willing to pay a great price for it, the sacrifice of their present ideal position of influence and happiness, and especially their 'highest prerogative of educating children.' Also, oddly enough, she points to the medical profession as one of the splendid privileges due to the old order, a profession that has been forced open within the last fifty years by the unremitting and much opposed efforts of Women's Rights women. As to the Education question, Lady Lovat quotes Plato in support of the view that to draw out the Divine Image in a human being is a greater work than the making of a beautiful statue. This is no doubt true, but there are few who would venture to assert that a man or woman of genius, an artist or a thinker, could not be as useful an instrument to awaken the Divine Image in another person's soul as an ordinary domestic person immersed in trivialities. Influence is no question of time. No women of any class really educate their children, they provide teachers for them or send them to school. Their own influence is confined for the most part to what they are and what they know the real source of all power. If anyone wishes to have influence, let her not forget Maeterlinck's fable about the man in the lighthouse, who gave away the oil in his lamp to the poor, and thus lost his power to save great ships from destruction. And it is one of the enduring happiness's of life that everything we learn and every strength we gain makes our lamp burn brighter and thus enables us to help other people. If women are going to be great educators they must not shut themselves out from any human activity, for all inventive and creative activity is not only good for men, it is good in itself: in fact, it is the condition of full human development and right doing. The idea that one power crowds out another in the human mind is surely based on a very false conception of the working of the laws that make evolution by a gradual widening of mental outlook, and the receding of horizons before a determined effort of the will. Women who willfully detach themselves from the energies and struggle and fight of the living world around them to pursue an ideal of the gracious seclusion of the family, and the sanctifying influence of passive existence, will too soon find that they have nothing to give their children, and that the young will go elsewhere for the generous inspirations of courage and heroic living. But nobody can escape the battle in the end. And nobody should.

'The garden and the cloister' (quoted from John Morley by Lady Lovat) are no doubt necessary and delightful for us all, but so are 'the dust and burning sun and shouting of the days of conflict' to every human being, man or woman, who believes in the high destinies of the human soul, but more especially to those who would be the means to awaken the Divine Image of heroism and power and hardly won wisdom in the soul of a child.

Love, Lady Lovat says, is the special prerogative of woman. But there are no special prerogatives. The world as God made it is free to us all. It is useless to tell women that the active life is the special prerogative of men; as useless as it would be to tell men that love is the special prerogative of women. These things are not so, simply because the Power that made the world did not make them so. In every contest since the beginning of history women have struggled and fought and suffered. In every great national movement, where those movements have come into the sphere of bloodshed and death, as in France, in Russia, in Italy, women have suffered and struggled and died in large numbers, and proved to the world a thousand times over by their deeds their possession of the heroic qualities of the active life.

As to love, surely it is a universal principle not to be narrowed down to any one section of humanity. Those who do not believe in the special prerogatives of sex can comfort themselves with the comprehensiveness of the ancient conception 'God is Love.' Lady Lovat allows that 'Love is the fulfilling of the law'; love is 'the only, the eternal foundation of the training of our race to humanity.' If these things are true, surely this Divine Principle, being her special prerogative, would prove nothing but the superiority of the spiritually enlightened woman's soul over the darkened soul of man. But this is not so; the sun shines on the good and evil and on the just and the unjust, and the great vivifying and purifying forces are the birthright of every human soul, irrespective of all accidents or 'prerogatives of sex.'

Now as to the present happy position and influence of women which is said to be threatened by their approaching emancipation. Lady Lovat thinks that what she considers the present ideal relations of men and women, and especially the private influence of women over men, are in danger. By all means lest we render unto Caesar the things that are Caesar's, but it is as well to remember that there are some things that are outside his jurisdiction. And our private relations to one another are not settled by the House of Commons, but by the deep working laws of our own natures. Lady Lovat thinks that men should reverence women and keep them on pedestals far removed from the contests and difficulties that go to make up life. But women are human beings, and not meant to live on pedestals; their place is in the midst of contest and difficulty, and there are some of us, men as well as women, who do not admire or revere or even tolerate the type of character produced by this St. Simeon Stylites attitude towards life, in man or woman. Anyhow, the doubtful privilege of a column is only possible for the favoured few of a leisured class. The mass of the female population have no time to dream of the very brittle influence which they are supposed to hide under a veil of weakness. They are not posing on pedestals, they are struggling and fighting through their lives, trying to earn their livings honestly and hold their heads above water in that world where there is no pity nor help for those who go under. If I venture to doubt Lady Lovat's generalisations of the great influence of politics on private life, I am also very far from sharing her opinion of the powerlessness of political forces to work out their results in the nearly allied world of industry. These forces are not so helpless as politicians would have us believe.

If Gladstone really thought that the 'terrible woes of this darkened world' could not be effectually dealt with by the State, why did he elect to spend his whole life as a statesman? Surely, in face of the many importunate problems that surround us, if he had really seen a more excellent way he would have taken it. Let us take courage. The Franchise is not a new and insidious method of overturning the lives and traditions and sentiments of the rich. It is not even a question of one political party against another. It is simply a means by which the mass of women in the professional and industrial worlds can defend their interests and their right to work. Practically, working men do not, as Lady Lovat thinks, contest inch by inch the idea that piece-work rates should be the same for women as for men, because they do not like being undercut, and the sympathy of working men for the suffrage movement is very much on the grounds of the indirect influence of political status on wages. They realise in a way that the leisured classes cannot, that it is the present outcast position of working women that forces them to pull down the rate for everybody by accepting such very low pay. And, apart even from wages, never before in the history of this country have women had more need of political power to protect themselves against injurious legislation. At this moment over 100,000 women are being threatened by Parliament with the abolition of their employment. We are told that a day will be given by the Government to the discussion of clause 20 of the Licensing Bill. It is by a sub-clause of this clause that the fate of these women will be decided. It seems that in a couple of hours' talk by unrepresentative legislators they will be deprived of their occupations, their incomes and their reputations, through no fault of their own, but simply because of their helpless unenfranchised position.

The President of the Local Government Board says openly that one of the great remedies for unemployment is the enormous curtailing of the work of women. This ingenious method of robbing Peter to pay Paul has no doubt its charm for a Government that depends for its very existence on Paul's votes, and has nothing to hope for or fear from Peter. Attempts are being constantly made to turn women out of their trades and livelihoods, whether it is the barmaids, the circus riders and acrobats, the pitbrow women, the married women of Lancashire (73,000), the married teachers, or the Cradley Heath chainmakers. Sometimes these things are done quietly, as in the case of trades like printers or florists. Here a simple application of the Factory Acts is enough to turn the women out of work, as the minute regulation of hours is quite impossible where the manipulation of perishable flowers is concerned, or where work has to be done at night, as in the printing trade.

The outlook is dark indeed for all working women, because the women's labour market is already overcrowded, and every displacement of labour simply adds to the competition in the lesser skilled trades, and, by making the supply of workers so much greater than the demand, brings down the already low rate of wages for all concerned. The franchise is a crying need to guard the interests of those who have to take part in the industrial struggle. It is easy to laugh at unmarried women for being faddists, and married women for being influenced by their husbands, but whether they are faddists or weak-minded people, if they are workers, they have need of the protection of the franchise, for they will have to fight their way in the world. Men are not disfranchised because they are faddists or because their wives influence them unduly. And Lady Lovat herself insists strongly on the tremendous influence of women over their husbands. Indeed, if a free mind were to be a qualification for voting, one imagines the electorate of this country would be reduced by a considerable number. In considering the question of adult suffrage, Lady Lovat says there are more women than men in this country. At first sight it seems a very odd contention to an ordinary mind used to democratic theories, that because a section of the populace are in the majority, that is a reason why they should not be represented in Parliament. The idea that all women would band together and vote against all men is absurd and inconceivable. Even in the present struggle for the suffrage, which you would think has been made entirely a sex question, by the exclusion of a whole sex, men and women have not been driven into opposite camps. There are plenty of men on the women's side, and doubtless many women who see no evil in the present state of things. The sentimental and speculative aspect of this subject has had its full share of attention; but one would like to appeal to those intellectual people to whom the franchise is naturally rather a matter for philosophic discussion than a vital need, as it is to the working classes, for the sake of theories and traditions, not to range themselves on the side of those forces that are making life so difficult and so squalid to millions of the poorest workers of this country.

In the course of a speech made by Mrs. Humphry Ward in proposing the 'Anti-Suffrage' Manifesto and published in the August number of this Review, she added the weight of her testimony to Lady Lovat's, and attacked the position of those who claim that the possession of the franchise by women will result in industrial equality between the sexes – a very practical gain, as it will work itself out in adjustment of wages to natural ability and capacity irrespective of the present artificial sex handicap. Everybody who is interested in labour questions from the workers' point of view, be they men or women, must wish for this result. Because infallibly and mechanically, by the same law through which women are underpaid, men are undercut, and the lamentations of trade unionists on the competition of what they call 'unfair' female labour are the commonplace of labour meetings and reports. Mrs. Ward indeed allows that women's wages are generally lower than men's, but, like Lady Lovat, she clings to the belief that political enfranchisement would be powerless to affect this economic evil, which is caused, according to her view, by five different reasons.

(1) 'There are more women than men.' While not disputing this statement as applied to generalities, it is impossible to deny that as far as the labour market is concerned truth lies in its exact opposite. There are far more men than women competing. And this is because at present so large a proportion of women's work is absorbed in the unpaid activities of married home life. People are apt to think that there are more women than men in industrial life because the competition for work is doubtless fiercer among women; but it must not be forgotten that this added competition is easily accounted for by the fact that women's labour is forced into a few restricted channels, because so many trades are artificially shut to them, while with men 'la carrière est ouverte aux talents' – 'the world of technical education and work is free to their competing abilities.'

(2) Mrs. Ward gives as one of the most important causes of women's low wages the backwardness of the organisation of women's labour. Now this is a confusion of cause and effect. Women's labour is badly organised in those trades where they are doing little-skilled and low-paid work. The same rule applies to men. This is no sex question. Any trade union secretary will tell you that it is almost impossible to organize men in an unskilled trade. Where men or women are doing highly skilled work they are usually well organized into strong societies. But women's societies are fewer and poorer then men's, because they are as yet excluded from the better and more highly paid parts of most trades. And where they are well organized the trade unions are crippled by their want of political status. It is not only the unskilled unorganized among women that do not get industrial justice. For instance, in every town in England the teachers employed in the elementary schools are paid by a fixed rate from the head master and the head mistress down to the pupil teachers,

in which it is carefully calculated, that, training and qualifications and hours being equal, a man gets so much more for being a man and a woman so much less for being a woman. And yet there are 30,000 women in the National Union of Teachers. Mrs. Ward considers low wages among unskilled men to be a proof that wages are not influenced by political forces. Nobody denies that among men skilled labour is, roughly speaking, highly paid and unskilled labour poorly paid. But the work of the political forces is to be found in the different payment obtained for the same or equally skilled quality of work by men and women. If the average of agricultural labourers' wages is low at present, it must be remembered that in 1872, 8s. to 12s. a week was the amount given by their leader, Joseph Arch, as a fair estimate of their ordinary earnings. After their enfranchisement their trade union, with the uncertainty attending all such organizations, gradually ceased to exist. The unquestioned improvement of the minimum 8s. to 15s. in the face of the industrial disaster like the collapse of the union can be traced to their improved political status. Just as so much of the amelioration of their social and industrial condition can be traced to the possession of what Joseph Arch called the 'political telephone of the vote' and in the working of those political forces in which he had such faith. Indeed, nowadays there is growing to be little doubt among trade union men as to the value of votes in the industrial world, and to this slow-growing conviction is due the modern development of the labour representation movement. Experience teaches, and it is noteworthy that the trade unions that fifty years ago received all suggestions of political action with cries of 'No politics' are now running their own special candidates for Parliament.

(3) Mrs. Ward says that marriage and the expectation of marriage affect the industrial value of woman's work unfavourably. There are two sides of this question. In trades and professions where women are stopped working on their marriage, and married women are not employed, such regulation no doubt takes the quality of stability from their work, and tends to the employment of very young girls, which is always a misfortune from an industrial point of view. But there are very few of these trades, and married women are specially useful members of trade unions (if their husbands are earning), as in times of industrial dispute they have something to fall back upon and this gives them independence and power. The same applies to their husbands, and many a man has been tided over times of struggle or unemployment through the help of his wife's earnings. Two incomes in a family lend security to the industrial position of its members.

(4) 'There is far more competition for men's labour' is Mrs. Ward's fourth reason for women's low wages. This is rather a cryptic saying, as competition varies so much in different trades, and in cases where it is a real factor it will usually be found to be due to easily removed causes, such as either the debar-

ring of women from technical training, or the old but fast dying tradition of women's inferiority as workers or human beings – a tradition which made it a few years ago, a distinct and marked descent in the social scale to employ a maid instead of a footman. So we come back again to the real root of all the economic mischief, the need of the mass of women for political life and energy to widen out this industrial outlook and strengthen their earning power.

(5) 'Men are stronger than women.' This is a generalization elusive and hard to test, for to measure strength is indeed a difficult task. The bearing of this statement on the problem of women's low piecework rates is hard to understand, because the strength of the worker, though it may affect the amount of his or her output, could in no way affect the value of the work per piece, provided that it is up to the standard of excellence required. If the employer's standard is not satisfied, the solution is easy; the incompetent worker, man or woman, is dismissed to make room for a more competent one. But, apart from the industrial point of view, this question of relative strength, and especially of physical strength, is a very important one, for here we come to what I would venture with all respect to call the root error of the 'Anti-Suffragists.' 'The modern State,' says Mrs. Humphry Ward, 'depends for its very existence on the physical force of men.' Now you might say with equal obviousness, 'the modern State depends for its very existence on the physical capacity of women.' Without going so far as the Christian Scientists, who tell us that matter does not exist, surely such a material point of view is hard to maintain in face of the accumulated thought and energy and will that has built up the difference between our own imperfect civilisation and the rude and brutal life-customs of a savage tribe.

Meanwhile we all know practically in our own lives that it is on our wills and our presence of mind, and not our fists, that we rely in any extremity. If it had not been so, the world might have been ruled by lions and tigers or even elephants. But the human will has conquered and rules over physical force, and the divine power of thought is the greatest power in the world. It is not even true that physical force, ruled and organized by will, controls our affairs. We do not choose our Prime Ministers and Governments because they know how to lead armies and win battles, and when our successful Generals come home from the war we may load them with honours and applause, but we do not entrust to them the destinies of the nation. The days of Napoleon and Julius Caesar and Alexander the Great have passed, and all who found their claims to rule on their superior physical force are building on the sand, and their claims must in the course of evolution crumble away into the same ruin, as the claims of the lion or the pack of wolves to terrorise the human race. We all know in our individual lives that willpower is no respecter of sex; women have the same capacity for strength as men; where they have not developed it as individuals or nations, they have been subjected through the hypnotism of fear and ignorance, and the penalties of such subjection are surely leading the way to a higher wisdom. It is wide of the mark to talk about the trained and specialised knowledge that men alone are able to get as a reason for women's low wages. With equal truth it might have been said when women were not allowed to qualify as doctors that it was impossible for them to practice because men alone were able to get trained in specialised knowledge. Monopolies in technical education are most certainly doomed, and even now this barrier is breaking down on all sides, and it will not be disputed that women are getting trained in specialised knowledge and qualifications in many and various fields. In politics, Mrs. Ward says, 'women are debarred by their mere sex from that practical political experience which is at least always open to men.' And she does not see the curious working of the law of reaction or compensation by which it happens that this very debarring and shutting out of women from politics has given them a practical experience almost unknown, among men. Just as, in a nation, want of success in war means concentration of national energy on questions of Army Reform, so the long political struggle against fearful odds, though it may have developed a tendency to disorder and mafficking among the less sober, has also given unique opportunities for political experience, and developed political faculties among the working and organizing part of the female population, faculties that cannot be crushed by physical force, for they are the stuff of which the political will to live is made, and as such they are a necessary part of the national life and carry in their very existence the complete assurance of their final victory.

In answer to the claim that it is inexpedient that what Mrs. Humphry Ward calls hygienic regulations should be imposed on the work of women, especially married women, without their own consent, she uses the curious argument that though the women concerned have no voice in the matter, other women who have neither worked in mills themselves nor been chosen by the workers to represent them have been consulted in the making of these laws. And here many of us would emphatically protest against the extraordinary theory that in political matters, while men must choose their own representatives, any woman can choose herself to represent all other women and no questions will be asked. The Anti-Suffrage Manifesto speaks of 'representative women' being brought into closer touch with Government departments. But, as far as Government is concerned, there are no representative women. There are no women with a mandate from their fellows to represent them in political matters. Whilst women have no votes they cannot have accredited political representatives. Labour questions are involved and difficult, and when factory laws are ignorantly and theoretically drafted, without due regard to the practical interests of some section of workers, it is no comfort to those workers to know that some 'distinguished' woman favoured among politicians has been consulted about their affairs. This sort of so called representation is no safeguard to anybody; if it were, men would never have felt the need for democratic institutions, and England might still be peaceably governed by irresponsible rulers who, by right of birth, consider themselves and one another fit to coerce the multitude for their good. Practically we recognise, as far as men are concerned, that the only safety for the governed lies in the fact that their governors in some way depend on them, and are therefore sensitive not only to their needs but to their judgment. A politician must have the countenance and support of his constituents, and it is to his constituents that in the last resort he must make his appeal. Without constituents you cannot have representation. Under a fair system if a woman wanted to be representative of the aspirations of a female factory population she would have to be prepared to stand up for what they really wanted, not her theories of what they ought to want, unless of course she could convert them to her theories. But until women have votes it is impossible that they should get true and honest representation from other women, who, however wise and cultured and distinguished they may be, can only have any influence as long as their views please the men in power. One of the lesser evils attendant on the present voteless condition of women is the fact that there is no test for the working value of women politicians, no means of gauging their influence and claims to be representative of other women. The truth is, the power of the few women of the upper classes who by their position and social influence are able to keep in touch with legislation is no comfort at all to the mass of the working women, who want to be governed by people who are responsible to them, and to whom it will therefore come as a matter of course to consider their interests and consult their intelligence, and the fact that men will anxiously consult distinguished and philanthropic ladies does not touch the point at issue. Nor does the example of American institutions. The strange thing about America is that it is often quoted to us as an ideal country where public opinion has such a high standard that barmaids would not be tolerated, and anti-suffrage societies flourish. And most splendid of all, the highly cultured and advanced State of Oregon has just defeated a woman suffrage resolution by 10,000 votes. But when one comes to inquire into the actual political and moral condition of American towns one begins to wonder whether anti-suffrage societies, barmen, and an enlightened masculine electorate are to be wholly congratulated on their political results, one hears bitter complaints of the public-houses as centres of political and moral corruption, and of the masses of ignorant and often alien voters whose vote and interest is for sale. The consumption of spirits per head is much larger in the United States than it is in England; over and over again lurid flashes of light have been thrown on the social and economic condition of the great American cities, a condition which is usually attributed by Americans to the influx of ignorant emigrants and the enormous foreign and often very retrograde element that has thus been introduced into the electorate. It is inaccurate to assert that the American women-suffrage agitation has been defeated, because as yet it is only partially successful; victory in four States may seem a very small thing, a little result for forty years' work, and yet this is perhaps a short-sighted and impatient view. Some of us were tempted to envy the swift revolution by which the Finnish women gained complete political freedom. But it may well be that here in England what we lose in speed we gain in stability, and Englishwomen who are slowly working forward towards the greater life may comfort themselves with the thought that much of the work of a rapid revolution may be undone by the inevitable reaction that dogs its steps, whilst the work of evolution, plodding steadily on through the storm of its own reactions, is founded on an everlasting basis of security.

Eva Gore-Booth,
National Industrial and Professional Women's Suffrage Society,
5 John Dalton Street, Manchester.

Barmaids' employment

The Times, 6 November 1908

Sir,

In view of the Government's abandonment of their attack on the barmaids' employment, may we take this opportunity of thanking those friends in and out of the House of Commons who have so effectually aided the Barmaids' Political Defence League in their successful campaign, by bringing the pressure of public opinion to bear on the Government through the House of Commons and the electors?[53] The trade of 100,000 women has been protected from arbitrary Government suppression, at the expense of much labour, agitation, and money, all of which have been necessary to make people realise what was going on and to focus public opinion.[54]

53 The Barmaids' Political Defence League overwhelmingly won their campaign: 294 out of 355 MPs rejected clause 20 of the 1908 Licensing Bill. Prime Minister Asquith removed the entire sub-section relating to women and children from the Licensing Bill on 2 November 1908.

54 This letter was printed underneath a letter from George Gooch, MP. In his letter to the editor Gooch disputed Gore-Booth's estimate that 100,000 women were then employed as barmaids, stating that the census figures identified 27,707 women employed in the trade in England and Wales. He warned that although the Licensing Bill was defeated in the House of Commons, 'the movement of opinion which has steadily gathered force during recent years is not likely to stop', *The Times* (6 Nov. 1908).

Surely any just person must see that such a struggle to protect an honest trade ought to be unnecessary, that in a free country such protection would be wholly mechanical. The question of suppressing a trade that absorbed the labour of 100,000 men could never arise in England at the present time, for the simple reason that the working men of England are the electors of England. Only when the working women are enfranchised will these questions cease to arise with regard to their right to legitimate work.

We are yours faithfully.

Eva Gore-Booth and Esther Roper.

Hon. Secs. Women's Trade Council Office, 19, Buckingham Street, Strand.

The Home Office and florists' work hours

Manchester Guardian, 25 November 1908

Sir,

With regard to your leading article of to-day, may we point out that the florists' assistants have already petitioned the Home Secretary for an exemption from the Factory Acts, and it was their own view of their case that probably weighed with Mr. Gladstone in making his decision to grant them the exemption order they asked for.[55] The petition was signed by a large number of employees and sums up the whole question.

May we also point out that it was only after the Act had been applied and some women had already lost their work as a result of it that the petition was sent to the Home Office. If the labour party depended on the votes of working women as well as men Mr. Henderson would not be attacking to-night the Home Secretary's wise and considered measure.[56]

Yours &c.,

Eva Gore-Booth, Esther Roper & Sarah Dickenson.

Manchester and Salford Women's Trades and Labour Council,

5 John Dalton Street, Manchester.

55 The Factories Act was expanded to cover many other industries and careers that were not solely factory based. In April 1907, Lord Chief Justice Darling found that since a room at the back of a florist's shop was mainly used for manual labour this constituted a workshop; the employment of florists' assistants therefore fell under the legislation of the Factory and Workshop Act.

56 Keir Hardie resigned as chairman of Labour in 1908 and was replaced by Arthur Henderson. In November 1908, Henderson requested that the exemption to the Factory and Workshop Act relating to florists' assistants be withdrawn. See: *Women's Right to Work*, p. 89.

Women's right to work

Manchester and Salford Women's Trade and Labour Council pamphlet

The last few years have seen one attack after another made by the Government on the employments of working women. Two years ago the Circus Riders and Acrobats were threatened with abolition. Last year the Barmaids were fighting for their lives. At present it is the Florists' Assistants who are to be abolished, through an unexpected application of the Factory Act and the refusal of the Home Secretary to grant an exemption order. It is hard to see why the Florists' Assistants should be forced into the fighting line. About two years ago the Lord Chief Justice decided that the florists' shops must come under the Factory and Workshops Act, because a bouquet was a manufactured article, and the place where it was made was therefore a workshop. The same process of reasoning might easily be applied to a private house, because a pudding is most certainly as much a manufactured article as a bouquet, and we live in hopes of seeing the day when Mr. Herbert Gladstone's kitchenmaid is not allowed to work after 8 o'clock. The result of the application of this particular ruling to the Florists' Assistants' trade is its abolition as far as these women are concerned. It is impossible for the florists to employ workers who are not allowed a reasonable elasticity in their hours.

This they represented to Mr. Gladstone, who at first granted them an exemption order which allowed them to employ women between 8 and 10 in the evening on condition that they made up to the women the two hours the next day. At the request of Mr. Henderson, this exemption order was withdrawn. It is hard to understand why the complicated machinery of Government should be used to crush so harmless a set of workers in a trade which is universally admitted to be a pleasant and healthy one. For the practical results of this regulation will be that a woman who has been decorating a dinner or ballroom will not be allowed under any circumstances to put the finishing touches to her work after 8 o'clock. The employers are agreed that with the new conditions they will not be able to continue employing women, but the work will be given to foreign men, as for some reason they do not consider that English men can do this peculiar work.

Obviously, these women are being sacrificed because they have no political power. It is easy to blame working men politicians for their hostility to women's labour, but it must never be forgotten that it is an undoubted fact that, under the present system, men's and women's interests in industry clash, and human nature being what it is, it is idle to expect people whose interests clash with yours to represent your cause in the House of Commons. Indeed, it is not given to very many people to be impartial on subjects that affect their vital interests. As John Burns once said in another connection, 'you do not go for an impartial opinion on the merits of cremation to the churchyard worm.' The present over-crowded state of the labour market is, of course, largely responsible for this antagonism. In the stress of competition the average man will welcome any excuse, sentimental and high-sounding or moral or sanitary, to reduce the number of his trade rivals, and so increase, as he thinks, his own chances of getting work.

When men say that the employment they covet for themselves is too unhealthy or unpleasant or degrading for women, behind their 'chivalry' you will find masquerading the ancient primitive desire to get something for oneself, cost what it may to others. Our methods now are not as crude as they used to be. If Ahab had been a child of this generation, he would doubtless have said that Naboth's vineyard was very damp and unhealthy, and that Naboth himself was getting consumption and must be turned out of it at once for the sake of his health. It is idle to blame working men for this state of things, and call them selfish. Work is scarce, and the difficulties of earning a living are very great, and the constant nearness of destitution drives people into desperate hostility towards their competitors. The upper class of men who are not faced by the fear of starvation nevertheless fight to the bitter end to keep all money-making professions in their own hands, and only yield inch by inch to the struggle for life of those whose industrial and commercial interests are still in some curious way considered by the majority of people not to really count. The working class is not more to blame in this matter than any other; only in dealing with industrial problems we must face realities, however unpleasant, and not gloss over the strange and impressive fact that most of the so-called sex hostility in England at this time is really and truly nothing but ordinary trade jealousy, taking advantage of any lingering social traditions, and of the fact of women's political subjection, to keep down the numbers of competitors in different trades. In the modern confusion and shipwreck of industry all the boats are over-crowded, and the men being protected themselves are trying to push the women out of the way, regardless of the fact that the sea is the only alternative. People are usually quite open about this; for women to be without work and without money does not matter.

Thus, John Burns openly proposed the other day as a remedy for 'unemployment,' that the work of women must be enormously curtailed. Here you see the doctrine of the inferiority of women pushed to its last logical extremity to cover the politician's natural and constitutional desire to help the voters in the industrial struggle at the expense of the voteless. The present masculine monopoly of representation is making the position of the women workers intolerable. Thus we have Mr. Shackleton, whose reason for existing in the House of Commons is presumably his connection with a Trade Union composed of a majority of women, openly daring to declare that his members if they are married should not be allowed by law to work. In the event of a re-arrangement of work between employers and employed, are the 74,000 married women in the cotton trade likely to get their interests fought for, and their end held up by, Mr. Shackleton?[57] Such representation is a simple farce as far as working women are concerned. Are the brass-workers likely to protect the women's interests in their trade, or the miners to stand up for the women at the pit brow, or the bookbinders look after the needs of the folders and sewers?

They don't even pretend to. The attitude of the miners is too well-known to need comment. They deprecate so much their own manners and language that they think all women should be turned out of the trade lest they might be contaminated by hearing it and they seem quite contented that this should be so. But, oddly enough, they do not seem to want to be separated from the very same women – their wives and female relatives in the much closer quarters of home; the language only seems to matter out-of-doors. The bookbinders are not quite so high-minded. They simply appeal to their members against the evil of female labour, and say 'each man should do his level best to keep the girls back.'

The trade jealousy of the brass-workers was also very frankly expressed at the last Trades Congress. Constant efforts are made in the cause of philanthropy to convert the Cradley Heath Chain-makers into the Cradley Heath Unemployed.

When an attempt was made this month in Parliament to take away the Barmaids' employment, the Labour members were divided on this subject, some of them quite openly wanting to turn out the women on the grounds that there would be more work for men. And indeed men really seem to think that it doesn't matter if a woman starves as long as a man gets work. This most extraordinary theory seems to have crept subconsciously into the minds of many, and to colour their thoughts on industrial problems, so that they practically end by thinking and acting as if work and money were a man's rights and women who wanted to live and to earn were thieves and robbers, who are only tolerated in a corrupt and foolish state of society; and because this seems to us unthinkable nonsense, we must not shrink from facing the somewhat appalling fact that a great many men both think it and say it. Wrapped in that strange egoism which is so blinding a force, they really do feel that women are only relative and only matter in so far as they are connected with men. A man should keep his wife, and it's dreadful for a wife to starve; we hear a great deal about working men's wives and little ones. But his sister is quite another matter, and at the bidding of a Trade Union he will refuse to teach his trade to

57 Labour MP David Shackleton was elected to the House of Commons with the financial support of female trade unionists on condition that he would pursue the cause of votes for women. Once elected Shackleton not only proved to be unsupportive of women workers, he later advocated for further restrictions to be placed on working women.

his own daughter. Now, in the long run, you cannot pick and choose, and the world will have to reckon with all the women there are, not only with men's wives and dependents. Men will have to learn to respect human life in itself apart from sex, and if they do not learn it through widening sympathy and developing intelligence, it will be forced on them by the logic of hard facts; and by being constantly undercut and turned out of their work by oppressed women, they will learn to understand the terribly dangerous power of the weak. They who are fighting the industrial battle on the women's side do not fear that women will ultimately starve or get the worst of it. It is the disaster for both sexes of the sordid struggle itself that they want to avoid. An unprotected country is in itself a source of temptation to its stronger neighbours. What we want is to give Naboth a chance of defending his own vineyard. And one wonders whether, if it had been strongly fortified, it would have been attacked.

It has been said that much can be done without the Franchise, and the recent victory of the Barmaid Defence League is quoted as proof that women without votes can apply enough pressure to cause the abandonment of a Government measure. This is like saying that because a certain man was able to defend himself against burglars with a revolver, it is quite right that we should all have to defend our possessions as best we can against such attacks. It is quite impossible that the Government should propose to sweep away the trade of 100,000 men from motives of sheer philanthropy, and force those men to spend money and time and labour in a long and wearisome campaign, the sole object of which is to protect their right to work, their reputations, and their daily bread.

The Barmaids have survived the attack that was made on them, but their capacity for fighting does not in any way justify a political system that excludes them from the Constitution and lays them open to such attacks. Unemployment is the worst industrial disaster that can befall anyone. In speaking of men, people seem to realise this, but as regards women they assume that an unpleasant trade is a more serious misfortune. This is of course to a practical person an absurd view, any work being better than none if you must earn money, and if not, why not give it up without waiting for Government to force you?

We are glad to read how in Norway the women in Government employ in the Postal Telegraphic Departments had their wages raised within a few months of their gaining the Franchise. Women need the Franchise for the sake of keeping up their industrial value. But if this were not so, if their wages were equal and paid independently of sex depreciation, they would still want it to protect them from the constant attacks on their work made by the House of Commons.

Eva Gore-Booth.

Manchester and Salford Women's Trade and Labour Council,

5, John Dalton St, Manchester.

The admission of women to Mr. Churchill's meeting

Manchester Guardian, 25 May 1909

Sir,

As a person who is immediately affected by the present Budget, may I protest against the fact that I was not allowed yesterday to hear the Government explanation of it because I am not a member of the Liberal party? The same natural and simple right of hearing what you will have to pay for and why is also at present denied to the majority of women in the gallery of the House of Commons. In saying this I do not mean to deny that a section of women have disturbed meetings and made speechmaking difficult. No doubt the arrangements for the admission of women were, in your correspondent's sense, a great success yesterday; in fact, there was no disturbance. But the absence of disturbance does not always mean peace. You kept out the five or six people you wanted to keep out, but you also kept out all thoughtful and responsible citizens who have not the good fortune to be men or members of the Liberal party. You also made the government of this country an entirely party matter as far as women are concerned; no non-party, Conservative, or Socialist woman is allowed the privilege of hearing a Cabinet Minister.

In the present method what impartial women resent is that you will not take the trouble to distinguish between the orderly and the disorderly among us. It is a principle of justice not to punish the innocent with the guilty. If the S.D.F. were to disturb a Cabinet Ministers' meeting in Manchester with shouts about 'unemployment,' &c. would you arrange that at the next demonstration no man should be admitted who was not 'guaranteed' by an officer of the Liberal Federation?[58] Of course not, and the reason is the root reason of the whole trouble – because men have votes and women have not, and therefore their approval, disapproval, or alienation matters nothing to practical politicians. You have avoided a row, and that is all you want, and you unconsciously allow yourselves to think it does not really matter to the prospects of the Liberal party whether independent women resent your present division of the female population into wives and daughters of members of Parliament, people with a character-note from an official of the Liberal party, and brawlers. There was a time when some of us would have thought such a classification would be impossible to a Liberal Government.

Yours & co.,
Eva Gore-Booth.
Cringlebrook, Victoria Park, Manchester.

58 Social Democratic Federation.

[Miss Gore-Booth talks as though it were quite an easy thing to distinguish between the 'orderly' and the 'disorderly.' She has not tried, or she might think differently. If women unknown to the party managers were to be admitted the task would become almost certainly impossible. There must also be a rather strict limit of numbers or again it would become impossible. None of our critical correspondents has a word of real blame for the 'brawlers' who make the whole difficulty. They reserve all their indignation for the means taken for preventing brawling. Ed. 'Guard.']

Admission of women to attend Mr. Churchill's meeting

Manchester Guardian, 26 May 1909

Sir,
I am afraid my letter has given you a wrong impression. I think that brawling at meetings is both futile and wrong, and I quite sympathise with the difficult position of the organizers who arranged this meeting. I have taken every opportunity, and so have the societies with which I am connected, to express this view.

As to the practical side of the difficulty, we can claim to have had some experience of it. For instance, before one of our large London meetings we were informed that an effort was going to be made to break up the meeting by young men students who had succeeded in breaking up a suffrage meeting the week before. The meeting was an important one, and it was proposed in the interests of order to exclude men. Somewhat against the feeling of the more nervous members of the Committee, we decided to sell tickets to anyone, and that the order of the meeting would be safe in the hands of our able stewards. The event proved us right. It may be said that this was an accident. But the principle on which we acted was 'nothing succeeds like courage, and nothing fails like fear.'

Yours, &c.,

Eva Gore-Booth, Cringlebrook, Victoria Park, Manchester.

[We are sorry to have misjudged Miss Gore-Booth's attitude, and are heartily glad to find ourselves in accord with her as to the futility and wrong of the policy of disturbances. We must all admire her courage and that of her friends on the occasion she mentions. The students wisely repented and behaved themselves; there is unfortunately not the smallest reason to suppose that the intending disturbers of Saturday's meeting would, if admitted, have done the same. Ed. 'Guard.']

Women and the nation; the workers III – no trades for women

The Englishwoman, June 1909

'There's no good talking as if men and women were equal in industry,' said a Government official the other day, 'because the fact is they are not. Their labour is subject to all sorts of legal disabilities. The law handicaps women and you've got to accept that to begin with.' Strange that the law about which such candid explanations were made was the much-vaunted Factory Act, dear to the hearts of so many innocent philanthropists, and supposed by multitudes of harmless people to be administered in the interests of the women workers. The official in question was defending the recent application of the Factory Act to the florists' trade, and explained to us with extreme and curious lucidity how little importance the Government attached to the almost accidental suppression of a very skilled and important women's industry. Women, often enough, do not realise their miserable position as regards industrial legislation, nor how the livelihoods of many hundreds, or indeed thousands, can be swept away at the whim of a few officials. Indeed, one often thinks it is only the strange ignorance of one half of the world as to how the other half lives that makes it possible for there to be an anti-suffrage movement in a great industrial country like ours. People are slow at finding out the meaning of things that happen. And when it was explained by those in authority to the two florists' assistants present, that it was no doubt hard for them to lose their trade, but, of course, their interests were not of importance to anybody, they were quite startled, and seemed at first unable to grasp the official view of the matter. It was not till they got into the street again that the recoiling idea struck them: 'I suppose it's all because we haven't got votes.' Indeed, in considering the position of women in industry, our official was right, it is no good talking as if men and women were equal, we must remember that all women labour under disabilities and disqualifications that are specially restricted to their sex, and quite unknown among men workers. Therefore, it follows, as the night the day, that it is women and not men who bear the utmost rigours of the industrial struggle.

Their political subjection and want of value are forces that work themselves out relentlessly in the industrial world. It is an undeniable fact that everywhere where women are employed in England, their wages are less than those of men in the same trade. Some people have imagined that the textile trades were an exception to this rule, and the textile operatives are doubtless better paid than most other women workers. But even here there are few women indeed who can earn as much as the ordinary man. The women weavers earn the same piece-work rate as men in the same process in Lancashire, and that is a great step in the right direction, and it is perhaps because of this that it is sometimes carelessly asserted that men and women are equal in cotton trade. But it must be remembered weaving is considered a poor trade for men.

Take another and better-paid process in the same trade – mule-spinning; there the men's rate is not different to the women's, because the women have no rate at all. They have all been turned out, and the process is most carefully and sedulously guarded from their competition by the men's Union. Few, indeed, are the women in the cotton trade who are able to earn the mule-spinner's ordinary rate of 2*l.* a week (in the Manchester district). It is absurd to jump to the conclusion that because, in one process, men and women get the same money for piece work that their position in the trade is equal. There are ways of killing a dog besides hanging him, and if most of the best processes are shut to you because you are a woman, it doesn't comfort you much to be told that because you get a decent piece-work rate in one process your position is ideal and equal to a man's. Of course the mule-spinners will say that mule-spinning is too hard work for a woman. Just as some Trade Unionists will tell you that the Factory Act should be applied to the florists, to save the most skilled and valued workers in the trade from being sweated. It has even been asserted that the overtime allowed under the Factory Act is enough for their work thirty days overtime are allowed, and this, indeed, would be enough if it was not for the fact that every time one person works overtime it counts one of the thirty occasions for overtime for every person working in the shop. This is a law of the Medes and Persians, and the Home Secretary himself cannot alter it. It renders the thirty days overtime, which is sufficient for the cotton trade, wholly insufficient for an industry like the florists, where everybody does not begin and end at once, as they do in a mill, but all depends on the liberty of individuals to go out occasionally after eight o'clock and finish decorating a room. And here, without dwelling on this subject, one would like to put in a word for honest investigation, and warn all those who would like to help women in industry, and who are not personally conversant with the technical details of different trades, to beware of accepting current theories and plausible-sounding explanations without a thorough first-hand sifting of facts. For even now, as in the days of Socrates, it is always easy, in dealing with outsiders, to 'make the worse seem the better reason;' and where people have no practical knowledge they are easily confounded by half-truths, and frighted [*sic*] by that false fire of sentiment which is so powerful in confusing issues. Public opinion is too often inaccurate, slipshod, and sentimental; but it is, on the whole, well-meaning, and legislation to handicap women's labour is always brought forward under a pretence of kindness and of 'protecting' the weak.

Not many have the hardihood of a Trade Union Secretary, who told me that, in a certain town, women should not be allowed to be 'drawers in' because the 36s. earned at this work is 'too good money for a woman.' But the 'too hard' work theory falls through when you watch women piecers [*sic*] doing the same work as spinners for 15s. a week, and the manager explains that there is no difference between them, except that the spinners have 'more responsibility,' for which you would think the difference of 25s. would very amply repay them.

As Mr. Haslam justly points out, the fact that men have captured the big women's cotton unions is responsible for a great many of the dangers and difficulties that beset the path of the woman worker.[59] But growing education and responsibility on the part of the cotton workers themselves is already stirring up dissatisfaction, and must end by securing for them their proper share of representation and consideration.

The case of women in the non-textile industries is widely different. Here, except in the few very skilled trades and processes, the whole average of wages is lower and the position more difficult. Everyone who has organized among them knows the comparatively helpless position of the hundreds and thousands of the lesser skilled, who work in the small workshops of those many obscure and swarming trades that crowd into the back streets of all great towns. The factory workers, who, working together under one roof form a solid body of several thousands, with the capacity of developing into an army or a mob, are in a different position to twenty isolated fancy boxmakers, or ten tailoresses, or thirty shirt-makers, or twenty machinists, or six waitresses, or five shop-assistants, or twenty clay-pipe finishers, or fifteen clerks, or thirty folders and sewers, who are trying to better their industrial conditions, and find it such an almost hopeless task. They are hampered on every side by trade union restrictions and oppressions; they are working in such small numbers and isolated positions that it is very hard for them to combine with their fellows; they have not the opportunities of acquiring that technical skill that gives value to the workers and strength to their organization, and they have as a body of workers no political value or significance. Now, all artificial restriction of the field of your labour must inevitably lower wages, because it increases the supply of labour on the market and decreases the demand for such labour.

It is a well-known fact that too large a supply of capable labour in one field makes organization well-nigh impossible; because when the labour market is overcrowded the labourer has not enough industrial value to make terms with his or her employer, but can be sent away without inconvenience. Organization is therefore no real solution to the problem of those multitudes who are cut off by arbitrary rules of sex from the apprenticeship and training so necessary for the acquirement of skill. It will be seen that every restriction and condition and exclusion to which women are subjected in England is intensified in the

59 James Haslam, originally a trade unionist and secretary of the Derbyshire Miners. Haslam was elected as MP for Chesterfield; he served from 1906 until his death in 1913, first as a Liberal Party member then as a Labour member.

case of this class of workers, and these causes, working round in a vicious circle, have the result of making the operatives' position well-nigh intolerable in its helplessness.

It is these workers and their like, with their increasing millions and their miserable average of 7s. 6d. a week, that are the great problem of the present labour world, for it is among their ranks that you will find the lowest wages and the much-quoted lesser skilled sweated worker, and it is in their name that much ill-considered and hasty legislation is suggested. Now, we have seen that for their underpayment there is one very direct and simple reason (much affected by political and social causes), the preponderance of the supply of this class of labour over the demand for it. Any legislation that is to help these workers must either lessen the supply of their labour by absorbing it elsewhere, or increase the demand for it. This you would think was an obvious-enough fact. And yet it is undoubtedly true that most legislation proposed with the express object of ameliorating the condition of these people must inevitably lead to an increase of the supply, or a lessening of the demand.

For instance, take the case of the florists' trade, now under discussion. By a judicial pronouncement it was decided some time ago that this trade must come under the Factory Act, and well-meaning people rejoiced that the florists' assistants should have the benefit of that which, when applied to women, is called 'protection.' This 'protection' means, in practice, that the better paid and most skilled of these women will lose their employment, because it is of the nature of their work that it should be done at a different hour from that which is legally binding on cotton operative women. For these very skilled workers are often employed in decorating rooms for balls and receptions between the hours of eight and ten in the evening, and this for a very simple reason: their decorations are made to a large extent with cut flowers, and great care must be taken that they should not wither before the hour when the ball, or supper, or party begins. These women designers do not want longer hours, they merely want latitude as to when they may take their hours, and they are most earnestly asking, hitherto quite in vain, for an exemption from the Home Secretary that will enable them to carry on their trade. Otherwise, directly the Act begins to be put into operation they will have to go, and foreign men will take their place, for Englishmen do not take to flower manipulation.

And what will be the economic result of these women's 'protection,' and the resulting displacement of their labour? The florists' trade will cease to be a skilled trade for women; all above the position of simple shop-assistants and young irresponsible workers will be thrown out of employment. The shop-assistants and young girls will go on as ever, but the skilled designer, or 'first florist,' or manageress will have to go. Now, beyond the cruelty involved to individuals, we have to realise the effect of the added competition of these workers, whose labour, hitherto absorbed in this very good trade, will now go to swell the supply in an already overcrowded market. If wages are, in the main, a question of supply and demand, will it help matters, from the workers' point of view, to increase the supply and lessen the demand in this wholly artificial and legal manner? This question is a very interesting one, because it is here you have a glimpse of the connection so strong, and yet so often denied, between wages – especially women's wages – and politics. By an application of the Factory Act the florists' assistants are turned out of work. The florists' demand for English labour is thereby artificially and politically stopped, the supply is in the same manner increased, and lower wages in other trades is the result of the increased competition caused by unemployed skilled florists trying to get unskilled work in other trades. Thus, in this concrete instance, we see the action of the two great artificial disabilities of women, the absence of political power to protect them from arbitrary interference and the limiting of their field of labour by restrictions and disqualifications.

In the face of these facts, it is strange that people do not more fully realise that the sweating of working women and their terrible industrial struggle is in reality but one of the experiences of their subjection. People nowadays have their consciences wakened more or less on the subject of extreme poverty, but they do not seem able to see that it is only the practical side of subjection and injustice. All attempts to deal with poverty, that do not include an effort for justice and liberty for the oppressed in the industrial struggle, are doomed to failure. Philanthropy without fair dealing is the kind of compromise that appeals to English people, but it is a most mischievous doctrine in practical things. People feel vaguely sentimental and uncomfortable about the conditions of women workers, so they feel they must do something. And it is so easy to do things. You can't force unwelcome restrictions down working men's throats, because they have votes. But women have no share in the resisting power of the nation. So when you vaguely think it must be horrid to be a barmaid, and spend your life in a public-house, or it must be dreadful to walk-on a tight-rope, or sort coal at the pit-brow, or hammer chains in a forge, you gather your friends together and start a Society to do away with or 'abolish' barmaids, or circus-riders, or acrobats, or pit-brow workers, or chain-makers, or whatever it may be, quite oblivious of the fact that your efforts, if they succeed, will result in an act of tyrannous cruelty by which many thousands will lose their livelihoods and many other hundreds of thousands will find it harder in consequence to earn, their livings.

We are slow to learn, but we shall have to learn in the end, that the terrible problems of the unskilled labour-market cannot be solved wholesale without patience and just dealing towards individuals. It is the last refuge of incompetence and hopelessness to put people into a class and say they ought to be abolished. Those who support the present movement for the abolition of home-work, and of the work of poor married women in factories, might pause if they would consider the practical result of the legal triumph of their causes. When no married women are able to earn a penny, either in the factory or in their homes, the suffering entailed on them and on their children is simply unthinkable. Every married working woman will be in a state of absolute dependence on her husband, cut off by law from the ordinary resources of the ordinary citizen, reduced to real slavery, and with no refuge from any industrial or physical disablement that may cripple her husband. The alternative proposal, that she should be kept by the State, is so fraught with practical difficulties and so expensive that we do not so much fear the carrying out of this more tolerable but no less final and hopeless form of enslavement. It is only a want of practical knowledge of the lives of the poor that can make people want to put the law into motion to cut off people from their last resources, and throw them on the mercy of the world for their daily bread.

From the ordinary man Trade Unionist's point of view the matter is a quite different one. John Burns suggested at a public meeting, as a remedy for 'unemployment,' that women's work should be enormously curtailed, and in every sentimental objection to women's work in any particular trade the ordinary Trade Unionist will see merely a splendid opportunity for getting rid of the competition of a few hundred or thousand workers. There is no secret in this. I remember a strike in Manchester in which the bookbinders went out against the employment of female labour, and in many trades there is a fierce battle waging between the men and women employees. In our revulsion against the harsh and unfair treatment of the women, it is difficult not to be too hard on the men who fight so determinedly to turn them out. A helpless, unenfranchised class of workers is a great temptation to the strong – and human nature is selfish. Work is hard to get, and if you can make a line of demarcation in your trade by which all the plums are reserved for the sex to which you belong, you would have to have somewhat rare mental qualities to refrain from using your power, because of the cruelty and unfairness of what you are doing. The same struggle goes on in the tailoring trade, and many other trades where men and women are employed, and the great poverty and low wages of women workers are, to a large extent, the result of the system of restriction and repression which it gives rise to. Of course there can be no doubt as to the end of these restrictions and repressions; already we are beginning to see their result. The Trade Unions refuse to allow the employers to have female apprentices. The women must live. The pressure of want drives them into having to bribe the employer to employ them by taking less money than men. Thus they get into the work. The men will not teach them, but they are quick and pick up the processes, and again bribe the employer by taking less money. It is useless to blame them for this, for everybody must and will live somehow, and if you shut the front door of industry against women, they have a nasty habit of turning round and going in at the back. This is not feminine perversity – no question of sex is involved; it is simply an economic fact that the mechanical result of oppression is undercutting. This is the terrible power of the weak, and it is thus that they revenge themselves on the foolish world that despises them. If Trade Unionists could only widen their horizon, and the Labour Party awaken to the danger of alienating and oppressing half the Workers of the country, they might gain a new and real hold on the multitude of the workers. A larger-minded policy might recognise that men and women of the working class should be comrades and loyal to one another. Competition may teach us that every worker is every other worker's enemy, just as in another class of life you may gain 20,000*l*. a year by your brother's death. But human nature is made for something better than calculating on other people's misfortunes, and the world is so constituted that any scheme that is founded on the sacrifice of one class to another is by its very nature one of the most perishable and fragile of things.

Meanwhile the women's struggle for existence in the labour world is waxing fast and furious. Hardly an annual trade conference can be held without resolutions and speeches fiercely denouncing the evil of female labour, and as the fight gets more hopeless the fighters get more desperate and extreme. It is no use for Socialists to have ideals that all women should wear nice clean caps and aprons, and cook dinners, and sew, and scrub floors, and rock cradles all their lives, because, rightly or wrongly, an enormous and ever-increasing multitude of women of all classes have wakened up to a wider view of human destiny, and to the perhaps Western idea of the necessity of independence and free will and choice of work for every human being, if they are to develop in themselves the qualities that will be of most service to the world. This is that profound instinct that many Socialists condemn as the abstract middle-class idea of liberty, and to respect for which we owe the fullness and variedness and colour of human life.

I hold no brief for the present conditions of women's labour. I do not want to minimise the grievance of their terribly low wages. That their work should lose its economic value is the natural result of their subjection, and of the constant injurious legislative attempts to restrict and hamper, or even put an end to, their labour for their own good. It would indeed be hard to overestimate the suffering thus caused to individuals and to families where women are the only, or even the principal, bread-winners. But this I do say, if any one wants really to help the women workers, their efforts will be to open all doors to them, both political and industrial, and they will not lend themselves through self-interest or mental confusion to a policy of handicapping their labours, and offering them sentiment when they ask for justice. At present women workers are too like the dogs that eat of the scraps that fall from the master's table. It is better to eat scraps than to starve. But those of us who realise the inexorable accuracy of the saying, 'Every dog has his day,' look forward to a fairer state of things. The forces that make for justice are intensely and extremely logical in their working. No privileges last, no monopolies can be kept up in the end.

People still have a fettling at the back of their minds that the world is made for men, and relatively for the women they support. Socialists are naturally prone to lose their grip of the great first truth of human life, the value and direct infinite importance of every individual. But they will find, as everybody else finds in time, that the world is made for every one of us; that you cannot lump human beings into classes and dispose of them wholesale; and that any scheme of the universe, however 'progressive,' that does not allow of the development of every individual life will break up and go to pieces before the fast-advancing wave of thought that extends the boundaries of human charity.

Eva Gore-Booth.

Women workers and the vote

Manchester Guardian, 14 July 1909

Sir,

With regard to Miss MacArthur's attempt to interrupt the women's suffrage meeting at the Queen's Hall, may we say that we were not able to enter into a discussion of the details of the Florists' Assistants' appeal, because the matter is at present under the consideration of a judge appointed by the Home Office to make an inquiry.[60] We were therefore instructed that it was not in order for us to discuss it.

With regard to the general question of Factory Acts, we go even further than Miss McArthur; we think nobody should work for very long hours, and we would gladly see the Acts extended to men, which would entirely do away with the difficulties in their application at present caused by the competition between men and women.

Yours, &c.,

Esther Roper.

Eva Gore-Booth.

Hon. Secs, Manchester and Salford Women's Trade and Labour Council.

60 Mary MacArthur, secretary of the Women's Trade Union League and founder of the Anti-Sweating League. The controversy over florists' working hours reached a height in May 1909. Judge Ruegg was appointed as a commissioner to examine the situation. Gore-Booth and Roper appeared at the inquiry to express the views of the florists' assistants. The Women's Trade Union League, represented by MacArthur, demanded that the restrictions be tightened and the number of hours women worked be reduced.

Running a suffrage candidate

Common Cause, 25 November 1909

The Industrial Women Suffragists in Lancashire have decided to take a hand in the political game at Rossendale in the event of the expected general election by running an independent candidate in the cause of Women's Suffrage.[61] This policy was determined on some years ago by a committee composed mainly of textile workers, who had collected and taken to the House of Commons a petition signed by 68,000 textile and other workers. They have, by long experience, come to feel the powerlessness of the unenfranchised in dealing with Parliament. Arguments, deputations, demonstrations, remonstrances, threats, demands, and even demonstration of physical force have all been tried by sections of Women Suffragists, and so far nothing has availed.

Many have become exasperated by the hopelessness of their task in trying, by direct appeals, to stir up the lethargy and persuade the indifference of those in authority.

As to reasoning with and threatening and talking to a Government that refuses to move, you might as well send deputations to a motor-car that has broken down. But although arguing and even more lively methods of persuasion have not produced the desired result, the position is none the less not by any means hopeless; a scientific adjustment is all that is necessary, a little careful setting to right of the action of the motive power on the machinery, and the motor-car is spinning down the road.

As the motive power and machinery are to the motor-car, so is the electorate to the Government. Without them it cannot move. It follows that the very men who to our claims are apathetic, indifferent, lethargic, become sensitive, sympathetic, energetic to help, when they are brought into touch with the machinery that makes and unmakes their positions.

Very rightly we have spent much time and labour and many years in trying to persuade and gain over our opponents. All this time behind our enemies the host of our friends has gathered and increased. The Government is not sensitive to us because we have no votes, and thus cannot affect the political situation. The strength of our position is that the ordinary people are with us – and by the ordinary people in an election I do not mean the politicians who belong to party organisations, and are loyal to their own side, and look upon the election as a game of football, and would never dream of considering the merits of a new idea. But the ordinary working men (as the miners, for instance, in Wigan) know the difficulties of women in the industrial world, and the

61 J. Malcolm Mitchell was chosen as the woman's suffrage candidate for Rossendale in the January 1910 general election. Mitchell was a journalist with *The Times* and he was founder and honorary secretary of the Men's League for Women's Suffrage.

sharpness of their struggle to earn a bare pittance, and are comparatively easy to persuade into the rough justice of 'It's time the women had a show.'

If we could focus and make Government feel the force of this opinion amongst working men; together with the active support of many men of all classes, we should supply some motive power to the machinery. Especially is this true in a three-cornered fight like Rossendale, where every vote detached from the parties has its value. For even if we do not succeed in the way we hope, we can at least disturb the balance and make our demand felt as a factor in practical politics. On the other hand, if Mr. Mitchell should get in, the Women's Suffrage movement would obviously gain enormous advantages. Not least amongst these would be to have a representative of Mr. Mitchell's abilities and proved sincerity, who would put Women's Suffrage before all party considerations and work for it with a single mind.[62] One or two elections may seem a small matter and Wigan and Wimbledon may not loom very large in the public mind as yet, but along this line there is the possibility of a great development. If in a few years' time the Women's Suffrage movement is in a position to put twenty candidates in the field, I will venture to prophesy that the existing Government, Liberal or Tory, will not be hard to satisfy that the majority of the English nation are 'demanding the enfranchisement of women with irresistible force and conviction.'

Eva Gore-Booth.

The women's suffrage candidate in Rossendale

Manchester Guardian, 13 December 1909

Sir,

May we point out that the Prime Minister's pronouncement on women's suffrage is a sufficient answer to those who in your columns and elsewhere have protested against our action in running a women's suffrage candidate in Rossendale.

It is true that in the event of a wholly improbable Reform Bill being brought out by the Government before they go out next time they will graciously allow the House of Commons, if so inclined, to insert a women's suffrage amendment. In fact, they will not order their followers to vote against it. We are told that the Government 'will not burke this question,' 'it is clearly one upon which the new House of Commons ought to be given the opportunity of expressing its views.' It is small comfort to those who are hungering for great reform to be told that in five years or so the House of Commons may possibly

62 Mitchell withdrew from the election at the last minute, pleading personal issues. Arthur Bulley stood as his replacement. He was owner of S. M. Bulley & Son, a cotton brokers in Liverpool, a member of the Independent Labour Party and of the Fabian Society.

have an opportunity 'of expressing its views.' Here is neither the spirit, the will, nor the force with which reform measures have ever been carried.

It is a strange thought for Englishwomen that the Ministers who have set their faces against the enfranchisement of the majority of the people are precisely the ones who talk most glibly about 'establishing upon an unshakeable foundation the principle of representative government.' The House of Commons is preaching the principles of democratic Government to the House of Lords. The lesson would carry greater conviction if the Commons set their own House in order first. Men trouble greatly about the unrepresentative nature of the House of Lords; to women the unrepresentative nature of the House of Commons is a far more deadly injury. In judging of women's actions in elections politicians must remember that men live in modern democratic conditions, whilst women are still, politically, under the old autocratic pre-French Revolution regime – tyranny that has always been the cause of much bitterness and suffering among the industrial classes in every country where it is tolerated. Our protest on this occasion is a small one, but we hope that it may be the first step on a road that will lead us far.

Yours &c.,
Eva Gore-Booth
Esther Roper
Hon Secretaries, Lancashire and Cheshire Women Textile
and Other Workers' Representation Committee,
5 John Dalton Street, Manchester.

Is the case urgent?

National Industrial and Professional Women's Suffrage Society pamphlet

Mr. Harold Cox gives us one of the chief lions in the path of Women Suffrage, the belief of politicians on different sides that various proposed measures of reform would work out against their party interests.[63] It is pretty generally assumed that an Act of Parliament that would simply make the law sex-blind would further the interests of the Conservatives, while adult suffrage is considered 'a Liberal measure.' This is an entirely baseless assumption. The propertied are not all banded together, as Conservatives, against the propertyless, as Liberals. If that were true we should always have a Liberal Government, for the poor are in the majority. Life is not so simple as that. There is such a thing as

63 Harold Cox, Liberal Party MP for Preston. Cox was an economist and became embroiled in the debate on women's suffrage in 1909 when he declared that 'there was no bias in English legislation against women, and that their economic position was not likely to be improved by the concession of the vote, but had improved without it'. 'A Famous Debate', *Star* (1909).

a Working Men's Conservative Association. Also there are Liberal Peers and merchants and employers. Prophecy is quite unwarranted: it is just as likely as not that working women will be Conservative; and professional and middle-class women are often Liberal and even Labour in their sympathies. Women who hold large property are so few that their votes would make no practical difference. As things are at present, even men must often change their minds between the elections: if they did not the same party would always be in power. In fact, everybody who has worked in elections knows the wave of feeling that seems to come over a community, and that carries one side or another to success on a flowing tide of irresistible impetus. The mass of men are not solid and grave students: divided into parties, they waver to and fro, and are influenced by many strange and unforeseen motives. Party is for politicians. Often enough the voters' feelings might be expressed by phrases like, 'It's time the other side had a show,' or 'We want a bit of change here,' or personal or local reasons.

Women are not less reasonable than men, but I see no reason for thinking they are more so. In fact, they are likely to be swayed by the same human motives, and therefore the effect of their enfranchisement on the balance of party would not be as great as politicians think. But even if it were, should we acquiesce in the judgement that politicians must always put the success of their party before their ideas of right and justice? Far, indeed, as we may be from the 'brave days of old,' 'when none were the party and all were the State,' surely there are some who will see beyond the mere party issues of the moment, that the Franchise is not primarily a weapon to secure the advancement of either party, but a means of defending the industrial and social interests of great classes of this struggling and, for the most part, poverty-stricken nation, in the midst of the confused strife of warring sections, where 'ignorant armies clash by night.' It may be that every party politician ought to believe that the 'success of his party is of the most importance to the well-being of the nation,' just as in old times the judges of the Inquisition no doubt believed that the success of the Church was of the utmost importance to the world. But it is from this idea that fanaticism springs. The end justifies the means: the massacre of St. Bartholomew established the triumph of the Church: the reprisals of Elizabeth were necessary for the security of the protestant faith. And people honestly thought this. Surely one touch of philosophy, or the religion of love, would save us from an idea which, through centuries, has deluged Europe in blood and filled the world with frenzy. It is true that the world's conscience refuses now to allow such dogmatisms to be carried out to their logical issue, and in England, at all events, by common consent, no party or Church is allowed to win its way to triumph through bloodshed or violence. But the attenuated form of this illusion is still in the mind of him who refuses to do justice and right because he fears it might prove bad for temporary party interests.

But we must believe that the resolute putting of the claims of party before granting of the franchise to women is really founded, in many cases, on a misapprehension of the women's case. Mr. Harold Cox obviously does not realise that he is dealing with a great industrial wrong, that causes much human suffering.

Women whose experience in different trades and professions has taught them the subtle, endless, entangled ramifications of this evil in the modern world, think that the urgency of this question, as illustrated by the condition and payment of working women, should give it a foremost place in the efforts of those politicians who have a kindly feeling towards the poor.

Mr. Cox says that the possession of a vote does not improve economic conditions. That is to say, with one stroke of the pen he sweeps away the whole foundation of the Labour Representation Movement and the Labour Party in the House of Commons. Not only this, but this saying strikes at the root of all modern political life. If the Government has no influence on the economic conditions of the country, why does it matter whether we are represented by Free Trade or Tariff Reformers? If Free Trade or Tariff Reform have no influence on wages and industrial affairs, arguments and speeches on both sides become nonsense, and it manifestly becomes a matter of no practical importance to working men which side they vote for. Fifty years ago Mr. Cox would no doubt have found supporters for his views on the non-connection of industry and politics among the Trade Unionists themselves, but it is noteworthy that the very unions, who at the time greeted all efforts to make a workingmen's franchise agitation with cries of 'No politics,' have gradually wakened to an understanding of the uses of national life, and are now voting large sums of money for labour representation, and often indeed straining every nerve to run their own candidates for Parliament.

Professor Dicey disposes of the whole matter with beautiful simplicity.[64] He says: 'No master raises his footman's wages because the manservant happens to be a voter, and he will assuredly not raise the wages of his housemaid because he finds, under some Women's Enfranchisement Act, she has got her name place on a Parliamentary register. Why in the name of common sense should a vote confer a benefit upon a woman which it has never conferred upon a man?'[65]

No sane person claims that the individual possession of a vote could in itself be a reason with an employer for raising an individuals' wages of either sex. Such an argument would indeed be easily checkmated. It is not the argument of serious women suffragists. Professor Dicey is welcome to win his game and defeat Professor Dicey. But any examination, however superficial, of the causes

64 Professor Albert Venn Dicey (1835–1922), jurist, originally a supporter of John Stuart Mill, he later became an opponent of women's suffrage.

65 Extract taken from A. V. Dicey, *Letters to a Friend on Votes for Women* (London: John Murray, 1909), p. 39.

that go to regulate the wages of a mass of people who are all paid at more or less the same rate, will show how sensitive these causes are to the action of political forces. If any one wonders why, from the top to the bottom of the social scale with few exceptions, women are paid less for their work than men, let them study the law of supply and demand and the amount by which it is influenced by political forces. The exclusion of women from vast fields of industry in the various professions and trades can only be kept up as long as they have no share in the national life. With the exception of a few factory and education inspectors and clerks, all the higher branches of Government service here and abroad are shut to them: also the 'learned' professions and most public employment, even in the medical profession, where they have won their way (because of the answering special need among women for doctors of their own sex). The result is that those whose labour would naturally be absorbed in all the various forms of human activity are artificially hampered and restricted.

Their energies, forced into a few narrow channels, go to overstock the supply of labour in the already crowded teaching, or nursing, or even type-writing professions, and thereby of course bring down the rate of wages in those professions. Those who are crowded out by this invasion flood into the labour market, and are forced to go down a step in the industrial world and overcrowd the already congested skilled trades. Here, again, is repression and restriction, and many trades and processes, such as spinning or bookbinding, are shut to women. These exclusions have their result in a tremendous over-supply of labour among the unskilled. The economic pressure produced by the want of scope is in itself enough to account for the lowness of wages, and it is through the reactions of this pressure that begins in the unskilled labour market that the oppression of women workers revenges itself on the whole industrial conditions of the nation.

Again, it must never be forgotten that the Government is the greatest employer of labour in the country, and as such has enormous influence on the labour market and the scale of wages. This influence has been turned to good account for working men by the Labour men in the House of Commons: but the example that the Government sets to the country in the relative values of men and women, as such, is accountable for much of the unfairness of the present state of things. There are other indirect ways by which the industrial position of working women is injured by Government, as for instance the law by which women are not allowed to work at night. By this regulation newspaper employment is shut to them, and the labour that would be thus absorbed is turned on to the market to increase the supply in other trades.

There is not much need to tell such things as these to factory workers because often enough they are men and women of a hard experience, who know well and realise fully that life is not made in water-tight compartments.

To people whose children are educated, and their daily labour minutely and often disastrously regulated by the State, the action and reaction of political, social, and industrial life is not a subject for argument, but a matter of every-day experience. How often have I lectured in a Labour hall in Lancashire, standing opposite to a large text in flaming letters of the walls, 'Political freedom must precede industrial emancipation.' In the labour world of to-day, this is indeed a generally accepted platitude.

But there are other causes besides supply and demand that admittedly go to regulate wages, such as workers' skill and the stability of their labour, the power of their Trade Unions and the position of the workers. It is easy to see how adversely the tradition of inferiority that goes along with political outlawry has affected the money value of women's work, so that a woman is paid less for her work even when it is exactly the same as a man's. The very piece-work rates are higher for men in the same trade, so that it must not be forgotten that in most trades women are simply fined for being women. Where the worker's skill is a factor, in many trades women are not allowed, by Trade Unions, to learn the skilled processes. Men's Trade Unions are strong political and industrial organisations, and they are able to bring pressure to bear even on public bodies to secure the exclusion of women from technical training as well as apprenticeship and skilled work.

In the Trade Union world, as in every world of industrial struggle, there is jealousy and the desire to lessen the number of your competitors. This very human desire is checked by certain laws between man and man, but in relations between the sexes in industry, the laws of justice and honesty have not yet been brought into operation. It is so easy and such temptation to take advantage of your competitor's weakness. Very few of us are so righteous in ourselves that we are fit to deal justly and generously with a subject race who at the same time are our competitors. This is one of the greatest arguments for the establishment of equality. I do not think that any fair-minded Trade Unionist will deny that many Trade Unions desire to repress women and get rid of their competition. You cannot blame them for this attitude of mind, as it is quite natural that in the confusion of the modern industrial world people should clutch at any means which they think may rid them of a certain amount of competition. But unless you kill people, or endow them, you cannot get rid of their competition. There is no kind, or just, or honest way of annihilating a rival, however disabled and helpless that rival may be, and no half measures can succeed. The only result of harassing restrictions and exclusions is to teach people ingenuity in undercutting – the mechanical revenge of the oppressed on Society. There is no need to dwell on the present standard of women's wages: the average of 7s, a week speaks for itself. Such a rate is a danger to the whole industrial world. Will bookbinders be able to command 36s. a week when employers realise fully the cheapness of female labour and the cleverness of female fingers?

Surely in the interests of men as well as women, it is very urgent that peace should be made between those who are at present struggling so bitterly in suicidal industrial warfare. And there cannot be peace till men have learnt to look on women not as aliens and intruders, but as English people, with the same right to earn their livings, and to fair play and justice, as themselves. This lesson will never be learnt by the nation at large till the Governing Body ceases to take their money and ignore their interests, and grants to them and to their Trade Unions and organisations the protection of the franchise.

Eva Gore-Booth.

National Industrial and professional Women's Suffrage Society,

5 John Dalton Street, Manchester.

Pit-brow workers

Manchester Guardian, 28 September 1911

Sir,

At the women pit-brow workers' protest meeting in the Albert hall, Manchester, on Tuesday evening, fifty pit-brow women from Lancashire coalfields will be present in their working costumes and three or four of these workers themselves will speak.[66] They will have the valuable support of the Mayor and Mayoress of Wigan, who have already taken a prominent part in the movement for their protection.

Besides these professional pit-brow workers, one amateur is also going to speak, a lady well known in Manchester, who in the course of investigation into this trade spent a fortnight 'shoving tubs' and picking out the dross from coal on the belt. Among the pit-brow women speakers is a certificated and medalled ambulance worker whose services during the terrible Pretoria disaster earned her the name of the modern Florence Nightingale amongst the miners in the district.

It is hoped that all those who sympathise with these women in their fight against the ruin that threatens them will join in this demonstration.

Yours & co.,

Eva Gore-Booth,

Esther Roper.

66 In 1842 women were banned from working below ground in mines, through tubshoving at the base of mines continued as an occupation for thousands of women in Britain. Similar to public houses, mines were often seen as unsuitable places for women to work. In August 1911, a select committee in the House of Commons proposed a bill to ban women working at coal mines altogether. The Miners' Federation supported the proposal.

Pit-brow women

Manchester Guardian, 5 October 1911

Sir,

In view of the resolution passed at the Miners' Federation to persist in their agitation against pit-brow women's work, may we call attention to a meeting arranged in London for October 31 to protest against Parliamentary interference with the pit-brow workers? It is essential that twenty or thirty of these workers should be present to remove false ideas about their dress and appearance.

Although, as pointed out in your leading article, Mr. Masterman has promised the support of the Government for the deletion of the clause annihilating this work, the workers are still threatened with restrictions.[67] As they have already an eight-hour day and the work is done under specially good conditions, the only conceivable restriction is a limitation of their sphere of activity. This is a very important matter, as that sphere has already dwindled down under the pressure of trade union action, and there is no work that they are engaged in at present that they would not feel the loss of most severely. Such a restriction would not mean loss of work for all, but it would mean unemployment for many. Mr. Masterman distinctly stated that some restriction might be substituted for the abolition clause. No restriction applying only to women can be anything but mischievous to these workers, who are working hard to prevent this unwelcome legislation being thrust down their throats.

An effort is being made to collect the £50 necessary to take a large party to demonstrate in London. Will anybody who is interested in the fate of these women send a contribution towards the 30s. a head necessary for railway fares. It will be easily understood that it is impossible for the woman to pay their fares, and there are as yet no funds available for this purpose.

Contributions should be sent to the undersigned at the Suffrage Office, 5, John Dalton Street.

Yours, &c.,
Eva Gore-Booth,
Esther Roper,
Hon. Secretaries Lancashire and Cheshire
Women Workers' Representatives Committee.

67 Charles Masterman, MP was responsible for the coal mines in 1911. The article referred to is 'Pit-brow women protest against abolition of their work; the vote as a defensive weapon', *Manchester Guardian* (4 Oct. 1911).

The insurance of domestic servants

Manchester Guardian, 30 November 1911

Sir,
May we explain why, as representing some working women's societies, we were obliged to withdraw at the last moment from speaking at the Albert Hall protest meeting tonight? After the important concession made by Mr. Lloyd George last night, which relaxed the iron rigidity of the bill and introduced the element of choice on the workers' side as to what kind of benefit he or she had to receive, we decided that the servants' cause, together with that of other workers, would be better served by the addition of certain other amendments than by the demand for their exclusion from the bill.[68] As we were unable to convince the Committee of the justice of this view, we were obliged regretfully to withdraw.

The amendments our society support are as follows:

(1) Friendly societies to be bound to take all lives, male or female (thus doing away with the necessity for the wholly unsound and practically non-existent Post-office insurance which will be the lot of the less healthy worker.)

(2) Contributions for servants should be graduated according to wages. For servants earning under 9s., 1d. should be taken off the worker's contribution and paid by the State.

(3) When a worker is out of work the employer's contribution should be paid by the State.

(4) Where men and women pay the same contribution they should get the same benefit.

(5) When the worker is in hospital and has no dependents the benefits should be shared between the worker and the hospital.

(6) The bill should not come into operation until sufficient time has elapsed to allow servants to form their own societies.

(7) The numbers necessary to enable a society to become approved should be reduced from 5,000 to 1,000, to admit new and growing societies.

(8) Death benefits should be allowed to relatives of deceased members out of their surpluses.

68 The National Insurance Bill was introduced in 1911. Manual workers were provided with medical protection through a weekly contribution from their wages. Domestic servants objected to the scheme on the basis that they had low wages and organised a rally in protest at the Albert Hall on 29 November.

(9) There should be some rebate of tax for employers in the case of schools, lodging-houses, working-class shops, and similar establishments where the number of servants required is no index of the prosperity of the employer.

Yours, &c.,
Eva Gore-Booth.
Esther Roper.

Rossendale and women's suffrage

Manchester Guardian, 1 March 1912

Sir,
In reply to Mr. Harcourt's repeated claim to have 'almost a mandate from Rossendale electors against women's suffrage,' may we state a few of the circumstances for the consideration of practical people accustomed to elections? As secretaries of the Textile and other Women Workers' Committee (the committee that initiated Mr. Bulley's suffrage campaign), we had opportunities of studying Mr. Harcourt's methods and propaganda.[69] No impartial person could possibly say that 'anti-women's suffrage' was a subject on which he founded the smallest appeal to the electors. Mr. Harcourt's campaign was carried on on quite other lines, and this fact could easily be verified by an examination of his speeches and election literature. His anti-suffrage views were kept very quiet, and in many cases glossed over entirely by his supporters. The argument used in the election was simply this 'a vote for Bulley (the third candidate) is a vote for the Conservative and the House of Lords.'[70] We were accused of splitting the Progressive forces at a time of great danger and difficulty, when the country was in such acute danger from the aggressiveness of the House of Lords, and we were told if only we would have a little patience we should get women's suffrage anyway, because, although Mr. Harcourt might not be in favour of it, the Government he represented would certainly give it, and the House of Lords, if it still had the power, would refuse to pass it.[71] Judging by the list of supporters of the Albert Hall meeting, the second

69 The sitting Liberal, Lewis Harcourt, ran against the Conservative candidate J. Kebty-Fletcher at Rossendale in the 1910 general election. The Textile and other Workers Committee were intent on removing Harcourt from his position as MP; he was viewed as an ardent anti-suffragist. The Committee put forward Arthur Bulley as a suffrage candidate.

70 The Liberal Party had an overwhelming majority. Harcourt received a total of 7,185 votes, Kebty-Fletcher received 4,695 and Bulley received a dismal return of 639 votes.

71 The 'people's budget', introduced in April 1909 by the Chancellor of the Exchequer,

part of this prophecy seems fairly justified, but the electors seem to have been mistaken in their estimate of the wide discrepancy between the views of Mr. Harcourt and of the other body of legislators 'by accident of birth' whose discomfiture was at the time the principal plank in his platform.

If there is any need to prove the democratic nature of the suffrage movement, it is only necessary to put beside the list of anti-suffrage peers in the Albert hall the list of trade unions whose representatives voted the other day at the Labour Conference that they will actually resist any extension of the suffrage that does not include women. Obviously if there is any mandate against women's suffrage it comes from above and not from below, and we surely cannot reasonably fear, after all the rhetoric of the last few years, that the Government will flout the often-expressed feeling of the great mass of women's organisations of all kinds, the repeated demand of the majority of the trade unions (male and female), and play false to the movement that has, in fact, shown itself to be, in its manifestations, the strongest and most widely democratic movement of modern times, for the sake of the protest of a few of those whom fortune has placed out of reach of the difficulties and problems of industrial life. Surely the Liberal party are not going to transfer their allegiance from the people to the peers.

Yours, &c., Esther Roper and Eva Gore-Booth.

National Industrial and Professional Women's Suffrage Society.

The anti-suffragist

Manchester Guardian, 30 April 1912

The Princess in her world-old tower pined,
 A prisoner brazen-caged, without a gleam
Of sunlight, or a window of wind… .
 She lived but in a long-lighted dream.
They brought her forth at last when she was old,
 The sunlight on her blanched hair was shed
Too late to turn its silver into gold;
 'Ah! Shield me from this brazen glare,' she said

Lloyd George. The budget promised social reform through taxation of wealthy landowners. It was rejected in the House of Lords. In support of the people's budget, Prime Minister Asquith challenged the power of the House of Lords, a move which eventually forced the Liberal Party to return to the people for a general election.

War and the subjection of women

Manchester Guardian, 2 December 1912

Sir,

Your correspondent's terrible description in to-day's 'Manchester Guardian' of the condition of the cholera-stricken patients in Constantinople must surely throw a sidelight on the things that are included in the price a country pays for the subjection of its women.[72]

I venture to say such an appalling state of neglect and indifference could not exist in a country where the women had even the most elementary form of personal freedom. It was not for nothing that one of the very first signs of the coming emancipation of Englishwomen was the hitherto unprecedented expedition and original courageous revolt of Florence Nightingale. Nowadays we read without surprise of Italian and Greek princesses fitting out hospital ships and going to the seat of war; we remember the armies of English nurses who were willing to brave any danger in the South African War, and we are beginning to realise the dependence of human usefulness on human freedom.

Initiative and free action (as shown by the Parisian women in the time of the flooding of the Seine) are of course impossible to those whose lives are spent in utter subjection and passivity. But it is surely a terrible sight to see a nation, however mutely and unconsciously, claiming help in times of calamity from those very powers in women which are the common heritage of humanity and which in times of prosperity their own social order has crushed down and destroyed. A nation that is content to breed a passive and dependent spirit in its women must inevitably suffer from the artificially produced helplessness of the 'sex that does not fight' in time of war.

Yours &c.,
Eva Gore-Booth.

Women's wages and the laws of supply and demand

Nineteenth Century and After, August 1914

The constantly repeated assertion that the rise and fall of wages has nothing to do with politics, but is determined by the laws of supply and demand, has such a specious air of likeliness about it that it often passes unchallenged among those who are unacquainted with the complicated network of cause and effect involved in our modern industrial system. It is, in fact, not a downright falsehood, but one of those half-truths, founded on an incomplete analysis,

72 Constantinople, capital of the Ottoman Empire, now known as Istanbul. During the First Balkan War a cholera epidemic spread through the ranks of the Bulgarian and Turkish soldiers in November 1912.

which are hardest of all to fight. The fact of the influence of supply and demand on wages is, of course, as true as the effect of the law of gravitation on every material object. But when human will intervenes, these undisputed natural laws cannot be taken as the sole causes of any event which in a certain sense may be said to be due to their influence. Thus, if it was not for the law of gravitation it would be impossible for one man to throw another over a cliff; but there is no court of justice in the world that would take the law of gravitation as a satisfactory explanation of murder. Such a crime, like any other human action, is ultimately a question of character, will, and opportunity. The amount of value attached by a violent robber to the object he covets, the amount of daring in his character, the amount of principle to be overcome, his skill in carrying out his project, and his concentration and quickness of mind are all factors that go to determine the event. So it is with the laws of supply and demand. We know that these are fundamental and indisputable facts without which no industrial event could happen. But we also know that they can do nothing by themselves, that their working is directed, interfered with, and modified by all sorts of other, just as important, factors incidental to human life and character. And this is so chiefly because the demand for any commodity is founded on human desire, the most variable and fluctuating of forces, influenced by caprice, fashion, physical health or weakness, the weather, war, famine, time and the historical events involved – indeed, by every accident which human life is heir to. Thus the value of an object may rise because the demand is greater than the supply, but it must be remembered that the demand cannot be greater than the supply simply because the supply is small, unless people have need of that particular object. Supposing the human race were to cease eating some particular fish – say, lobsters – it would not matter in the least how rare they were and how hard to find, a lobster would at once become as valueless in the market as a rat. If, at the dictates of fashion, women's hats became like men's, and at the same time they ceased wearing silks and satins, as men have already gradually done, the value of artificial flowers, feathers, and costly stuffs would decline in direct proportion to the decline of the demand. Then, in times of war, the simplest necessities of life gain a great artificial value; the supply of bread may be cut off in a siege, but the demand remains steady. In the late coal strike the price of coal went up for the same reason. Such a strike in summer, or in the West Indies, would have had no such violent effect on prices. For the supply was cut off artificially at the same time that the cold weather heightened the demand. Then in a country without railways or factories the whole relation of the supply to the demand would have been different, and the result of cutting short the supply would have altered in proportion.

The prices of things, then, may be said to be regulated by the relation between the amount of the special need at any given moment for any particular article and the ease or difficulty with which this need is gratified. And all those factors that influence human will in desiring, or, on the other hand, human action in obtaining, have their direct influence on the price of commodities. It will be seen that this definition covers also all differences in prices caused by local or general rates of wages paid to those engaged in producing or transporting the particular commodity, and by their fluctuation increasing or diminishing the difficulty by which the commodity is obtained. Political and historical considerations are included, such as the effect of different tariffs on prices, an effect that has given rise to endless disagreement among those, who wish to arrive at the net result of the contradictory working of a force, that seems at the same time to put up the price of commodities and to increase the wages paid to the labourer. The problem of weighing good against evil results is further complicated by the fact that the labourer is always also a buyer, and so seems to gain with one hand and lose with the other, also by its effect on the shipping and transporting trade. Thus we see that a political measure can produce in its effect on prices a problem that, in its many-sided complications, has so far defied humanity to furnish a universally acceptable solution.

Now, as labour is a commodity bought and sold like any other commodity, anyone wishing to understand the cause of specially high or low wages gained by any special section of the community, men or women, must not be content with putting down these differences to the action of the law of supply and demand, but must examine carefully and weigh, on the one hand, all the human factors controlling and regulating the wish to use such labour by which the demand is governed, and also the forces that tend to an increase or decrease of the supply. Taken on the surface, without such an examination, the market of human work presents a strange and indeed baffling spectacle. Those who tell us that wages are entirely a matter of competition, that if there are fifty people wanting to do one piece of paid work they will undercut one another and so bring down the rate of payment, whilst if there are fifty pieces of work going begging, and only one worker available, that worker could command his own price, have not gone far in their effort to analyse and solve the manifold problems that present themselves to our minds. Taking an instance from the industrial experience of the upper and privileged classes, we find a member of the Government paid 5000*l.* a year for his work. Can we explain this by saying that there are so many Cabinet Ministers needed by the nation and so few people willing to do such work, that, in fact, the demand is so much greater than the supply that the Cabinet Minister, however incapable a worker he may be, can command a price for his labour of such proportionately large dimensions? On the contrary, when we look into the matter we find, first of all, there are six hundred men in the House of Commons, most of whom would eagerly desire such a position, and all of whom would consider themselves quite as capable of filling it with distinction as the present Cabinet. Then outside, the House of Commons there are thousands all over the country ready and willing to compete for such work, and yet this competition is no danger at all to Mr. McKenna or Mr. Lloyd George, nor does it in any way reduce the remuneration attached to their present positions. This is, of course, an extreme instance, but cases crowd into the mind of so-called 'jobs,' posts that are paid so highly as to be out of all proportion to their usefulness to the community or the difficulty of finding someone to fill them adequately. They are, as it were, shelters built through history by the favoured few to keep out the competition of the gradually evolving and self-emancipating multitude. The multitude, as it struggles forward in its slow, sectional, yet inevitable advance, has swept away many, barriers and filled with the strife and fury of competition many hitherto sacred spots reserved for generations as the heritage of a few distinguished names. But often this advance has only meant a widening of the ranks of the powerful to admit a few turbulent newcomers into the inner ring. Still all around us we see the influence of the past and the unassailable position of the first-comers, social prejudice, class precedent, interfering with and impeding and changing the direction of the laws of supply and demand. A Government clerk whose work requires no special training will earn his traditional eight or nine hundred a year. He may be a very useful member of society, but it will hardly be contended that, if the laws of supply and demand had been allowed their unimpeded way, his clerical labour could have commanded so much larger a reward than the skilled and trained engineer who is glad to earn 3*l*. a week. If we look into history we shall find everywhere under many guises the same constantly recurring struggle between the buyer and seller of labour fluctuating to and fro, and inspired by the two great clashing human desires, the desire to buy cheap and the desire to sell dear. We begin in the primitive physical-force days with the result of that warfare which, in prehistoric times, gave power to the victorious fighter and caused the dominance of a few chiefs, who were thus put into the position of buyers of labour. Thus was evolved the victory that first enabled the buyers to compel the labour of slaves for the (then not so small) price of subsistence and a kind of safety; the buyer's victory, of course, lying in the fact that for that price he bought not only labour but entire submission and dependence, and the now rightly unsaleable and invaluable quality of human life, depreciated and dethroned from its real sovereign position of infinite possibility.

The victory of the seller who becomes a buyer can be seen again and again in the annals of the past. We can trace it in the person of the general of a victorious army: David, who kills his tens of thousands, whilst Saul kills his thousands, and, prevailing thus against his competitors, commands, as the price of his labour, the power and revenues of the head of the State; or, to take a more modern instance, Napoleon, who, because of his many victories, is able to sell his labour, at the same high price, to the French nation. In all such cases an astute use of the laws of supply and demand has placed the user beyond the power of these laws. For when the seller of labour wins in the battle, his first care is to shield the fruits of his victory from the levelling action of these laws. He becomes, like David, the Lord's Anointed, or, like Napoleon, the Emperor who distributes a catechism to instruct his subjects that his will is as the Will of God, with like penalties for the rebellious. So has grown into being 'the divinity that doth hedge a king' and has been able to protect dynasty after dynasty through so many vicissitudes of the world's history.

Again we trace the same victory on a smaller scale in every country where an aristocracy has been evolved out of the turbulent elements of society on its way to organisation. The subordinate officers, generals and captains, demanded and obtained a high position, with lands and money, as a price of their labours. When they had obtained it, they managed to shield it from competition by the introduction of the hereditary principle. In this way, not only the King, but the upper classes have, at all events in England, been able for hundreds of years to shelter themselves and their descendants from the frightful severity of the laws of supply and demand. They grasped in their hands, for a time, all political power, and laws were made by them to protect their property and uphold their position.

In the industrial struggle of later days we see the same forces at work. From the ranks of the sellers of labour has emerged a class of buyers. It is a question whether the original founder of every great industrial enterprise in England was not a member of the working or professional class, in other words, the sellers of labour. The truth of this fact will be seen in the evolution of the new rich middle class, who are divided from the old aristocracy by the traditions of a different origin, and whose position and influence as buyers of labour is as powerful as theirs, and guarded in the same way by the laws of property and heredity. This new feudalism is indeed one of the most powerful forces of the present age, and here again we see that the victory of the seller of labour has simply resulted in changing him into a buyer of labour. But the world moves on. The sellers of labour have begun to think of themselves as a permanent and valuable section of the community, and in the present day we are in the midst of a labour problem which, in its efforts after adjustment in the relations of capital and labour, is convulsing society, and which might be defined as the growing struggle on the part of the sellers of labour to protect themselves from the laws of supply and demand, without changing their position as labourers – the attempt, in fact, to substitute a trade-union rate of wages for the supply-and-demand rate. This relatively new claim of democracy is quite distinct from, and often indeed at open war with, the old claim of a free passage and an easy ascent between the ranks of buyers and sellers. It is not enough for us nowadays that a grocer's assistant may become a capitalist and an employer of labour. It is not even enough that certain classes of 'professional' labour have established their right to high rewards. The same spirit that has enabled lawyers, doctors, and politicians to keep up their prices artificially is at present rapidly developing among the multitude of obscure and innumerable manual workers faced, in their struggle for existence, by the stubborn and difficult fact of an enormous supply of labour and a relatively small demand.

The revolt has two sides, as there are two ideas, often antagonistic, struggling for supremacy among the somewhat chaotic elements that go to make up our present English labour movement, the sectional and the universal. The idea of sectional advancement inspires an attempt to protect certain portions of the working class from the competition of their fellows, so that at all events some of the workers should be sheltered from the severity of the laws of supply and demand. The Trade Union movement is, of course, responsible for the development of this spirit. All this is natural enough. As a trade union is a body of workers in one particular industrial process, it is limited in its sympathies, and the first instincts of such a body tend to create a sort of corporate selfishness, which works out in an effort to keep up wages by reducing the supply of labour. It is thus likely to develop into a disintegrating force, responsible for much antagonism between different sets of workers. In its essence it is an attempt of certain classes of sellers of labour to keep up their own prices at the expense of other workers, to evolve, as it were, a new aristocracy of labour. Its application in the repeated and ever-recurring attempt to cut off the supply of women's labour, by rendering the employment of women in certain trades impossible or illegal, either by trade union action or by special Act of Parliament, has given rise to a most deplorable condition of sex war in industry. The same remarks apply to the feud between skilled and unskilled, the regular and the casual labourer, with the difference that different sections of men find it impossible to use the terrible weapon of political disablement against one another. This latter method of interfering with the law of supply and demand is, of course, only possible in dealing with the unenfranchised. Politicians will not entertain a proposal that, if on the other hand, any trifling and hollow excuse of philanthropy or propriety is enough to form the basis of an attack on the livelihood and wages of women. Thus in the past few years we have seen Parliamentary attacks on the employment of women acrobats, pitbrow workers, barmaids, and florists' assistants. The law against the employment of women at night is of course a tremendous handicap in the wages struggle and is an immense help to men trade unionists, in the printing trades more especially, in their efforts to make impossible the competition of women in the better-paid processes. When we compare the wages of the compositor earning 40*s.* a week and those of the woman folder and sewer who never can hope to make more than 15*s*., it is idle to say that this difference is due to the law of supply and demand, because it is really a result of artificially interfering with the action of this law; the compositors having protected their trade from its action by not allowing a great section of workers to compete, and thus strictly limiting the supply of labour. At the same time the competition in the lesser-paid processes is, of course, intensified, the supply is increased, the demand remains steady, and consequently wages go down. This result has not been obtained without fierce struggling among the workers, and it was only after a long but unequal fight that the Edinburgh compositors were able to get rid of the women who had been engaged for many years in the work. Another triumph of the same kind was scored last year by the brassworkers in the Midlands. In many ways these exclusions and repressions bring their own retribution. For years the mule-spinners were able to keep up their wages to 40*s*. a week by not allowing the competition of women. They have held persistently to this point, but the advance of civilisation has defeated them. The new process of ring-spinning has been invented, and is gaining ground every day; improved machinery, with women to mind the machines, is gradually taking the place of the old high-paid labour, which, of course, the employers are delighted to dispense with. The ups and downs of the struggle for sectional protection produce varying results, but to the careful observer the end seems inevitable. A house divided against itself cannot stand, and it is easy to see that no permanent solution of the problems of competition, satisfactory to the seller of labour, can be found along these lines of internecine warfare. It has been said that when thieves fall out honest men come by their own, but it is truer to say that when honest men fall out thieves come into what is not their own. When any set of workers are excluded from their trade a mass of unskilled labour is turned adrift on the market. It is unskilled because it is a rough practical truth that no working person is skilled in more than one trade. It goes to swell the supply of unskilled labour. So that while competition is reduced in the skilled trade, it is made proportionately more severe in the unskilled trades. And the net result is that the already well paid are better paid, and the badly paid are worse paid. The men whose trade is thus protected from the law of supply and demand earn artificially good wages, whilst the excluded section bring down the rate for all women.

But this is not the end. The mass of these workers struggling for industrial existence fall easy victims to the class of unfair and sweating employers, cheap processes and machinery are invented, and the men with their high prices and protected position suddenly find their whole trade cut away under their feet by a multitude of helpless, outlawed, unorganised, and half-starved workers. The old individual aristocracy found the means to shelter their position by heredity and law, the new aristocracy of labour, sectional instead of individual, cannot find any means of permanently sheltering themselves from the ruthless laws of competition, from which they have temporarily escaped. Instance after instance crowd into the mind of cases in which the buyer has eventually defeated the seller in this unequal struggle. As taxation and the loss of political power is gradually reducing the fortifications of the feudal aristocracy, so surely will modern forces, such as the growth of machinery and the emancipation of women, break clown the class distinctions that have gradually formed themselves inside the working class. As for the effect of the present state of warfare on the position of the women workers themselves, it will be seen that it accounts for a great deal of the undoubted hardship involved in their present industrial position.

The extremely low rate of remuneration earned by women has caused much discussion of late years. It is maintained that the reason why women's wages are so much lower than men's is because the supply of labour is so much greater than the demand; but it must never be forgotten that this is not because the supply is large, but because under present conditions the demand is bound to be small. There are not nearly as many women as men in the labour market, but most of the better-paid trades and processes are inexorably shut against their competition, and thus, whilst their labour is artificially forced into a few channels, it is inevitable that these channels should be swollen and overcrowded, and that in them the supply of labour should far exceed the demand. At present they are not allowed to be lawyers, clergymen, or politicians; the Stock Exchange is shut to them, so are all good Government appointments, and all the best work in the Civil Service, together with the best-paid trades and the better processes in the poorer trades. This artificial suppression of the demand for women's labour in the majority of paid employments is, of course, bound to have its effect on prices in the trades where they are admitted. It must be also remembered that as the demand for any commodity is determined by all the influences that condition human desire for that commodity, the demand for women's labour has been in the past, and still is, widely influenced by the world-old tradition of their inferiority and subjection. The factor of the social value of the labourer in determining the rate of his wages must never be left out of count. Trade unions by their combined action may do something to put up the industrial value of the individual. But it is easy to see that they can do nothing when confronted with an artificial suppression of the demand. And this because they are the result, not the cause, of good employment. If men were not allowed to be bookbinders or mule-spinners there could be no societies of men in these trades.

The traditional inferiority and subjection of women has made possible the task of those trade unionists who hoped to keep up their own wages by keeping, down the supply of labour, but such a position can only be temporary, depending as it does on the subservience and outlawry of a class that is gradually but surely gaining in independence, education, and force. Indeed, it is gradually being forced on the minds of many that the trade union position is inadequate to the growing needs and development of *The Times*. The sectional protection it affords is indeed only temporary: it is a half-way house in the evolution of the individual into the universal. As the result of this conviction we see the stirrings of a new idea in the minds of many workers, an idea that among men has taken to itself form in those often clashing elements and ambitions that have gone to make up the Labour Representation movement, with the consequent evolution of a Parliamentary Labour party.

Without any particular or reasoned scheme of Socialism, which indeed seems alien to the present trend of ideas in England, workers of all classes have joined together in a new effort to add to the industrial value of the labourer, without cutting down the supply of labour, by indirect means, such as pressure on public bodies, especially Parliamentary departments, and also by that improvement in the status of the worker, his position and his education, technical or general, which is bound to open up new fields for his activities and increase his earning power. This movement, in spite of the fact that it is so much wider than the trade union movement, cannot be called universal, as because of its Parliamentary nature it has so far limited its action to protecting the interests of the enfranchised – often, indeed, at the expense of the still excluded class of women workers. The characteristic of the new idea of protection is that it is a political protection; therefore, as it is, it is only partial, but with the enfranchisement of women it would automatically become universal in its protective action. Hence the place and usefulness of the women's suffrage movement in our industrial development, pointing the way as it does for the first time in history to industrial protection for the most defenceless class of workers. And surely, in view of the suffering caused by the present state of things, this is no vain dream. A society all of the members of which were protected from the ruthless working of the laws of supply and demand has perhaps never yet been seen on our planet, but none the less in one form or another it seems to be the goal towards which our modern society is slowly evolving. Year by year one class after another is added to the list of those who are allowed to benefit by the growing movement towards universal protection. Meanwhile the problem of the unprotected is slowly growing more and more difficult, try as we may to tackle it with anti-sweating and minimum-wage legislation. Because as surely as more and more workers are protected from competition, so does competition become more acute among those who are left out. The position of the women workers is unique. They are, in fact, in the gradual evolution of an ever-growing and widening system of industrial protection, among the last victims thrown to the wolves of supply and demand. But it will be said that if protection is universalised it will cease to exist. So it will in the relations of one worker to another, because there will be nobody left to be protected from. But trade unionists need not fear this state of things. What the working class needs is not protection from one another, but protection from the evils of poverty. And this is the new ideal towards which all social and industrial reformers are slowly feeling their way.

What the world seems slow to realise is that no solution of the labour problem can be even approximately satisfactory that does not include in the general amnesty and balance, towards which evolution seems slowly working, that class of women workers who are at present the only class of the community shut out from all the age-long protection, political and social, devised by humanity to circumvent the ruthless cruelty of the laws of supply and demand.

Eva Gore-Booth.

Women at the pit-brow

Manchester Guardian, 2 February 1914

Sir,

May I protest against the so-called 'amicable settlement' by which thirty poor women have lost their work at the New Charlston colliery, for no fault of their own except, of course, the initial one of having been born women? The strong protest of the Miners' Association has been successful. To the manager the whole matter appears a 'storm in a tea-cup'; pit-brow women have been deprived of their work, and everything is smooth again. The men did not even want the work; the management dwelt on the difficulty of getting boys to do it. There seems to have been no reason behind the violent action of the miners' official, besides the wanton bitterness of sex prejudice.

It seems almost like having a double political life, with a foot in both camps, that these men should go straight from this cruel attack on the liberty of women to earn their living to speak in London, not at an anti-suffrage meeting, but at an Albert Hall meeting organised to support the women's new claim to live their life in their own way – political, industrial, and social. For surely this is the real meaning of the women's suffrage movement. And in the light of this larger interpretation, the President of the Miners' Federation can surely be only regarded by women's suffragists as an opponent.

Yours & co.,

Eva Gore-Booth.

National Industrial and Professional Women's Suffrage Society.

Women teachers and the vote

Manchester Guardian, 9 April 1914

Sir,
Referring to Mrs. Fawcett's letter in the 'Manchester Guardian' to-day in support of the action of the Women Teachers' Franchise Union at the forthcoming Conference of the N.U.T., may we appeal to all conference delegates, whether men or women, to show their sympathy with the plucky fight that has been carried on by the suffragist members of the Union for the last year or two by joining in the demonstration organised by the Women Teachers' Franchise Union, in the Wesley Hall, Lowestoft, on Saturday, at 7.30p.m, as well as by supporting the women's suffrage resolution at the Conference itself?[73] Anyone who realises the splendid work of women teachers and the scant recognition that they receive from the State in the matter of pay and promotion must sympathise with these women in their struggle for the status and prestige of citizenship.

Yours, &c.,
Esther Roper.
Eva Gore-Booth

A medical loan fund

Manchester Guardian, 29 July 1915

Sir,
The letter which appeared in your paper yesterday signed by the Prime Minister, Mr. Balfour, and Lord Curzon drew attention to the great and pressing need for more women doctors, and appealed to the public to support the London Women's School of Medicine.

Now, of course, there is no need in Manchester for special women's schools, as we have at the University and Infirmary one of the best training schools in the country. The great need here is money for maintaining students, and thus enabling them to take advantage of the facilities already existing. Many exceptionally gifted women students are quite unable to afford the whole expense of this long training. A medical loan fund has been started, and there are several women anxious to avail themselves of this help. We earnestly appeal to all those who realize the grave urgency of the situation to send contributions in time to help a few women to start their medical course here in September.

73 The president of the National Union of Women's Suffrage Societies, Millicent Garret Fawcett's letter to the *Manchester Guardian* was published on 8 April 1914.

Cheques should be sent to the treasurer, Mrs. Alfred Haworth, Woodend, Altrincham.[74]

Yours, &c.,
Esther G. Roper.
Eva Gore-Booth.
Elizabeth A. Haworth.
5, John Dalton Street, Manchester,
July 27.

'Women's Rights'

Poems of Eva Gore-Booth

Down by Glencar Waterfall
There's no winter left at all.

Every little flower that blows
Cold and darkness overthrows.

Every little thrush that sings
Quells the wild air with brave wings.

Every little stream that runs
Holds the light of brighter suns.

But where men in office sit
Winter holds the human wit.

In the dark and dreary town
Summer's green is trampled down.

Frozen, frozen everywhere
Are the springs of thought and prayer.

Rise with us and let us go
To where the living waters flow.
Oh, whatever men may say
Ours is the wide and open way.

Oh, whatever men may dream
We have the blue air and the stream.

Men have got their towers and walls,
We have cliffs and waterfalls.

74 Elizabeth MacGowan (Mrs Alfred Haworth) worked with Gore-Booth at the Manchester University Settlement and later supported her many causes.

Oh, whatever men may do
Ours is the gold air and the blue.

Men have got their pomp and pride –
All the green world is on our side.

'The Street Orator'

Poems of Eva Gore-Booth

At Clitheroe from the Market Square
I saw rose-lit the mountain's gleam,
I stood before the people there
And spake as in a dream.

At Oldham of the many mills
The weavers are of gentle mind;
At Haslingden one flouted me,
At Burnley all the folk were kind,

At Ashton town the rain came down,
The east wind pierced us through and through,
But over little Clitheroe
The sky was bright and blue.

At Clitheroe through the sunset hour
My soul was very far away:
I saw Ben Bulben's rose and fire
Shining afar o'er Sligo Bay.

At Clitheroe round the Market Square
The hills go up, the hills go down,
Just as they used to go about
A mountain-guarded Irish town.

Oh, I have friends in Haslingden,
And many a friend in Hyde,
But 'tis at little Clitheroe
That I would fain abide.

Criminal Law Amendment Bill

Manchester Guardian, 22 February 1917

Sir,

At this time of rapid legislation there is a great danger of the Criminal Law Amendment Bill being passed into law without the public being aware of its real nature.[75]

This bill calls for special consideration, as it involves the sweeping away of a reform accomplished after years of agitation and work and the reintroduction of the worst feature of the Contagious Diseases Act.[76] According to Mrs. Josephine Butler's view, compulsory physical examination of prostitutes was the keystone of these Acts.[77] Under clause 2 of this bill power is given to the magistrate to order the medical examination, with a view to the discovery of venereal disease, of any person convicted of 'loitering or importuning passengers for the purposes of prostitution or solicitation.' This clause also applies to people found guilty under such Acts as the Indecent Advertisement Act, the Vagrancy Act of 1898, and many others, and to people found guilty of 'aiding or abetting the commission of any offense' under the Act itself.

The experience of every country in Europe proves the absolute futility of compulsory examination as a precaution against the spread of disease and doctors as well as social reformers have pointed out the danger of creating a false security in people's minds by a measure that is as ineffective as it is outrageous. Infection can arise shortly after examination, by which the object of the examination is entirely defeated.

It has been argued that it is a mitigation of the evil effects of the bill that it is supposed to apply to men as well as women. Without allowing for one moment that it would be any mitigation if this were in practice true, the circumstances of the case make the provision entirely theoretic. The clause is aimed at the weakest and most helpless class of the community, and as only a very strong and quick effort will prevent its becoming law, we appeal to all

75 The Home Office introduced a new Criminal Law Amendment Bill in February 1917. The Bill classified sexual intercourse or solicitation by any person suffering from communicable venereal disease as a criminal offence. The Bill also granted magistrates the power to order the detention of women under 18 who had been convicted of soliciting. Frank Mort, *Dangerous Sexualities: Medico-Moral Politics in England since 1830* (London: Routledge, 2000), p. 207.

76 Contagious Diseases Acts passed between 1864–69 to control the spread of venereal disease among the armed forces. On arrest, women were forced to undergo a medical examination.

77 Josephine Butler launched a campaign to repeal the Contagious Diseases Acts in 1869 and the Ladies National Association for the Repeal of the Contagious Diseases Acts was established.

those who care about clean living, human kindness, and liberty to use at once every means of urging its deletion.

Yours & c.
Eva Gore-Booth
Sarah Dickenson
Esther G. Roper
Manchester and Salford Women's Trade and Labour Council.

The coalition majority

Manchester Guardian, 7 January 1919

Sir,
It has been stated by Mr. Bernard Shaw and by other Progressives that the reactionary results of the present election are due to the votes of the newly enfranchised women.[78] On examining the figures it seems that this result is not due to the voters, men or women, so much as to those responsible for the present system of Parliamentary representation. If five million odd voted for the Coalition and over 4,500,00 voted against, it is surely childish to argue that there was an overwhelming majority in favour of the Coalition, or, indeed that the country was swept by a great wave of pro-Coalition feeling. Rather it is fair to say that the overwhelming majority of Coalition members in the House of Commons is a result of the failure of the machinery at present employed to give any effective expression to the will of nearly half the voters.

Sometimes one is inclined to think that on the solution of this problem depends the future of centralised representative government in this country. If nearly half the electorate is represented by 221 members and the other half is represented by 484 members, then one sees how easily the present system may work out into a state of things that in theory might seem farcical but in practice is a real danger to democracy.

Yours &c., Eva Gore-Booth.

78 This was the first general election to take place after the Representation of the People Act 1918 was introduced. The act vastly reformed the British electoral system by removing virtually all property qualifications, enabling men over 21 years of age to vote and women over 30 who adhered to some property qualification.

PART II

Pacifism and conscientious objection during the First World War

The First World War vastly changed the face of both the trade union and suffrage movements. Days after war was declared in August 1914 the Home Secretary, Reginald McKenna, announced an amnesty releasing all suffragettes imprisoned for anti-government and militant activities. Mainstream suffrage organisations suspended their campaign for the vote, joining forces with the government in support of the British war effort. The National Union of Women's Suffrage Societies (NUWSS), under the leadership of Millicent Fawcett, proved their commitment to the British war effort by establishing support facilities such as Red Cross centres and hospital units at the front. Leaders of the Women's Social and Political Union (WSPU) toured England on a recruitment campaign actively promoting the introduction of enforced conscription to military service. Emmeline Pankhurst proudly proclaimed to Edith Shackelton of the *Daily Sketch* that 'we are doing everything we can to help recruiting'.[1] Mrs Pankhurst adopted what can be described as an extreme patriotic stance, evident in her decision to rename the WSPU journal, *Britannia*, complete with the slogan 'For King, for Country, for Freedom'.[2]

The patriotic activities of such women soon stretched to publicly humiliating men of military age who did not voluntarily join the army. A favoured activity was to target young men not in uniform and publicly present them with a white feather as a sign of cowardice.[3] Admiral Charles Fitzgerald initiated the scheme in Folkestone at the onset of war. Fitzgerald condemned young men who did not join the military as 'slackers' and 'loafers'.[4] His scheme for public humiliation was soon employed by women across Britain as an active recruitment tool.

Initially young British men rushed to answer the call to war. On 7 August 1914 Field Marshal Lord Kitchener, newly promoted to the position of Secretary of State for War, submitted the first public appeal for 100,000 men to volunteer for war service with the infamous call, 'Your King and Your Country Need You'.[5] Several more such calls would soon be made.[6] The high levels of

1 Laura Mayhall, *The Militant Suffrage Movement: Citizenship and Resistance in Britain, 1860–1930* (Oxford: Oxford University Press, 2003), pp. 121–2.

2 The WSPU launched their first journal in October 1912, entitled *The Suffragette*. The journal was renamed *Britannia* in October 1915.

3 Mary A. Ward and Emma Orczy promoted the scheme to women in Britain.

4 Andrew Lambert, 'Fitzgerald, Charles Cooper Penrose (1841–1921)', *Oxford Dictionary of National Biography Online Edition* (Oxford: Oxford University Press, 2004).

5 Peter Simkins, *Kitchener's Army: The Raising of the New Armies, 1914–1916* (Manchester: Manchester University Press, 1988), p. 39.

6 *The Times* (28 August 1914), p. 6

recruitment to the armed services was also driven by women who encouraged, inspired or humiliated their male folk into joining the armed services.

By 1915 the numbers of men volunteering for war service was not enough to replace those killed or maimed at the front. Propaganda posters soon appeared, imploring men to sign up in order to protect their women and children at home. Recruitment posters became increasingly more emotive. After a German bombardment on Scarborough in December 1915 a poster depicting a small girl holding a baby outside a bomb-damaged building was widely distributed. The caption implored 'Men of Britain! Will you stand this? 78 women & children were killed and 228 women & children were wounded by the German raiders.'[7] The recruitment campaign was also increasing in Ireland: Figure 7 shows the crowds gathered for a Royal Dublin Fusiliers recruitment parade in 1915. An estimated 80,000 Irishmen had enlisted in the British army during the first twelve months of war.

As war dragged on, the economic consequences on the home front were soon realised. The NUWSS reacted by establishing an employment register to organise the replacement of male labour with female. On 17 July 1915 thousands of women who had previously marched against the patriarchal establishment took to the streets of London in a woman's-right-to-serve demonstration. The *Illustrated London News* admiringly described how 'the demonstration will be historic, and when the story of the World War comes to be written, the patriotic part played by women of the Empire, of France, of Belgium, of Italy, of Russia will be chronicled, and this great demonstration of women craving to work for the war will find honourable place'.[8]

Women would, however, also become the key instigators of British anti-war campaigns. When the number of men volunteering for war service began to subside, Gore-Booth turned her efforts to the anti-conscription movement in England. Her activities would later influence anti-conscription activities in Ireland to great effect. Adopting a pacifist stance in England at this time was a particularly defiant act. Gore-Booth was at risk of being labelled unpatriotic or even worse viewed as a German sympathiser in the midst of anti-German propaganda in Britain. Yet from the onset she was prepared to make anti-war statements publicly. By now Gore-Booth and Esther Roper had moved to London. The smog-bound air of industrial Manchester was worsening Gore-Booth's already rapidly declining health. The two women moved into the top floor flat at 33 Fitzroy Square in the fashionable area of Bloomsbury (see

7 The sub-caption reads, 'No. 2 Wykeham Street, Scarborough, after the German bombardment on Dec. 16th. It was the home of a working man. Four people were killed in this house including the wife, aged 58, and two children, the youngest aged 5.' Prints and Photographs, Library of Congress Division, Washington, POS – WWI – Gt Brit, no. 39.

8 *Illustrated London News* (24 July 1915), p. 109.

Figure 7 Dublin Fusiliers recruitment parade, 1915

Figure 8). Gore-Booth was now residing in the capital and was best placed to conduct public speeches against war and to become involved with emerging pacifist groups.

Part II contains copies of Gore-Booth's speeches, pamphlets, letters to newspapers and journal articles promoting ideals of pacifism. The first entry is a speech delivered by her on 12 December 1914, only months after war was declared. Gore-Booth addressed a meeting of the National Industrial and Professional Women's Suffrage Society in London and like many other speeches in Part II it was later published as a pamphlet. In this instance the pamphlet was printed by the Women's Printing Society which had been established by Emma Paterson with the help of Emily Faithfull in 1876. The Society employed female printers and typesetters when the trade normally excluded women.

The next year Gore-Booth spoke at the Pacifist Philosophy of Life Conference at Caxton Hall, London in July 1915.[9] The conference was significant for numerous reasons. The programme of speakers included many notable figures including the philosopher Bertrand Russell (third Earl Russell), the peace campaigner Arthur Ponsonby (first Baron Ponsonby of Shulbrede) and writer

9 A full report was published: *Towards Ultimate Harmony: Report of Conference on Pacifist Philosophy of Life, Caxton Hall, London, July 8–9, 1915* (London: Headley Bros. for the League of Peace and Freedom, 1915).

Figure 8 33 Fitzroy Square, Bloomsbury, home of Eva and Esther during the First World War

Violet Paget (pseud. Vernon Lee.) Over four hundred people attended the conference and it was reported that they were 'keenly attentive and sympathetic' and the papers were of 'high intellectual quality'.[10] The conference

10 As reported in the *Labour Leader* (15 July 1915), cited in Bernd Frohmann, Mark Lippincott and Richard A. Rempel (eds), *The Collected Papers of Bertrand Russell, Volume 13: Prophesy and Dissent, 1914–1916* (London: Routledge, 1998), p. 145.

resulted in the formation of the League of Peace and Freedom, an organisation with which Gore-Booth instantly became involved. The organisation was described as offering a 'socio-psychological critique of war as "the result of a false attitude towards life in the individual and the community"'.[11] Attending this conference had a lasting effect on Gore-Booth; while there she befriended Fenner Brockway, founder of the No Conscription Fellowship. The Fellowship offered protection for men who refused to take up arms on moral, religious or political grounds.

By the time that Gore-Booth met Brockway the Great War had been raging for just one year and already it had claimed an enormous loss of life. The numbers of British soldiers at the front was declining rapidly. Not enough men were volunteering for war service and those killed or maimed were simply not being replaced. One week after the pacifist conference was held at Caxton Hall, Prime Minister Asquith proposed a national registry to record the details of everyone living in Great Britain between the ages of 15 and 65. The compulsory registry revealed that two million eligible men had not yet volunteered for war service.

For the first time in history, military conscription was introduced in Britain, coming into effect on 2 March 1916. The Military Service Act contained a section allowing for individual exemptions due to conscientious objection. However, the process for gaining an exemption from war service would prove to be particularly challenging. Over 2,000 local tribunals and seventy appeal tribunals were established across England to hear cases. Tribunal members were generally elderly, middle-class men. The work was unpaid and seemed to attract enthusiastic supporters of war.[12] If a man failed to gain an exemption from a tribunal and still refused to take up war service he would face a court-martial and ultimately a prison sentence. The law did not exclude the possibility of a death sentence, although such sentencing was not enforced.

The high level of arrests depleted the male membership of the No Conscription Fellowship. The female members oversaw a highly organised press department to expose the injustice and brutality of the way conscientious objectors were treated. As part of their propaganda campaign the fellowship launched a weekly newspaper, *The Tribunal*, in March 1916. Initially the journal was printed by the National Labour Press, the same printers of the *Labour Leader*, the Independent Labour Party's journal. Fellowship members monitored the

11 League of Peace and Freedom, *Towards Ultimate Harmony: Report of Conference on Pacifist Philosophy of Life* (1915), pp. 171–2. As cited in Martin Ceadel, *Semi-detached Idealists: The British Peace Movement and International Relations, 1845–1945* (Oxford: Oxford University Press, 2000), p. 218.

12 As identified by Thomas C. Kennedy, *The Hound of Conscience: A History of the No-Conscription Fellowship 1914–1919* (Fayetteville: University of Arkansas Press, 1981).

activities of appeal tribunals. Hundreds of volunteers attended trials across the country recording personal details of conscientious objectors, remarks made by tribunal members, perceived illegal activities and the outcome of cases. These fastidious details were published in their newspaper on a weekly basis. Gore-Booth travelled across the country attending as many tribunals as possible in her role as a 'watcher'.

Due to the contents of *The Tribunal* military authorities made persistent attempts to disrupt the publication. The National Labour Press offices were raided and their printing presses dismantled. The No Conscription Fellowship simply organised more printing equipment. The fellowship offices were raided and a member, Joan Beauchamp, was arrested. Beauchamp eventually served a prison sentence for her anti-war activities but not until 1920. The General Secretary, Violet Tillard, was sentenced to sixty-one days in prison for refusing to divulge the whereabouts of the printing equipment. Edith Smith was sentenced to six months in prison for printing a leaflet without submitting it to the strict scrutiny of censorship.

Gore-Booth was undeterred by such criminal prosecutions. She dramatised a day in the life of a 'watcher', a day she spent in an 'ugly airless' room. The stark story was published by the National Labour Press as a pamphlet. Her account provides a rare glimpse into the oppressive process involved in seeking an exemption from war service. Gore-Booth's account, originally entitled 'At the Military Tribunal' was published simply with the same title as the Fellowship journal, *The Tribunal*.[13]

Many of the writings in Part II relate to the plight of conscientious objectors. The writings were published as pamphlets by the League of Peace and Freedom, the National Labour Press and the Women's Printing Society. Gore-Booth wrote letters on the issue to the *Manchester Guardian*. Short articles were published in *The Flame*, the official journal of the League of Peace and Freedom and a longer prose text in one of the most distinguished theosophical journals of the time, *Service*. During the war years Gore-Booth became involved with the Theosophical Society and formally joined the Hampstead branch of the Society in 1919. Theosophy is a New Age esoteric religion which combines science, eastern religions and spirituality. Theosophy was amenable to feminist politics and opposed to war in all its forms.

The final writings in this section are taken from Gore-Booth's poetry collection, *Broken Glory*, published during the end of the war in 1918.[14] This small volume, published by Maunsel Press in Dublin, is packed with strong political

13 Pennsylvania State University Libraries, Eva Gore-Booth Collection, box 1, folder 15: AX/B40/RBM/00139, original handwritten manuscript 'At the military tribunal', by Eva Gore-Booth.

14 Eva Gore-Booth, *Broken Glory* (Dublin: Maunsel, 1918).

sentiments and was surprisingly passed by the British censor. *Broken Glory* contains anti-war poems but also crosses over into Irish nationalism which is treated in Part III of this book.

Whence come wars?

A speech delivered at a meeting of the National Industrial and Professional Women's Suffrage Society, in London, 12 December 1914

I think I may assume that none of us at present need any convincing as to the intolerable and squalid horror of war. We read in the papers every day, as a matter of course, of thousands of brave people of all countries shot dead or mutilated for life; we hear terrible tales of hardship, of the cold and wet, and the unbearable filth of the trenches, and of the frightful illness caused by privation and suffering, the brain affection that is the result of staying for days with your feet in water, the tetanus that comes from poisonous conditions, the pneumonia and fevers, and the thousand and one cases of mental and nervous collapse that must be the result of the unnatural and hideous conditions of life. Then we hear of a devastated country, towns bombarded, villages burnt, crops destroyed and thousands of people face to face with all the miseries of famine and homelessness. In our country we are surrounded by mourners, by people who have lost all that made life worth living, whose nearest and dearest are lying dead among the unspeakable horrors of what is called the field of honour.

Instances of heroism self-sacrifice shewn by soldiers on all sides have been quoted as a justification for war. But it only adds a little to the general tragedy to think that such fine qualities should be lost to the world, and lives that might have been so useful swept away in the universal and intolerable carnage. For indeed in normal times of peace, Society has much need of the heroic virtues, in the present difficult and complicated struggle to build up a more ideal industrial and social civilisation. Consideration of and liking for the individual soldiers can only deepen our horror at the orgy of death and destruction that is going on around us.

But I do not want to dwell on this side of the question; it is far too real already to most of us. The thought that forces itself on one's mind is that this state of things is not like any other great catastrophe, a mine disaster, or a pestilence, or a famine; it is not an accident or the consequence of some uncontrollable elementary force; it is the deliberate and calculated result of human will power and intelligence, determined by some extraordinary paradoxical impulse on the destruction of everything that is of value to human life.

I think one may say at present that public opinion has reached this point: very few people have a good word for war in itself, they often detest it, but they look upon it as a terrible necessity, a dreadful means to a righteous end.

Now almost every problem of modern morality results from the different views that people take of this fundamental question, how far the end justifies the means.

We no longer sell our souls to the devil: we make an instrument of the devil and use him to fight against evil. When we go to war we must convince ourselves somehow that we are fighting in the cause of righteousness and justice. It is idle for Mr. Bernard Shaw to rail against English people for what he considers their hypocrisy in justifying the present war as a noble struggle undertaken in defence of a small and weak nation fighting for existence against fearful odds.[15] If he goes to Germany he will find the same sort of thing, the peasants defending their beloved Fatherland against the aggressive militarism and tyrannical oppression of Russia. For Turkey on the one side this war is a holy war just as much as it is for Russia on the other. Without some such pretext no nation could nowadays face the horrors and miseries and universal suffering of war. When we send people out to kill and be killed we must feel that the cruelty of our deeds is redeemed by the nobleness of our purpose. We have long passed the days when we could injure one another light-heartedly and glory in it. We justify ourselves by phrases. For a great right we will do a little wrong, as if a great right was ever helped by a little wrong. And then there is that other phrase quoted in the reviews and papers, and I think responsible for much muddled thinking. 'Righteousness backed by force.' I should like to set against this quotation another one that seems to me truer; then 'because right is right to follow; right wore wisdom in the scorn of consequence.' If you want to get rid of the tyranny of a phrase, the only thing to do is to analyse it. What is this force that is the ally of righteousness? The most direct way to find out is to go to France or Belgium and see for yourself. Failing that you can read the newspapers and talk to wounded soldiers. You will find that force means practically the power of killing, wounding, and disabling masses of human beings. Now alter the phrase a little. Say 'righteousness backed by massacre and mutilation.' When you put it in plain words doesn't there seem something; a little incongruous in such an association?

At all events there is nothing new in the idea. A large percentage of the admittedly worst deeds done in the more modern history of the human race, have been done as force to defend righteousness. Every heretic murdered in the Massacre of St. Bartholomew, every priest tortured and burnt at Smithfield, every harmless old woman persecuted and hunted and finally burnt as a witch, every innocent mortal beheaded in the French Revolution, was a

15 The Irish playwright, George Bernard Shaw, was an outspoken opponent of the war. He published an essay 'Common sense about the war', *New York Times* (Nov. 1914), in which he criticised 'the British civilian [who] does not allow his perfect courage to be questioned'.

martyr to the delusion that you can defend righteousness with force. We look back with horror on what are to us the foolish atrocities of the Middle Ages. Yet we seem to have changed in little except in our idea of righteousness. We no longer defend religion by force, but we are still ready to kill and destroy in the name of those things we hold sacred, such as science, the good of the State, our country, and even liberty itself. In the time of the Inquisition we tortured people's bodies, not to wreak our anger, but to save their souls, and no doubt the inquisitors honestly regretted the terrible necessity of inflicting pain for even such a glorious end. Nowadays we vivisect animals, not for the pleasure of torturing them, but for the sake of the knowledge that may in the end, we think (erroneously or not) help science to combat disease. We hang murderers, not because anybody really thinks nowadays that revenge of an 'eye for an eye' and a 'tooth for a tooth' kind is right, or because we like doing what we think wrong, but simply because we think such revenge is necessary for the good of the State. Those people who wish to regulate vice will tell you that they are taking a morally dubious but necessary method to secure the health of the community.

I could give you many instances of the deep-rooted conviction that is the basis of so many people's thinking, that to do evil that good may come is not to do evil at all, but to do good in a very painful manner. For indeed the whole work of such organisations as the Humanitarian Leagues might be defined as to attempt to prove to the world that no good ever really comes out of doing evil, that it is a foolish and vain dream to think that you can train the devil and force him to serve God, and that no amount of noble purpose can justify a cruel deed.

Of course the argument depends altogether on what view you take of evil. Perhaps I have taken it too much for granted that people will take the New Testament view of it, that is an absence of love or goodwill in one's dealings with life outside oneself. To those who deny the existence of good and evil I would suggest that the same result would be reached by speaking of goodwill and hate as opposites. To those who take the Old Testament view of evil as disobedience to arbitrary regulations imposed by Providence, and who can look upon religion as obedience to authority, I can only say l hope that the result of blind obedience to authority may horrify them into disbelief in the divine nature of external powers.

This question has another side. It is quite obvious that if you really believe good will result from evil doing, you will be equally ready to believe that evil will arise from doing right. How many social reforms have been checked by this fear among politicians of doing good lest evil should result.

I think those of us who worked in the Suffrage movement must be interested to note a curious psychological fact that the very people who were afraid to do what they acknowledge to be good and just because they were sure it would bring an evil result on the world, were ready enough to undertake the evil business of war, not from love of evil, but from their sure conviction that as a good deed would have an evil result, an evil deed would have a good result. The world seems strongly convinced that the true way to ensure justice and righteousness is not by being just and right oneself, but by going out and killing other people for failing in the same virtue. We deplore the militarism of Germany, we think by defeating her we shall put a stop to it, whereas all we can really possibly do is to convince her that we too put our faith in militarism and our militarism is stronger than hers. For allied to the theory of doing evil that good may come there is another doctrine that may not be so openly recognised but haunts the dark corners of most people's minds. Again in the varied ups and downs of the Suffrage movement it became clear to many of us that (expediency apart) the very real obstacle that stood in our way was the very strange and unreasonable superstition that physical force is the right and sensible basis for society. Now physical force is not a possible basis for society; it is the destruction of society. To found society on physical force is like founding it on a volcano. We see the logical result of such a foundation in the present catastrophe. Mr. Bernard Shaw points out that the only way you could really crush a nation is by killing all the women, and of course the stability and strength of a society in time of war depends on the amount of its population it is able to keep outside the physical force arena, for it is on there the future depends; they are the true foundation of the civilisation of to-morrow. Society is really based on a contract of mutual help and goodwill among certain individuals, very likely a peace for interested motives, but still peace, and the use of physical force involves the cancelling of this contract, and consequently the break-down of society. Society and civilisation exist in England to-day, not because of war, but in spite of war.

I am purposely not entering into the question of the unfortunate European diplomacy that led to the war. We have, many of us, personally, to begin with, too long and sad experience of the standards and ideals of politicians to wonder at the breakdown of their powers of negotiation. I have no doubt if I had been the warlike ruler of a powerful nation instead of a humble representative of a peaceful Suffrage Society, I could have found it in my heart to declare war over and over again against any one of the Cabinets that have ruled over us in my time. And I feel sure that other nations must have had the same kind of experience of their own rulers. I don't go quite as far as the distinguished critic who said he thought 'that at the end of the War every country in Europe ought to hang all its politicians,' but I do think that the present deplorable state of affairs is due to the spirit in which international diplomacy has been carried on.

It is the idea that physical force and the implied life and death struggle of contending interests is the basis of life, with its consequent admission of enmity as a natural and right relation between human minds, together with the idea that you may do evil that good may come, righteousness backed by force, that have made the present state of things possible.

We have surely reached the logical result of some wrong doctrine when we find the Governments of ten civilised nations forsaking their proper functions of caring for the welfare and happiness of the governed, and straining every resource of science and knowledge to cause as much pain, on as big a scale as possible.

People are always saying the Christian doctrines of non-resistance, of turning the other cheek, of returning good for evil, are impractical and impossible. I cannot see how people can say that because they have never been tried, the doctrines of force and resistance have been tried ever since the world began, and the results have been so disastrous that most of us are in our hearts longing for a change of some kind.

I think we have a clear proof that difficult international questions can be settled without an appeal to arms in the history of the disarmament of the United States and England on the Canadian frontier. It seems to us now a quite natural and easy thing that there should be no friction here, but it isn't so long ago that this enormous frontier of 4,000 miles was in a state of armed suspicion, very much like the frontier between France and Germany. It was only after the war between America and England that rose out of the Napoleonic wars, when part of Canada had been taken, and retaken, and England had been defeated once or twice at sea, that by the determined and repeated efforts of President Munroe and Mr. Adam, a treaty was concluded which had for its main condition the dismantling of ships of war on both sides that were patrolling the lakes, and general disarmament on the frontier. Note we see the result of the disappearance of armed force on both sides in the present relations between England and America, relations which however they may go up and down between friendliness and coolness, have yet somehow managed to eliminate altogether the possibility of real physical warfare. This story would seem to prove that to get rid of irritation you must abolish the armed force while the irritation is still there.

Then again Sweden and Norway have been able to separate without a fight. If this had not been actually done everyone would say human nature being what it is, it is quite impossible. The fault is not in human nature itself, it is in the false ideas to which human nature has somehow adapted itself. It is a mere get-out to speak of the necessity of war and say to the non-resister, 'if you had been in Mr. Asquith's or Sir Edward Grey's position, at the beginning of August, would you have declared war or not.' Because the answer is, if Mr.

Asquith and Sir Edward Grey had been non-resisters they never could have got into such a position and the problem for them would never have arisen.[16] If people would give half the will and brain power and scientific work that they now lavish on the problem of trying to defeat Germany, to the problem of how to avoid war, we should soon be delivered from this appalling curse.

Human nature has been, I think, very much wronged in the whole controversy; war is not due to the passions of the multitude. The multitude's passions are roused after war has begun, but what passion was there on the subject of the Austro-Serbian crisis in England before the beginning of August? The soldiers indeed fight often enough without any angry passion, merely because they think it their duty, their minds are full of courage and self-sacrifice, their only fault is that they have submitted their wills and their consciences to the dictation of other people. The life and death struggle and clash of interests is not between the nations, nor between the soldiers, but between the politicians.

Indeed the majority of peace people are telling us now to cure war we must get democratic control of our foreign policy. There must be no more secret treaties and back stairs diplomacy. Everything must be done in the light of day and in the glare of public criticism. I think this is absolutely true as far as it goes, and in so far as the very admission of the democracy tends to create a new spirit among us. But if it only means the admission to power of a new class with the same ideals as the old, a class with submissive and uncritical minds, easily distorted and deluded by the thoughtless savagery of the daily press, it won't carry us very far. What we want is more than a new organisation of diplomacy, it is a new spirit of friendliness and goodwill.

People also think that the entrance of women into political life and responsibility will make a difference to our way of thinking and there are two very strong reasons for hope along these lines. Firstly, although individual women are just as savage and ready to fight as individual men, for a variety of reasons women do not form themselves into bands and go out and take life, and collectively they have absolutely nothing to gain and all to lose by war. They have no share in the honour and glory of war, although they have in the danger; indeed, in the Boer War for instance, 20,000 Boer women and children lost their lives as compared to 4,000 men. We do not yet know how many women have been killed in France and Belgium, but we do know that guns bombarding a town are no respecters of sex, and that wherever there is a war some country is invaded, and wherever a country is invaded women are killed. They are also victims in the same degree as men to the frightful pestilences and diseases that are bound to follow war. When their country is not invaded they yet suffer if not from the loss of life itself, from the loss of all that makes life worth living.

16 Sir Edward Grey, British Foreign Secretary from 1905 to 1916.

In no case do women gain anything at all by war. Men tell them that soldiers are protecting their hearths and homes, and even lives from destruction. If this were true it would be intolerable to any high-spirited woman to be asked to buy her life and safety at such a price of suffering and death to others. But it is not true. As far as safety and comfort goes, who would not now rather be a woman of Luxembourg with no army to protect her, than a woman of Belgium protected by the armies of France, England and Belgium. The protected Belgian women are at best homeless fugitives, at worst murdered victims of war, whilst the unprotected Luxembourgers whose country is occupied by the German soldiers, are alive and well in their own homes.

But I have another and a stronger reason for thinking that when women have their share of political power, there will be no more war. I have tried to make clear in the course of what I have been saying that the reasons that have prevented men politicians in Europe giving women Suffrage, are the same reasons that made them able to steer their countries into war. I have even suggested that other iniquities, such as vivisection, capital punishment, much of our penal system, as well as war, and women's repression, are all the result of the same mental mistakes, a great many beads, different in themselves, yet threaded on the same string.

The enfranchisement of women would mean that the string was growing too weak to hold beads together. That politicians were beginning to trust that part of the race most removed from the exercise of physical force, that they were beginning to do what they knew to be just, to do right without fear of producing wrong. Such an action would shake the ancient rule of force and expediency to its foundations.

When people really understand that it is the action of a lunatic to do evil that good may come, and that goodwill is a truer basis for society than physical force, then war will be abolished, and woman enfranchised, and people will try to live with one another, and with animals, in friendly sympathy and kindness.

During the last fifty years all over the world women have struggled and worked for Women's Suffrage. And the Governments of Europe have tacitly said to them over and over again, 'We can do quite well without you, thanks; men can manage the affairs of the world; we have no need for your assistance.' They have had it all their own way. And now look what they have brought the world to. They have absolutely broken down in their proper function. They have turned the world into a vast slaughter-house. They are spending all their science and money, the fruit of ages of toil and self-denial on engines of destruction. They have failed hopelessly in their task. The blind have led the blind, and we are standing by to see the result. Isn't it time that women, who feel the burden of all the present death and horror and mourning, should free their minds and enlarge the scope of their actions, and make the force of their thoughts felt in the sphere of foreign diplomacy, the sphere in which our men politicians have most dreaded and deprecated the influence of women, and in which they themselves have failed most utterly and hopelessly.

Eva Gore-Booth.

National Industrial and Professional Women's Suffrage Society,

5 John Dalton Street, Manchester.

Religious aspects of non-resistance

A paper read at the conference upon the pacifist philosophy of life, Caxton Hall, London, 8 July 1915

'Where the mind is without fear and the head is held high;
Where knowledge is free;
Where the world has not been broken up into fragments by narrow domestic walls;
Where words come out from the depth of truth;
Where tireless striving stretches its arm towards perfection;
Where the clear stream of reason has not lost its way into the dreary desert sand of dead habit;
Where the mind is lead forward by Thee into ever-widening thought and action.
Into that heaven of freedom, my Father let my country awake.'

Rabindranath Tagore.

All of us who have been thinking about the present war must surely have been struck by two facts that at first sight seem to contradict each other. First of all there has never been a war in the world's history in which have been engaged so many kindly, humane and enlightened people, who hate the whole horrible business from the bottom of their hearts, and who are anxious to civilise war and carry it on with as little cruelty and as much humanity as may be. Secondly, in spite of this, this war is a specially fearful, destructive and cruel war, it affects non-combatants on a larger scale and more terribly perhaps than war has ever done before in history. It is, in fact, causing the most gigantic accumulation of pain and misery and death that the world has ever seen.

And this seems to be chiefly because we are cleverer than our ancestors. Now to my mind it is not the least of the condemnations of war, that, the cleverer you are at it, the more intolerable it becomes. It is only if you are very stupid and primitive in your methods that it is at all endurable to humanity. Take, for instance, the fact, that we have all read in the papers, that one shell from a naval gun has killed 500 people and destroyed six months' stores, and contrast that with the amount of damage done by the bows and arrows of our ancestors. When we think how imperfect is our present understanding of scientific forces, and yet what we can do with it, we must realise that unless we make some vital change in our way of looking at life, every step in our advancing knowledge of science is a new danger for the human race, and that perfection in that knowledge might really and practically work out at the wiping out of humanity itself.

Now it is no wild Utopian theory but a hard practical fact that those among us who think life worth preserving as in itself a good and beautiful thing, who have some kind of faith or interest in the human race, have only two courses open to them, to make war on science and to save ourselves through stupidity, or to make war on war. To try to stop the progress of science, as the churches found in the Middle Ages, is a desolate and hopeless enterprise, as it is making war on that progress and evolution which is an essential part of life itself. To stop scientific development and research, even in the interests of the survival of the race, is of course an absurd and impossible idea, and, if it were not, which of us would care to survive at the expense of our brains?

When people in the Middle Ages found that there was beginning to be a clash between their scientific and their religious ideas, their first impulse was to try and stamp out this science which they felt to be a danger to their religious life. When they found fire and sword could not stop the growth of knowledge, they began to readjust their religious views to such good purpose that, nowadays, it would seem quite absurd to us to think that the fact that the earth goes round the sun could upset anyone's religious faith. Has not our knowledge, like theirs, outgrown our wisdom, and is not therefore the necessary task before us not to decrease our knowledge but to increase our wisdom. Whilst our science is the science of the twentieth century, our morality is the morality of the Middle Ages. Is there not some understanding we might attain to, which would allow us to profit from the wonderful discoveries of Sciences as regards the annihilation of space, the resulting drawing together of the race, whilst resisting the temptation of using them to destroy our neighbours?

Now, personally, I do not believe that the human race is going to rush to its own destruction. We are not Gadarene swine, animals rushing headlong over a precipice at the mercy of some blind and infatuated instinct of self-preservation, but human beings, with minds and capacity for thought, and it only remains to be seen how much suffering it will take to stir our minds into activity on unaccustomed lines, to force us to question the philosophy and traditions of the past, the host of suggestions that have surrounded us from infancy.

It is useless to think you can ameliorate or civilise war. If Science discovers more effectual means of destroying masses of human beings, those means will be inevitably used. For the object of war is to maim, kill, weaken, and cripple your adversary into a state of helplessness, savagery, and unscrupulousness will help a nation to win, whilst humanity, scrupulousness or pity must inevitably tend to failure. As a matter of fact, the standard in war must always be set by the most savage combatant. The kingdom of hell as well as the kingdom of heaven is like a grain of mustard seed. We may begin by making resolutions to be moderate, civilised or humane. But standards are quickly lowered by the pressure of an iron necessity, passions develop by the way, and those who are carrying on war will soon find that they are carrying on a crazy competition in destructive cruelty, and that when once the grain of mustard seed is planted, it grows swiftly and inevitably into a great tree that overshadows the earth and hides the sun.

Faced with this appalling calamity of present cruelty and destructiveness of war and the unthinkable horror of its future development, we are justified in trying to find some way of thought, some change in our ideals, that will make war impossible. I hope nobody thinks this is a mean motive, like being driven into a religious life through the fear of hell. We know that no religion could be founded on fear. And yet, on the other hand, nobody could think it mean or cowardly, when in a community, after some frightful experience of the ravages of cholera, small pox or typhus, people are driven to reconsider their way of life in the light of the laws of hygiene and cleanliness.

Now I want to take all this, for a moment, from the point of view of the wisdom to be found in the New Testament. I suppose the key to every religion is to be found in its conception of God. In the New Testament one finds two conceptions of God, one is Light, the other is Love. I do not think it will be denied that Light and Love are the same things as knowledge and humaneness. If it is true that every advance in knowledge makes war more intolerably anti-humane than before, and every advance in humanity must make it more unsuccessful, how can anyone who believes in the Divine Nature of light and love or knowledge and humanity not see that there is something utterly irreconcilable in the essence of war itself, with that conception of Divinity, no matter in what cause the war is begun?

Those who think that force is allowable in a good cause, as what has been called high-handed righteousness, though not in a bad one, have to face the fact that this theory would justify almost every violence in history. Agamemnon sacrificed Iphigenia for the purest motives of patriotism. In the Middle Ages, all sorts of people, such as Joan of Arc, Giordano Bruno, Latimer, Father Campion, and thousands of others on both sides were burned or hung in the cause of religion. Christ was crucified to save disorder and rioting, and because it was necessary one man should die for the people. Socrates was poisoned because his teaching was considered a danger to the State. Every war that has ever been fought, civil or international, has been fought for at least two good causes, one on each side, because naturally every cause is a good cause to its adherents. For indeed whatever the cause of violence may be, its result is always the same, no amount of good motive makes any difference to the amount of pain, suffering, and death brought into the world by violence. 'Oh, Liberty, what crimes are done in thy name,' exclaimed Madame Roland, and, indeed, one often thinks that the cruellest deeds of the world have been done by those human beings who have been able to convince themselves that strong measures are justified in the defence of all they hold most sacred, be it religion or patriotism, or liberty, or even the safety of those they love.

The question is, are we going on for ever with all the cruelty and destruction of war, saying that it is inevitable that we should do evil in a good cause, or are we to find some other way of serving liberty and justice and noble causes, that does not involve the wholesale massacre of human beings. If it is true that violence for righteousness sake results logically and surely in a measure of suffering and destruction, not the least lessened by the goodness of the cause, but in exact proportion to the amount of violence used, it must surely be true that in some way or other our popular standard of right and wrong has been mistaken, that the fact that we have fallen not into a ditch but over a precipice, means undoubtedly and truly that the blind have been leading the blind. Now it sounds paradoxical, but is nevertheless true, that nobody will arrive at the idea of non-resistance unless he has most strongly cultivated his powers of mental resistance to suggestion. For to arrive at the substitution of goodwill for force in human relations one must be able to resist the sway of a host of ideas and assumptions that have come to be an integral part of the sub consciousness of a great many people. Ideas such as, 'You must be ready to fight in a great and noble cause,' 'You must stick up for your friends and crush your enemies,' 'If you see the strong attacking the weak you must go and knock down the strong,' 'You must help your side against the other side,' 'You must be ready to face fearful odds in the defence of all that is dear to you.' You must in fact use force and coercion, though with regret, when it is necessary to secure the triumph of good against evil.

I think all these ideas get their influence on our minds from the fact that they have a certain amount of truth in them. For instance, if you are going to fight at all, it is better to fight in a good cause. If you must crush your enemies, it is a step in the right direction to stick up for your friends. If you must take sides in a fight, it is less mean to help the weak against the strong, than to help the strong against the weak. If you must kill, it is more generous to do so in defence of other people's lives than in defence of your own. If you feel it necessary to use force and coercion in your relations to the world, it is better to strive consciously for the triumph of good than to fight for the possession of money or power. If you are going to use a wrong method it is perhaps better to do it for a right motive. The idea that lies behind all these phrases, inspiring and justifying them, is one that has caused great havoc and suffering in human affairs. Most people, indeed, take for granted, without discussion or insistence, that a human being is naturally a fighter, and that a criticism of causes and methods is the only concern that morality can have with the question of war. And this again is a half-truth, because each human being is indeed, naturally a fighter, but not a fighter against other people. Our brains and arms are weapons indeed in the great struggle of humanity with adverse forces, mental and physical, but to use them to destroy other people is to turn our weapons against our friends, and by doing so lose ground in the real battle, the battle of evolution, by which the human race is seeking to wrest knowledge and unity, happiness and beauty out of a world of stubborn and adverse forces.

To concentrate all our force and courage and heroism in this struggle is the opportunity that comes to those who refuse to use these qualities in a struggle against other living beings. To those who believe in the oneness of the Spirit of the Universe, whether in its old Eastern form as the doctrine of the unity of all things, or put into modern theological language as the unity and Fatherhood of God, such a change of the field of battle will seem natural enough. It is curious to note how the foundation of this idea has been strengthened by the discovery in modern science of the unity of all physical life, involved in the idea of evolution, and popularised as a vague insistence on our relations to the monkeys. The fact of this physical brotherhood makes more real to us what many people look upon as a mystical Eastern dream, that sense of unity which is the inspiration of all art, whether it is expressed in the subtle relations of the vibrations of colour and form, or the mysterious movements and affinities of rhythmic sound, or the strange new values and sympathies and identities involved in poetic imagery. Again and again this haunting sense of the oneness or reality has inspired revolutionary genius in the attempt to bring new values and relations into our mental and moral outlook. Indeed, the two great religions of the world that have been founded on a logical conception of the unity of all life, Christianity and Buddhism, have also been united in their effort to set a new ideal before humanity. Instead of the mighty and successful warrior, the knight errant rescuing the distressed, rewarding his friends and punishing his enemies, we have, in Buddhism, the ideal of the friends of all the world, the enlightened and all-powerful man who, as Buddha says, 'neither contends nor kills, who desires not to get the victory, who is moved by goodwill to all the world.' The conception of a character who, when he was reviled, reviled not again, and when he suffered threatened not, who loved his enemies, did good to those who hated him, and would not allow his friends to strike a blow in his defence, or in the defence of the cause he represented, but suffered the last extremity of pain and death without a struggle or even a protest, seems far removed from what we know of the stormy fighting gods of the Celtic, Teutonic, or Scandinavian nations. On the whole, such an ideal seems also foreign to the orthodox religions of Egypt, Greece and Rome, though here and there among the Greeks we find traces of such thoughts. They are also to be found in the writings of the Chinese philosopher, Lao Tze, a contemporary of Buddha's, whose belief in the power of gentleness is one of his most characteristic thoughts. There is something very human and modern about his complaint of the unreasonableness of people: –

> 'Nothing on earth is so weak and yielding as water, but for breaking down the firm and strong it has no equal. All the world knows that the soft can wear away the hard and the weak can conquer the strong, but none can carry it out in practice.'

It was perhaps in ancient India that the sway of the gods of force and conquest was first disputed by the foreshadowing of a new philosophy, a philosophy put into form by Buddha five hundred years before the birth of Christ in words such as these, 'If a man foolishly does me wrong, I will return to him the protection of my ungrudging love, the more evil comes from him the more good shall go from me,' and again, 'what now, brothers, is right action, a man, brothers, has given up killing, without stick or sword, compassionate, full of sympathy, he cherishes kindness and pity for all living things.'

The story of the pilgrims and the lion is an illustration of the logical completeness and unflinchingness of Buddha's point of view.

From the Dhammaphada

Two pilgrims journeyed through a desert place
   To find the grove where that world-honoured one
Preached unto men and Devas, by God's grace
   A lion met them at the set of sun.

Unto the love of all things bound and vowed
   One pilgrim dared to die nor drew his sword,
And his white soul, winged like a silver cloud,
   Stood with the Deva throng before the Lord.

The other, gazing on his brother's clay,
   Longed so for the Lord Buddha, that he slew
The lion standing on the Holy Way,
   Nor any gentle dream of pity knew.

But stumbled on the path and wandered far,
   And toiled across the sandy desert wide,

And found our Lord under the evening star
  And a bright Deva standing by his side.

And knew his comrade by the lion slain,
  And marvelled much and longed to see him there,
Deeming him rotting on the distant plain
  Who dwells with Buddha in the inner air.

Whence come you brother, whom I left for dead,
  Such worlds away by that fierce lion torn?
Ah, long I wait for you, the Deva said,
  Here by his side who waits for all things born.

And gently on those brave companions smiled,
  The Lord of all things at the inner gates,
Where through long centuries with blood defiled
  Gotama, dreaming, for the Lion waits.

The idea of the unity of life and its capacity for perfection is expressed very strikingly in this story, where the three persons of the legend, the one pilgrim in his self-defence, the other in his non-resistance, and even the lion himself in his aggressive fierceness, are represented as all journeying by degrees to the same goal of universal love and unity, the goal that Buddha himself has already attained to after many lives in different forms.

Again we read in the Dhammaphada, how Buddha, in explaining the reason of a misfortune that has befallen some seemingly innocent person, tells that in a past life the sufferer has been guilty of causing the same pain to someone else, as he says, 'that which I now do in my body hereafter shall I myself receive,' or of the mercy earned by another man, because of the mercy he has himself shown, as in the story where he explains his own kindness to a very revolting mendicant after appealing to the general principles of mercy and deliverance, by telling how, in a past life, this very mendicant was executioner to a wicked king, and that he had shown mercy in one particular case to a man who begged for it, and Buddha ends the story by saying, 'As I was the man who begged for mercy, my lot is now to help this wretched man as he had mercy on me.' The theory seems to be that, because of the unity of life, you can never escape the consequences of your actions, for what you do to another you do potentially to yourself. This is no question of a punishing God, but, as the future flower is contained in the bulb, or to use a modern illustration, as the photograph is contained in the undeveloped film, so does every deed of force involve future force against yourself, every cruel action means a future suffering from cruelty, every act of rigid justice against some offender works out in the end as an act of rigid justice against yourself, and every action of kindness or mercy means kindness and mercy earned by the doer, in the midst of those circumstances produced in a future life by one's present actions. And this, because it is part of the little understood nature of things, that as all life is one, all actions one does are really and practically done to oneself. This doctrine of the justice and mercy of the Universe is indeed founded on a deep conviction of the unity, of the goodwill, the slow inevitable evolution, and what one might call the interchangeable sensitiveness, of all things human and divine.

The same idea may be found very strongly expressed in Christ's teachings, as for instance when he identifies the suffering of a sparrow with the consciousness of God, or in sayings like, 'Inasmuch as ye did it unto the least of these my brethren ye did it unto me,' and the repeated assertion that what you do unto others shall be done unto you, whatsoever measure you mete it shall be meted unto you, also, 'Blessed are the merciful, for they shall obtain mercy,' also in the often quoted, 'They who take the sword shall perish by the sword.' It is very noticeable that this saying might be put as a moral at the end of many of the stories in the Dhammaphada that illustrates the Buddhist doctrine of Karma by explaining how an injury done to another person is always in the end suffered by the doer of the injury, even after many years and lives. 'That which I do now in my body, hereafter I shall myself receive.' But perhaps the great force of Christ's doctrine of non-resistance, as expressed in the Sermon on the Mount, is due to the fact that, in his justification of it, he appealed not only to this doctrine of the unity of all nature, which has indeed been the essential belief of mystics of all ages, but he added to that an idea which must have been strange to his hearers. After he had attacked the ideals of his time, and indeed of our time, the old instinctive defensive standard of the nations, 'Love your friends and hate your enemies,' and the old ideal of justice, 'An eye for an eye, a tooth for a tooth,' he expressed his own ideals in words so familiar that I need not quote them, about not resisting evil, and turning the other cheek, and so on. And then he justifies his position by a startling appeal to his conception both of the nature of God and the divine nature of human life. To those who have been taught to conceive of God as the Lord of Hosts, the Judge and Avenger of the Jews, it must have been rather shocking and startling to be appealed to to prove their identity with an unflinching, logical, impartial force of kindness and goodwill, to be asked to show themselves the children of 'your father who is in heaven, for he maketh his sun to rise on the evil and the good, and sendeth rain on the just and the unjust.'

This appeal to our identity with the divine impartiality leads of course straight to what one might call the foundation idea of non-resistance, for it implies that one should treat other people according to what one is oneself, not according to what they are. And that self must be without variableness or shadow of turning. 'Perfect as your father in heaven is perfect.' Some of us are accustomed to feel uneasily that there is a certain amount of loss of fine qualities of determination, endurance and courage involved in non-resistance, but is it not rather a gain in strength of character to act always unswervingly according to what is in yourself, independently of outside circumstances or the deeds and passions of other men. To those people who wanted to call down fire from heaven to consume those whom they honestly felt to be the enemies of God, Christ answered, 'You know not what spirit you are of.' Violence, force and hatred in public or private life only become possible when we have mistaken our own nature, and have allowed ourselves to be swept away by the pressure of circumstances, from the truth that is in us, till we are out of touch with the overwhelming inevitable purpose of all things, that spirit of unfaltering goodwill what we call God, the light and love that is also the deepest principle of our own minds.

'Utopia'

Broken Glory

Cruelty, bloodshed and hate
Rule the night and the day,
The whole earth is desolate,
To what God shall one pray?

Is there a force that can end
The woe of the world's war?
Yea, when a friend meets a friend
There shall be peace once more.

For love at the heart of the storm
Breaks the waves of wild air,
And God in our human form
Is life's answer to prayer.

The death penalty

Manchester Guardian, 20 January 1916

Sir,

With regard to the refusal of the Government to eliminate the possibility of the death sentence from the Compulsion Bill, may I point out that, as the bill now stands, if a man fails to convince a committee nominated by the local authority not only that he is a bona fide conscientious objector, but also that a conscientious objector ought to be exempted, he may pay with his life for the private militarist views of members of his district council. For the district council is not bound to exempt conscientious objectors; it is only allowed to do so if its members approve of such exemptions. To judge by what one reads in the press, many people have, quite honestly, lost all their respect for a man's right to his own soul and conscience, and are ready to try to force anyone by threats and even extreme punishments to do what he thinks wrong. Of course in many cases men of local standing and influence may be able to gain consideration, but what is going to happen to the poor and friendless man, who has surely as good a right to his own conscience and life as the son of a local magnate?

It is idle to tell us, as Sir F. E. Smith did, that the death sentence has not been carried out on soldiers in this country, when large sections of the working classes believe that offenders against military discipline are sent to France and then dealt with by the 'humane' tribunals that (according to Sir F. E. Smith) carry out the appalling penalties that are legalized by the Army Act, penalties such as death for disobedience to an officer.[17]

Your, &c., Eva Gore-Booth.

The Tribunal[18]

'Conscientious Objectors'

For the Hidden One in every heart,
Lost star in the world's night,
Fire that burns in the soul of art,
The Light within the light –

For the gentleness of Buddha's dream
And Christ's rejected truth,
The treasure under the world's stream,
Pearl of pity and ruth –
Before six ignorant men and blind
Reckless they rent aside
The vail of Isis in the mind ...
Men say they shirked and lied.

The tribunal

The ugly airless room with its hot-looking glass roof seemed to be strewn with wreckage and haunted with memories of vain appeals and helpless protest. It was just 3.30. The watcher in the gallery, whose head was beginning to ache from bad air, was engaged in counting up from notes, taken by her next door

17 Frederick Edwin Smith, 1st Earl of Birkenhead, then Attorney General.
18 Published as a pamphlet by the National Labour Press *c*.1916.

neighbour, how many small businesses had been wrecked since she came in at 2 o'clock. It was like walking down a street looking at the remains of the shops after a Zeppelin raid. One old man, particularly, it was impossible to get out of one's head. He was a working man whose two sons had started a little tailoring business three years ago. One of them was already at war, and the old man had come to claim an exemption for the remaining son. He was so obviously frail and broken that you would have thought his case would have wrung pity out of a drum-head court martial. He had brought with him a solicitor, who explained that if his son had to go the business would have to be shut up, and the old man and his wife of 68 would have to go to the workhouse. For a moment one felt sure that even these men, with their merciless mania for destruction, must feel a touch of human sympathy and understanding. There was a moment's pause. Then the Military Representative looked up and said decidedly, 'We want that man,' and in a moment the Chairman was pronouncing his strange formula, 'The Tribunal have carefully considered your case, and find they cannot grant you any exemption.' The old man, who had stood up all through the proceedings, turned and groped out of the room with a sort of lost and baffled look that was very painful. After that came a conscientious objector. He was a very young man, obviously sincere and intensely nervous. You felt that never before in his life had he dreamt of telling the public about his religious convictions. The watcher noticed that her neighbour (she who took the notes) was praying for him with concentrated force and energy. He was fair game for the Tribunal, especially for its clerical representative, who seemed to pursue him with the relentless animosity of the professional for the enthusiastic amateur. He was quickly reduced to pulp. It was found out that he was not really a Quaker, that he only went to the Friends' Meeting-house because he agreed with their views about war, and he did not even subscribe to their funds. Of course, after that he had no chance. Then the Church intervened, and the clergyman floored the poor young man with the inevitable Sphinx riddle, 'If a German attacked your mother, what would you do?' The young man hesitated for a minute, then he said in a very low, uncertain voice, 'I would try to make terms with him.' 'How I wish the Government would do likewise,' was the thought that passed through the watcher's mind as she craned her head over the gallery railing, and very nearly dropped her umbrella on the clergyman's head (quite by accident) in her endeavour to hear better. But down below in the Tribunal the remark was received with general derision. The clergyman stuck to his point, 'Would you rather kill a German or allow a German kill your mother?' The woman with the notebook drew in her breath and prayed hard. The young man did not answer. Over and over again the clergyman repeated his question, doubtless convinced that his foe was utterly defeated, not knowing as indeed men of his kind never do know, the difference between silence and defeat. Quickly, though after the usual 'careful consideration' of a minute-and-half, the man's claim to a conscience was dismissed, and he himself was hustled out. At the door, in his nervous hurry he managed to collide with the next applicant, a large and somewhat heavy-looking merchant. He had come to protest at the ruin of his business. The Tribunal were much politer to him, he was a publican, and one of them actually chaffed in about being one of his best customers. One could see they respected him as an honest, upstanding Englishman, not one of these wretched, shivering cowards hiding behind their humbugging consciences. But still for all that, his doom was sealed. The usual formula was said over him, and he went away protesting. After that two or three conscientious objectors got very rough treatment. One man, who looked refined and rather delicate, and said he was studying architecture, was asked in the good old hearty English fashion, 'How often he had a bath?' and 'if he lay in bed all Sunday' and advised by the Tribunal 'to get up early and go to bed early, and his conscience would soon cease to trouble him.' The whole attack was quite unprovoked, the assumption seeming to be that the possession of a conscience indicated the presence of an unhealthy mind in an unhealthy body. Anyhow, for that young man the cross examination began with insult and ended with injury. And all the time he was quite unmoved and gentle, yet sticking firmly to his belief that war is against the spirit, teaching, and example of Christ in the face of the Church and its official representative.

There was another applicant who gave the nerves of the Tribunal a very bad shock indeed by the crudity of his answers. He was a pleasant smiling young man with an imperturbable temper, much at his ease, and obviously full of friendly interest in his fellow-creatures. He was asked 'Why do you consider Christ was opposed to war?' He leant back in his chair and considered for a moment. 'Well, you know,' he said, slowly smiling at the Tribunal, 'one can't exactly picture Jesus Christ taking a bayonet and sticking it into a German soldier or an English one either, for the matter of that.' A distressed flutter passed over the Tribunal. 'Oh,' said the Chairman tactfully trying to cover up such an unexpected lapse from good taste and good feeling, 'I don't think we need consider such an extreme case as that.' Afterwards the same young man electrified the Tribunal by allowing that some time before the war he had lectured on 'The Hypocrisy of Patriotism.' By that time, of course, his case was hopeless, but he filled up the measure of his iniquities by letting out the disgraceful fact that he dared to live, and lecture too, in the sacred precincts of the Y.M.C.A. Not even content with this, when asked why he ventured to live there he said, quite unconcernedly, that it was called Christian, and therefore he thought it was a very suitable place to shelter a man with his views. Of course he had no chance, but then nobody else had either, and, at all events (the watcher thought to herself) he got a real run for his money.

At any rate, there were three types – the nervous young man who had no fluency, but whose sincerity broke through the strain of his uneasy manner, and was quite unquestionable; then there was the other, quiet and determined; and lastly, the straight-looking young man with the pleasant face, who knew so well how to hold his end in that rather one-sided debate, where his adversaries had been rehearsing their parts over and over again for endless weeks of weary afternoons. Two things they all had in common, they were all sincere, and they were all dismissed as imposters by the Tribunal. The watcher had just remembered that that was the last conscience case that was going to be heard that afternoon, and was beginning to calculate how she could go without threading on her neighbours toes, or making too much noise, when she became aware that a new claim for exemption was being read out, which seemed to be based on rather an old assertion, 'that the spirit of God in the hearts of men has no power to hurt or kill anyone.' The Clerk read this out in a rather puzzled voice, whilst the new applicant sat down and looked with apparent interest at each member of the Tribunal in turn. The watcher noticed the manner of the Chairman stiffen as he allowed he had been out of work for some years and had no permanent address. 'A regular loafer,' he murmured aside to the clergyman, who nodded back to him with a kind of I know-the-sort-of-fellow expression. Then the Chairman began his usual conscience-searching questions. The applicant had a very peculiar voice, clear and rather high, with a curious, almost tragic, sound to it. After a few minutes the woman who took notes and had begun writing again, suddenly shut up her book, sat bolt upright, and gazed over the heads of the Tribunal, with a look of astonished interest at the young man's impassive face. He looked up, and a glance of recognition passed between them. At the moment one was glad to see he had a friend in the gallery. He seemed a man of very decided views. When the Chairman asked him what church or religious society he belonged to, he said, 'I am not here for any church but for the sake of Reality and Truth.' When the clergyman asked him to explain his rather blasphemous-sounding assertion that the Spirit of God had no power to kill or hurt anyone, he said, 'Power to hurt is an evil thing, therefore the Spirit of God has no power to hurt anyone.' 'Well, I'm not a theologian,' said the Chairman, 'but I don't see what that's got to do with your objection to defending your country.' 'Don't you see,' said the applicant, 'that the truth in a man's soul is the Spirit of God. Therefore, as man who knows his own soul can never hurt or kill a living thing. It is only they who do not understand themselves who can do such things.' The Tribunal obviously couldn't understand what he was driving at, or what all this talk had to do with conscientious objections to military service. 'Any way,' one member remarked, 'too much conscience seems to have a very odd effect on the brain.' The young man said nothing.

But when the Chairman asked him 'how long he had held these views,' his emphatic answer, 'Always,' provoked some laughter among members of the Tribunal, and one member asked him, 'was he born a Pacifist or did he feel it coming on after being christened?' The clergyman frowned as if he felt this remark was derogatory to one of the most important ceremonies of the church. But the young man answered the question at once, as if he had been waiting for it. 'These ideas,' he said, 'are not yours or mine to come and go, and be taught to one person and not another, the spirit that has no power to hurt is your own soul, only you do not know it. When you have found your own soul you will understand my words, but not till then.' The clergyman got rather red, 'Since when' he said hastily, 'has the Spirit of God prevented a young man like you doing his best to help his country and his friends,' 'I am here' said the applicant, 'to show others the Reality I have found in myself, not to help them kill each other.'

'That's not what you're here for,' said a member of the Tribunal rudely, 'You're not thinking of helping anybody. I don't suppose a man like you ever helped anybody in his life. I take it you're here to get us to help you to get out of doing your duty and defending your country.'

Now came the time for the clergyman's coup. 'If,' he said, 'your mother was attacked by a German with a bayonet, would you not kill him to save your mother's life?'

'May I ask you a question in return?' said the applicant. 'Do you believe in God?' and he looked straight in the clergyman's face. The clergyman was irritated. He answered sharply, 'Look here, young man, it won't help your case to be impertinent, you must know I am a clergyman … '.

The young man answered without apologising but without anger, 'Then you do believe in God,' he said, 'well, if that is so, do you not think my mother's life would be safer in His hands than in mine, stained with my brother's blood.' 'I suppose you'd leave her to fate and run away,' said a member of the Tribunal, with a kind of vague spite. The young man did not answer. Another member of the Tribunal, who seemed a little friendlier than the others, asked the applicant if he would not help his country by doing non-combatant service? In this way he could help his friends without injuring his enemies. To this he answered with a friendly smile, but with a decided shake of the head. 'The only work I will do is the work of the spirit that is within me.'

'In fact,' said the Chairman, summing up, 'You won't help your fellow-citizens, and you don't recognise your duty to the State that provides for you and defends you from your enemies, don't you think you're rather selfish?' The young man said, 'It is God, not the State, who defends us and provides for us, and all the people in the world are our fellow citizens, I help everyone whom God gives me the power to help.'

By this time the clergyman was really angry. 'Do you ever read your Bible, young man?' he said. The applicant smiled, 'Not often,' he said. 'I thought so,' said the clergyman, 'then you probably don't remember that Christ told us to render unto Caesar the things that are Caesar's.'

'Yes, but so few things are Caesar's,' said the young man, 'some metal coins he has minted, the house he has built, the land he has seized, but never my soul or yours. My soul, my life, my conscience, my mind have nothing to do with the State. They are free as the sunshine and the air, for they belong to God alone.' 'You seem to me to repudiate all your most sacred obligations,' said the clergyman, 'do you really think we can claim to be called a Christian, in any true sense of the word?' He had taken up the telephone book, and was turning over the leaves as he spoke. There was a moment's pause. Then the applicant answered, 'You may call me what you will,' he said, 'I am one who lives the truth he has found in his soul.'

'He says he has a conscience; why, he isn't even a Christian,' said a member of the Tribunal. About three minutes later the Chairman announced the decision of the Tribunal in the usual formula: 'The Tribunal has given your case the most careful consideration,' he said, 'and owing to your refusal to help your country in any way, they have come to the conclusion that your conscientious objection is not genuine, and therefore they refuse to give you any exemption whatever.' The young man said nothing, and turned to go out of the room. As he did so, the woman with the note-book got up suddenly and leaned over the railing staring at him. He looked up, and there was something in his face, seen at a new angle, that startled me. I had a sudden attack of curiosity. 'Who is that queer young man?' I said to her, 'I seem somehow to have heard him speak before, but I don't know when or where ... 'Oh do you not know,' she said, 'it is Someone I have been hoping all my life to meet – people said He would come here again, but, indeed, I never thought to find Him here.'

The faith of the conscientious objector

Manchester Guardian, 18 March 1916

Sir,

A man was refused yesterday total exemption at the Holburn Tribunal on the ground that he was not a Quaker. Another man at the same Tribunal who had proved to any impartial person a conscientious objection of a religious and moral nature was told that because he had asked for a total exemption and was not willing to undertake non-combatant service the Tribunal did not believe in his sincerity and refused him any exemption at all. At Tunbridge Wells a well-known conscientious objector was refused exemption on the ground that he was not a Christian. Mr. Clifford Allen, who is widely known as a conscientious objector, was also refused all exemption.[19] Another man was refused, in my hearing, because the chairman said he could not consider his conscience, but must subordinate it to the conscience of the country he lived in. These are only a few examples of what is going on all over England.

The result of this action of the tribunals must, of course, be that the majority of the conscientious objectors will not in the eyes of the law be conscientious objectors at all; the conscience clause will become, as far as they are concerned, a dead letter. Take this in conjunction with Mr. Tennant's amazing and sinister answer to Mr. Snowden, that the words of the bill that 'a man who failed to obey an order calling him up from the reserve for permanent service under the Military Service Act shall not be liable to suffer death' really only applied to 'conscientious objectors,' and we are face to face with the full horror of the situation.[20] Men whose only crime, even in the eyes of their enemies, is that they take the words and example of Jesus Christ in too literal and overpowering a manner for six or eight men among their fellow-citizens are at this moment in England in danger of being shot for their adherence to these ideas. Yours & c.

Eva Gore-Booth.

33 Fitzroy Square.

'To J. W. in Winchester prison'[21]

Broken Glory

Yet once again the barred and bolted gate,
The smiling face seen through a wire cage,
The foolish tools of state-entrenchèd hate,
The prisoner's dream beyond all fear and rage.

Outside men's maniac fury shrieks and raves,
And dark submission chained in sunlight dwells,
The only free souls in a race of slaves
Live in strange solitudes and prison cells.

19 Clifford Allen helped form the No Conscription Fellowship and was an active anti-war campaigner. He published his controversial speech 'Is Germany right and Britain wrong?' in 1914. Allen contested his conscription in 1916 and was arrested and jailed in August of that year.

20 John Tenant, under-secretary of the War Office. Viscount Philip Snowden openly supported the No Conscription Fellowship in Parliament.

21 Written to an unknown conscientious objector in Winchester Prison where many COs were incarcerated during the First World War.

Rhythms of art

League of Peace and Freedom pamphlet number 12

As the word Art has many meanings I had better begin by explaining not what I think it ought to mean but simply what I mean when I use it. I mean 'the true expression in form of a human being's perception of one of the hidden rhythms of the Universe.' You may say this is only an analysis of Mr. Clive Bell's definition 'significant form,' but for my purpose the analysis is necessary, as it is only through analysis that one can get to the hidden ground of unity under the varieties of outward form.[22] It will be admitted that to create new and significant form you must understand the forces that are behind form. No amount of sticking out in an unforeseen direction will make form significant to you. Put an ordinary inartistic person down to draw a willow, he will produce a more or less accurate copy of the form of the tree. But let an artist want to re-create the significant form of a willow in a picture. The hidden rhythm that is the essence of the tree's life will take hold of his soul and haunt his sub-consciousness till out of the insistency of the rhythm the form emerges reborn in his mind, not a copy of a tree, but a true and living expression of his own perception of, and close affinity with, the hidden force and rhythm in things that rushes forth into exact and accurate expression in the form and character of a willow.

Such a painter we call instinctively a creative artist, as distinguished from a mere copyist, as we feel that for his work he is in touch with, and able to draw upon, that creative force and essence of life that is behind all outward form, and by its mysterious rhythms builds up the living, breathing, coloured world of every-day experience. But Art does not only deal with visible objects. The rhythms that express themselves in thoughts and ideas in the human mind can also rush forth into individual manifestation at the will of the artist. Thus there are two ways of writing verse. It is easy for anyone to produce passable verse by imitating the style and method of some real poet. But real poetry springs from the same foundation as real painting, real sculpture, real music. It is the outward expression by a poet of one of those strange essential hidden rhythms of the Universe that has haunted his soul and maddened his brain, until he found relief in projecting it into the world of thoughts and words that seemed to be his world, waiting in chaos and inherence to spring into living form at the rhythmic touch of creative force. 'Here is the finger of God, a touch of the Will that can, existent behind all laws, that made them, and lo they are! and I know not if save in this, such a power be given to man, that out of three sounds he frame, not a fourth sound but a star.'

22 Clive Bell, an English art critic.

It is doubtless true that many people are still deaf and blind to these creative rhythms of the Universe that are the Spirit of God moving on the face of the waters, and the wind blowing wheresoever ... But I think we are every one of us potentially artists, with a star to create, a star that remains a mere nebulous mass of chaotic impressions waiting for the formative force and sureness of rhythmic movement to whirl it into being, as a new and shining light in the heavens of manifested life. It is the attempt of the copyist in every art to reproduce the surface of things, whether it is a scene from nature, an anecdote, or the expression of an idea, that is responsible for the hostile criticism that brings into disrepute the purpose or moral in literature, and the meaning or story in the arts of colour and form. We all know how easily a literature with a purpose ceases to be Art. For the artist in thought is concerned not so much with the idea, but with the rhythm behind the idea. And this is the explanation of the puzzling paradox that confronts us. For, if a purpose leads Art to destruction, so the want of inner purpose and unifying rhythm leads to utter incoherence, a sort of nebulous limbo made by souls without even force enough to build a hell for themselves, let alone a star. As the rhythm behind the tree, the flower, the mountain, or any other visible thing is the painters concern, so the rhythm behind the idea, the thought, the feeling is the poet's concern.

This handling of essential rhythms is what makes an appeal to rite distinctively aesthetic emotions in us. Take Keats' lines in the 'Ode to the Nightingale':

> Thou wast not born for death, immortal Bird,
> No hungry generations tread thee down,
> The voice I hear this passing night was heard
> In ancient days by Emperor and clown.
> Perhaps the self-same song that found a path
> Through the sad heart of Ruth, when, sick for home
> She stood in tears among the alien corn,
> The same that oft-times hath
> Charmed magic casements, opening to the foam
> Of perilous seas in fairylands forlorn.

These lines preach no morals, they tell no stories, they explain no ideas, but you feel in them the touch of those rhythms that are behind a thousand myths, legends and ideas. You might express some such idea in conscious thought as the tragedy and mystery of human life, and the rapture of contemplation, bound together through the ages by the immortal beauty of a song. But such explanations are inadequate and foolish set beside the star that Keats created.

To give another very well-known instance. In Pater's famous lines about the 'Mona Lisa' you can see how a critic can turn suddenly into a creative artist, for he looked at the picture as Shelley might have looked at a thundercloud, or Keats at the moon or Wordsworth at a primrose, and was so fascinated by the hidden rhythm that is the law of its life, that instead of talking about it, he gave expression in his own medium to that mysterious and fascinating rhythm that is the enchantment of so much of Leonardo's work.

Many people who write must be conscious of the deep, inner relation of all Art as an expression of rhythm. In fact this consciousness is so vivid that, from the writer's point of view, it is a fascinating speculation as to what colour the inner vibrations of certain poems would work out at in the world of the vibrations of light. I remember discussing this point years ago with an Irish poet. I remember we agreed that 'Paradise Lost' has a purple colour. I wonder if you will think me too fanciful if I say that for me the purple is too red I prefer the deeper and bluer violet of some of the short poems, or the hot silvery mauve and green of 'Sabrina Fair,' or the sunny blues and golds of 'L'Allegro.'

Certain critics nowadays, Mr. Clive Bell for instance tell us that it is not natural for many people to be moved by the same aesthetic emotion for a natural object as for a work of art. If that is true it is surely nothing but the sign of some strange natural insensitiveness to the rhythms of beauty. It is hard to believe that anyone who is really stirred by Puvis de Chavannes, 'Pauvre Pecheur' or by a play of Maeterlinck, would not get the same aesthetic emotion from a white rose in the twilight. The morning hush in the woods when the dew is on the grass and cobwebs glitter on the low branches of the trees is as moving as Shelley's 'Adonas,' and the blue and gold walls of San Clemente, Torcello, or San Marco, can rouse in one but the same emotional ferment that you can feel many evenings by the sea while the waves are breaking whitely in the twilight, and the common air we breathe seems to be the veil of some great secret. There is indeed a deep truth hidden in the old Irish legend of the Durdabla, in which the world was supposed to be upsung into being by the magic harp of the Gods. This harp had three strings: the iron string of sleep, the bronze string of joy, and the silver string of sorrow. From these strings came the melodies manifested in the Seasons of the year and all visible form as well as emotion and thought.

After this poetic leap into the dark I would ask you to look at the whole question in the light of modern scientific ideas. Naturally I can only touch the outer fringe of this subject, but I often think it is strange how modern science seems to play into the hands of ancient poetry. To take a small instance, 'a world upsung into being' does not seem half as irrational and fantastic a conception if you know that the vibrations of different musical notes will fling a loose heap of scattered sand into definite, regular forms and patterns. Someone has defined architecture as frozen music. It would be interesting to follow up all the sidelights that Science has to throw on the relations between the Arts. The dethroning of the atom of matter from its place as the foundation stone of the living universe and the setting there in its stead of the unit of electricity has cut the solid ground of materialism from under our feet, and has put in its place the rhythmic movements of perilous forces.

The more we probe into the heart of things the more we find ourselves depending on fierce elemental forces, balanced in a clash of fiery energy, our very material life itself perhaps nothing but the result of a vortex in the ether. Our feet tread the whirlwinds, the tempests that rage through our hearts and minds are, as every poet has always known, one with the cyclone, the earthquake, the hurricane. We can no longer say as something final, 'We go as we came to the earth,' for we know that physical life is not the child of the dust, but our bodies and the dust alike are the children of those great elementary forces that fill with tremendous vibrations, movements, rhythms and explosions, that mysterious underworld in which Science is slowly groping its way, and that lies behind all the simple, quiet seeming phenomena of everyday life. We live in the midst of mystery. The very poker with which we poke our fire is a marvelous conglomeration of rhythmic, ally whirling atoms, none of which touch one another, but are held together by an unknown and mysterious substance which we can control by electricity, and use to alter the position of the atoms, with the strange result that the bar of steel becomes charged with magnetic power, and our common poker becomes a Moses' wand for the working of miracles.

The conception of the identity of those forces that hold the world together in the dark, with the strange, vibrating rhythms that arc the underworld of Art, leads straight on to a study of those mysterious movements in the realm of will and thought that hide the secret foundations of character. Do we not feel the same rhythms at work behind human lives and actions. Incidentally, the existence of this subconscious underworld of rhythmic forces, uniting in their foundations art, life, and nature, seems to be a simple enough explanation of the magic and glamour of poetic imagery, which is after all nothing but the discovery of hidden relations, an inspired guess at unknown unities.

Does not the fascination of some of the noblest of human lives reveal to us at once their kinship with the most beautiful of the world's colours and the immortal forms of the loveliest art? In reading the story of the life of Christ or Buddha, or even the death of Socrates, who does not feel an aesthetic emotion and know himself to be in the presence of great works of art? Lives like these are living tragedies, where strange and deeply buried rhythms have never yet found complete manifestation in any material except the material of human life though a touch of those rhythms may be found here and there in some Greek play, or perhaps Leonardo's pictures, or the works of some of the poets but most of all in Greek sculpture. Oscar Wilde was haunted by the idea of the essential Greekness of Christ, and one feels that, though one may doubt some of his deductions, his sensitive perception is right and in those living and vibrating rhythms that surge upward into manifestation in the strange living and dying of Christ, one recognises the completion of that subtle suggestion that haunts and eludes and promises in the smile of an archaic Apollo.

On these lines one would say that the evils of life exist for the same reason that people prefer bad art to good, second rate to first rate, the primitive, fourth vibrations of the sorting out and conglomeration of matter to the more subtle rhythm of the upward struggle of human thought and feeling. We tolerate wars for the same reason we prefer Rudyard Kipling as a poet to Shelley, or Pinero to Ibsen, or a musical play to a Greek tragedy, 'God Save the King' to Wagner.

Thus the 'Dark Rosaleen' is a far more beautiful poem than 'Rule Britannia,' because the rhythm that finds vent in rebellion, imperfect as it must be, or else it could not find vent in violence, is still a more subtle and beautiful rhythm than the vibration that expresses itself in the ponderous pomposity and violence of Empire.

Here we come face to face with the problem of what we call beauty and its relation to Art and life and nature. Much of a contradictory nature has been thought and said about the meaning and origin of beauty, ranging from the gross materialism of the politician, like Burke, who said that war was the source of the sublime, and sociability and the sex instinct the source of beauty, to the idealism of Hegel, who looks upon beauty as the manifestation of God in nature and art. Personally, the divine nature of beauty seems to me a far more plausible theory than the sexual one, as it seems to be one of those great forces the working of which you meet everywhere in every corner of the Universe, personal or impersonal, at every moment of life. What has social life, or sex, to do with the whirl and rush and glory of an Atlantic wave or the colour of a cloud floating in the sunset? People have materialistic ideas of Beauty, because as Beauty moves us to aesthetic emotion they have come to regard a beautiful thing as a thing that gives pleasure; but is it not, at all events, just as likely to be true that the intense thrill of impersonal ecstasy, that we call aesthetic emotion, and that we got from Beauty, is a touch of that sense of living unity which is the Joy and perhaps the true life of the spirit. This is no pleasure of the personal senses, it is the impersonal delight of the Spirit in a sudden awareness of the Universal Spirit. For aesthetic emotion is one of the few emotions that has in it no desire for possession, or even for the return of emotion. The purest emotion inspired by another human being usually implies, and is often wholly made of, a desire for the impact of the other person's affections on one's own consciousness. But nobody expects the flattery of personal love from the mountain, the sea and the sky. Such emotion asks for nothing in return, it casts aside the personal will and throws itself out into the Universal. It knows nothing of jealousy, hatred, or the desire of destruction, tyranny, or submission. If it has any desire at all it is the divine desire of creation. Such an emotion is obviously the enemy in the human mind of hatred and slavishness. In its passionate embrace of the Universal it leaves no room for fear. For there are no dark corners peopled with dangerous and hostile forces for those who have once felt the touch of the Universal Spirit in the magic of beauty. This is why I think sensitiveness to beauty or aesthetic emotion is one of the great regenerative forces in human character. I know this subject has become confused in many minds because of the undoubted fact that hosts of writers, painters, sculptors, and even musicians, are indifferent to and, indeed, rather scornful of beauty, and seem to be wholly incapable of aesthetic emotion. And these people are as sensitive as their neighbours, the shopkeeper, the idle rich, or the worker, to the infection of fear, hate, slavishness and greed, that have their outward manifestation in the disease of war. But these are those who have felt the desire to reproduce rhythm and yet have not known the enchantment of beauty. And as religion without beauty loses its touch with reality, and ends by creating the evil illusion of her, so Art without Beauty can only produce unreal and rather hateful incoherencies.

It is hard to define Beauty. We only know it as one of those divine omnipresent forces of the Universe such as wisdom and power, that were the gods of many ancient religions, and whose existence denied by those whom insensitiveness has made sceptical. In the old Irish legend, when Niamh, the spiritual beauty, threw her spell over the heart of Oisin, the hero, he left his fighting and his feasting and followed her, riding over land and sea to Tirnanogue, the Country of the Young, the Gaelic Paradise. But Cuhoolin, who also fell under the influence of Niamh, and was for a while proof against the false ideals and glamour of the war spirit, in the end mistook a deceitful and treacherous stranger for the true Niamh. Falling under the spell of illusion, he dreamed (as so many, alas, have dreamed) that the spiritual beauty was calling him to battle, and followed a false god, to find his doom amid hatred and bloodshed and agony.

I know indeed there are many powerful ways of helping the world in the heavy task of regenerating its broken life and thought, through reasonable argument, education, example, and social reform, but in thinking of this Society and its special concern with the ideals that lie behind our activities, one seems to feel a great need, among even some of the idealists of our time, for the rediscovery of beauty as a tremendous mental force, and of aesthetic emotion as the soul of religion. For as the false glamour of martial romance and beauty have been the means of leading many bewildered people to death, slavery, destruction and cruelty, so the understanding of the real truth of beauty must show us the meaning of that horror of perverted energy that surrounds us on every side, as well as the true proportion of that self-sacrifice and courage that is willing to kill as well as be killed, to maim as well as to be maimed.

With the light of real beauty in our minds we shall not be dazzled by the rays of military glory, and we shall shrink back from that hideous vice of obedience that deforms the free splendour of the human soul growing up towards the light in the beauty of its own divine image, as the body of a child might be deformed and stunted by a poisonous atmosphere or a paralysing drug. At present the world seems bewitched by the malign powers of fear, cruelty, and obedience; slowly, indeed, do we fight our way towards our far-off ideals of peace and freedom.

To anyone who is considering how the life of men can struggle into the sunlight out of the whirlpool of evil forces that seem to be dragging it down into chaos, I would like to suggest the symbolism of one of those ancient ideas embodied in the Kabala. That the two great forces of life, Power and Mercy, or Intellect and Religion, can only be joined together by passing through the sphere that is called Beauty.

Eva Gore-Booth.
League of Peace and Freedom
180 St Stephens' House, Westminster, S.W.

'The sanctity of conscience'

Manchester Guardian, 25 March 1918

Sir,

Bishop Welldon says that the sanctity of conscience is 'an established principle in the modern world, the dearly bought result of a spiritual conflict extending over three or four centuries since the Reformation.'[23] He then amplifies this statement by explaining that it is only a certain kind of conscience that is sacred, what he calls an enlightened conscience, 'a conscience void of offence towards God and man' that deserves universal respect. By this phrase St. Paul could certainly not have meant a conscience that does not bring you into collision with the authorities of the State or the sense of right and wrong of the majority of your countrymen, as he himself suffered imprisonment and death because his loyalty to his conscience was an offense to the State under whose laws and what Bishop Welldon calls 'advantages' he happened to live.

If the only conscience that is still held worthy of respect is the one that is approved by the majority and sanctioned by the State, then we have gained nothing by what Bishop Welldon rightly calls a spiritual conflict extending

23 James Welldon, Dean of Manchester until 1918.

over three centuries. Because even before the Reformation the conscience of those who agreed with those in authority was universally respected. Even the Roman Empire did not persecute the Christians because the Romans objected to any particular form of religion. In this matter they were entirely tolerant. But they regarded Christianity, as perhaps it is, as a danger to any well-organised State.

We shall all agree with Bishop Welldon's desire for an enlightened conscience; it is with the implied definition of enlightenment that runs through his letter that I venture to disagree. There are not many people who will be ready to put their deepest convictions on one side for fear of 'injuring by words or actions the efficiency of the State.' Rather, if they find the State at war with all that they conceive (perhaps wrongly) to be noblest and best, many human beings will cease to wish for its efficiency in what to them is a tragically mistaken course that leads only to death, misery, and destruction, and it at once becomes a matter of conscience with them to help in a change of ideals that will lead to life and happiness for its citizens.

If this point of view seems intolerable to Bishop Welldon, I should like to remind him of what a distinguished Free Churchman once said: 'You cannot be said to have learnt tolerance till you can tolerate that which seems intolerable.'

Yours, &c.,
Eva Gore-Booth.

The messengers

The Flame, March 1920

God sent a Snake to bring a message to Adam. But Adam was afraid of the Snake, so he killed it, and thus he did not hear the message. Then God sent a Worm, very feeble and harmless, but Adam despised it, and trod it underfoot. And thus he did not hear the message. Then God sent a Brown Deer, beautiful in swiftness, ranging through the forest. But Adam was hungry, so he made a bow and arrows, and shot the deer, and made it into venison. And thus again he did not hear the message.

Then God sent an Elm tree, with leaves of such a living vivid green, that no man could despise it. And it was neither dangerous nor good to eat. But Adam cut it down, and made it into boxes and coffins. And still he did not hear the message.

Then God sent a White Rose that was so fragile, nobody could use it for anything. But Adam cut it at once and put it in a vase. And still he did not hear the message.

Then God sent a Dog. And the Dog loved Adam. But Adam cut a hole in its head to see how its brain worked. And still he did not hear the message.

Then God sent him Two Children that he might learn from his own flesh and blood. But Adam gave them his blessing and sent them out to kill one another. And still he did not hear the message.

The messengers II

The Flame, May 1920

At last, when the children had killed one another, and the dog was dead, and the rose faded, and all the trees cut down, and they that were left of deer had fled in terror to the mountains, God sent to Adam the Messenger from Within, and the Son of Man was lifted up in his heart.

Then Adam was afraid and tried to cast him out. For he said 'Here is the Snake I destroyed come back to torment me.' But the Son of Man only smiled at him.

And in his smile was the Wisdom of the Serpent and the Treasure of the Humble.

Then Adam was contemptuous and tried to tread him under his feet, saying 'This is merely the Worm I killed, coming to life again.'

But again the Son of Man only smiled at him.

And in his smile was the gentleness of the Wild Deer of the Forest, and the beauty of the Rose, and the glory of the Elm tree.

But Adam carved the mystery of his smile into a great statue, and sold it for much gold.

Then the Son of Man wept, and through his tears shone the eyes of the Dog that had died in agony, and the souls of the Children who had killed one another,

But Adam said, 'This is only a phantom of the imagination, caused by some nerve repression in youth.'

And he rose up in anger and terror, and tried to strangle his tormentor. Then the Son of Man spoke. And in his voice was all the sorrow and the beauty of life, and the Divine love in the human soul.

And, at the sound of it, blindness fell from the eyes of Adam, and he knew his own spirit. Falling on his knees in the dust, he stopped his ears that he might hear the Voice of the Everlasting Mercy, and covered his eyes with his hands that he might see the Inner Light of the Universal Truth.

A sketch in Florence

The Flame, July–August 1921

On our way to the Uffizi[24] we passed a silent crowd standing on the banks of the Arno and gazing with concentrated attention at the dull green ripples of the slow river, swaying under the shadow of its many bridges. Two boats were moving up and down, stirring heedlessly the ancient brown and yellow reflections that had lain for over seven hundred years on the water staring back at the piled-up muddle of houses on the Ponte Vecchio. Restlessly the boats came and went; it seemed as if they were waiting for something that was going to happen, looking for something. The crowd watched them with breathless attention. The idea of a boat race passed quickly through my mind and faded. For there was something fixed, anxious, almost agonised in the attitude of the watchers. That is not the way that people watch boat races.

'What has happened, what are you looking at?' I asked a man who was standing beside me, leaning over the parapet.

'A man drowned himself last night,' he said; 'they are looking for the body.'

He spoke in a rapid, intense way, without the emphasis that comes naturally to so many Italians.

'Why did he drown himself?' I asked

'The motive?' he said. 'Ah, he was called for military service. He was a young man of twenty-four; it was not the first time – he knew exactly what he was going to.'

My neighbour was speaking hurriedly with a concentrated quiet bitterness in his voice. He paused every two minutes to wipe the tears from his eyes and the sweat from his forehead with a dingy red handkerchief, as he poured out his story of the evil slavery of military life and told how terribly the young man had suffered, how he was 'nervoso, ma molto nervosa.'[25] He spoke too, of his family, and what the shock had been to them, and he said hard words against the Government and the army. And all the while the brown boats moved to and fro over the water, green as chrysoprase, in a futile, hopeless sort of way, and the crowd watched absorbed, breathless, waiting for something, spell-bound by the horrible fascination of violent death and the last dreadful activity of despair. I thought 'Alas, for those who are born into this iron age of ours. For everywhere in the world the leaders of men's wills are the devoted and industrious servants of death, the blind battalions follow the blind leaders to destruction.' And strangely the old words rang in my ears, 'Lord, if thou hadst been here my brother had not died.'

24 The principal art museum in Florence, Italy.

25 'Nervous, but very nervous.'

Ten minutes afterwards I was standing in the Uffizi gazing at the radiant tranquillity of the 'Adoration of the Shepherds,' painted five hundred years ago by Lorenzo di Credi. Like the crowd outside on the Lung' Arno, the seven people in the picture were all looking for something, waiting for something to happen, breathless, absorbed, pre-occupied. The kneeling girl, in her eagerness, did not even seem to see the angels who prayed beside her. The old man had laid aside his weariness. The shepherds had forgotten their distant mountains, and the long road and the straying sheep. Long ago they, too, had wandered over the hills, amid steep rocks and dangerous precipices, seeking in the starlight the dawn of the eternal truth. And now they had found what they sought. And each intent, down-bent face was lit by the same luminous mystery.

Behind them the night had faded, the hills were blue in the dawn wind. But day and night were nothing to them who knew the secret of Eternity. It seemed that they had been here for thousands of years, and for thousands of years that still ivory light had transfigured the pale bent faces with a dream of peace. Only a few yards away the body of a young man, driven mad by the cruelty of men, washed to and fro in the restless waters of the river. But here was the ultimate meaning of all things. A mysterious child lying defenceless, pillowed on a sheaf of corn, the Eternal Peace and Divine Pity moving, in the gentleness of Eternal things, among the blood-stained dreams of this bewildered star.

The death penalty

Manchester Guardian, 8 June 1922

Sir,

The refusal to reprieve Jacoby has startled many people.[26] There are two different points of view among those who support hanging. They look upon it either as a punishment for a murder or as a necessary deterrent to protect society from other murderers. In this case it is hardly necessary to argue the first point. The medical aspect and the age of the criminal, together with jury's recommendation to mercy, have been made the grounds for a quite convincing appeal for mercy. But the other consideration remains: is capital punishment likely to deter others and stop the present epidemic of crimes committed by youths?

To hope for this result is to pin one's faith to fear as the protection of society.

26 Henry Jacoby was one of the youngest people to be hanged at Pentonville prison. He was executed on 7 June 1922, at the age of 18. He was charged with the murder of Lady Alice White. Jacoby battered the woman to death in the course of a robbery.

Now fear works in many ways; and not always as a deterrent. If anyone doubt this, let him try the old experiment of walking along a narrow plank on the ground and then propping the same plank 30 feet above the ground and trying the same walk. He will find especially if he is a nervous person, that when he is confronted instead of attacking the will with threats of violent death, as it has been the custom in past ages, would it not be possible for us to begin to work at the suggestion side of the problem so that the struggle may not arise, at all events until the will has been reinforced by the constant exercise of mature life? The victory of suggestion over will in extreme youth is one of the difficult weaknesses of human nature, most potent in the manufacture of criminals. It will never be conquered by fear. The only true protection of society along these lines would be built up by a reinforcement of the will with real constructive motive, and not by a weakening of it through fear; and also by a real attempt to change the suggestions now so plentifully thrust on to immature minds by our present social environment. The effect of the war suggestions in the last few years has been trenchantly analysed by the secretary of the Howard League for Penal Reform, who shows why crimes among boys would naturally follow a childhood spent amid the inevitable mental accompaniments of war.[27]

Yours, & c.,
Eva Gore-Booth.
14 Frognal Gardens, London, N.W.,

'The Artist in War Time'

Broken Glory

Oh, shining splendour of the human form
That takes my heart by storm,
Strong as a river, subtle as a prayer,
Or the first moon ray in the twilight air,
Line upon line of moving silver light,
Building our dreams up to the spirit's height,
Enfolding the grey dust and the earth's green
In coloured ecstasies of light unseen!
The Spirit that moves among the forest trees
Has doubtless built this shrine,
That erring men may fall upon their knees
And worship God and man, one soul divine –
Yea, and the little children of the earth
That make the world sweet with their wanderings,

27 Margery Fry, secretary of the Howard League for Penal Reform.

And wild-willed pilgrims of mysterious birth
Gliding across the sky on silent wings.
Ah, surely no man born dare rise and slay
Eternal Beauty wrapped in robes of clay,
Or break and blast and utterly destroy
Life's little ivory tower of fragile joy!
Loud answerèd the black and stupid guns,
'We are the darlings of man's heart, the wise
Call us the world's Redeemers, mighty ones
Have bid us clear for them the troubled skies,
And holy souls have blessed us, for we stand
For God Almighty in a godless land.
God, Who art feeble grown and blind and dumb,
Take heart, through us Thy Kingdom yet shall come.'
Labourers in mad mechanic purpose bound,
They dig in vain Immortal Beauty's grave,
And bury the very starlight underground,
And crash above the song of wind and wave
Their monstrous rhythms of fire and steel and lead.
On some red field or battle-blasted hill
Men dream the Eternal Beauty lieth dead,
And all our souls are subject to their will.
Most ancient Beauty, scorned and thrust aside,
Who doth yet in white peace and silence dwell,
Pity us tortured slaves of bloodstained pride,
Lean out once more from the invisible,
Let fall from thy dream-haunted obscure throne
One ray of moonlight in earth's broken brain.
Our souls are thine, Belovèd, thine alone,
Behold thy lost world at thy feet again.

Art and peace

Service, January 1926

An ex war-minister has been writing, in glowing terms, in Nash's Magazine, of the joy he experienced, when, after months spent in organising the whole-sale destruction of war, he lost his office, and took refuge in what he calls a hobby. A subtle instinct urged him to take up oil-painting. This he found, strangely, was far more absorbing than golf, or even polo. He ceased to be conscious of the passage of time. He was absolutely happy. And this is really not the least to be wondered at. For art is construction, war is destruction. And the man who had been immersed in the organisation of the most ghastly wholesale destruction that the world has yet seen, showed a natural human impulse, in turning for relief to his over-strained brain, to the constructive work of art.

Construction is the most natural and delightful of all occupation. The joy of making something is one of the most natural and fundamental of human joys; in it one of our deepest instincts is gratified. A pudding, a chair, a hat, a dress, a table, a picture, a poem, it does not matter what we make. So long as we are conscious of the power of making it well; the act of making is pure joy.

Destruction itself seems to be an instinct with some people, we have all had experience of the child, who would rather smash the piano key-board with the poker, than play the most beautiful music; and do we not all know sight-seers at an Exhibition who will pay sixpence for the pleasure of 'smashing up the happy home.'

But just as, what we call art is a peculiar kind of construction, so what we call war is a peculiar kind of destruction. And the peculiarities of both have made them eternally antagonistic to one another – thus the constructiveness of art has filled the world with significant forms of beauty and truth, whilst the destructiveness of war not only breaks up existing forms of beauty, but it creates indescribable ugliness, and fills the world with that atmosphere of falsehood and hate which is necessary for the spread of international propaganda, but absolutely paralysing to the creative imagination in man. Everybody instinctively demands truth, even those who are indifferent to beauty. And how shall truth come at the call of those whose minds have become the home of unkind falsehood. Thus the artist may lament the destruction of beautiful forms, the blowing up of the Acropolis,[28] the defacing of Rheims Cathedral[29] or the bombing of Damascus.[30] But how far more subtly antagonistic to the interests of creative art, is the mass of perfectly necessary less than poison the minds of all combatant nations. War cannot exist without falsehood. During the last war I remember reading on the advertisement board of a peculiarly monstrous atrocity film, an invitation to people to come in and learn to hate – the advertisement ended in large letters 'if you do not hate you cannot kill.'

28 The Parthenon, part of the Acropolis in Athens, was blown up during a Venetian siege in 1687. The Greek government began restoration of this important symbol of Greek culture in the twentieth century.

29 The cathedral was built *c.*1211 in Reims, France. In September 1914 the German army, convinced that the cathedral functioned as a French watch tower, fired on the building, severely damaging the roof. After extensive restoration work, funded by the Rockefeller family, the cathedral was reopened in 1938.

30 In 1925 the city of Damascus was bombed during the Druze Revolt. The old part of the city was almost burned to the ground.

Now corporate hate cannot be developed without slander, because no nation is entirely bad or hateful. If you tell the truth, you only make your audience realise how like one nation is to another. Indeed people are, in the main, good-natured, and do not learn to hate easily. It really seems true that, to hate another person satisfactorily, you must form a false idea of them. Continued war cannot exist without the constant renewal of hate.

It is not that hate is characteristic of armies, it is characteristic of the war spirit, and it is a matter of common observation that people at home often seemed to have more war-spirit than the soldiers. I do not think this is accounted for by any peculiar characteristic of the civil population, but partly by the fact that they did not know their enemies, and believed what they were told about them, whilst the soldiers, often enough, found the wild bogeys created in men's minds by their passions, became simply ridiculous when applied to the very ordinary, and sometimes agreeable, individuals who were their prisoners. 'Our friends, Fritz and Hans, will now oblige with the Hymn of Hate' was the English sergeant's announcement at a trench concert, overheard by an officer.

But at home things were very different. There was a real atmosphere of hatred and contempt, fed by a stream of fabricated atrocities. And one cannot doubt but that it was the same in every other combatant country.

If hate is necessary to war, it is fatal to art. For the world of art is simply the world seen in the light of love. Every poet is a lover, every real artist an enthusiast. No creative genius is negative. To develop the hostile side of your nature is to develop the negative side, to cramp and cripple the creative force of imagination. You cannot create anything with hate. To make a thing live outside yourself you must love it. No real living art comes into existence any other way.

Hate is the spirit that denies. By the initiative power of love alone can the sculptor pour some of his own life into the stone he is hacking at, or the poet make words luminous with the inner flame in his mind.

Hate is the opposite of love but love is something far more than the opposite of hate, or the opposite of anything. It is an atmosphere of mind, a temperament, a way of living, a force, but, in its relation to war, you might call it peace.

People will, naturally, quote Homer to prove that great poetry can be inspired by war. But really you cannot prove anything of the sort from Iliad. It is certainly a description of a war, but such a war as never was on land or sea. It is a war of gods and goddesses, who use unfortunate human beings like Robots, to carry out their purposes. More like the story of a succession of duels, than the record of a war, the Iliad is full of conversations between gods and men, friends and enemies. It is curious to see how these mortal enemies mix praise with defiance, and seem to kill one another, without much anger, at the behest of the gods. If Homer is no pacifist, he is yet neither a partisan or a hater, and the atmosphere of the Iliad is full of enthusiasm and pity.

It is obviously not patriotism in the cause of Greece or Troy, but the love and admiration he has for the beauty and courage of his heroes, both Trojan and Greek, that inspire his splendid imagery, and shine out on every page. You feel the 'magnanimous Hector' is as dear to him as the 'noble Achilles.'

It is to the gods, whose playthings we all are, that he attributes men's misfortunes, rather than to the wickedness of their enemies. 'Alas without doubt the gods have summoned me to death,' says the dying Hector to his 'iron-souled' foe. And it is not Jove, 'delighting-in-arrows,' who 'orders Agamemnon to arm the long-haired Greeks with all their army, to take the wide-wayed city of the Trojans.' Apollo, not Hector, is really responsible for the death of Patroclus, while Hector himself, in his last speech attributes his death to Pallas Athene, rather than to the enemy he apostrophises as 'god-like Achilles,' at the same time prophesying how Phoebus Apollo and Paris should kill Achilles himself, at the Scoean Gate.

Euripides, who was a pacifist, goes much further than Homer, in this direction. He tells (in 'Helen') how the cause of the Trojan war was nothing but an illusion; Helen never really went to Troy with Paris. But the Gods made an image, exactly like her, out of empty air and a cloud, to deceive Paris and Menelaus. And it was for this illusion that the war was fought, and that for ten years Greeks and Trojans killed one another.

The Greek writers do not seem to resent what we should call the cruel and despotic actions of the gods. Indeed they do not seem to resent anything, but to look on the evil deeds of men as the result of the incomprehensible force of some mysterious fate. It is perhaps in this that their greatness lies, their attitude and the atmosphere of their work is not hostile to gods or men, but full of pity, admiration and awe. They may rejoice in the beauty and strength of heroes, and mourn for their misfortunes, they may tell of the vengeance of Orestes and Electra, the sacrifice of Alcestis or Antigone, but their pre-occupation is always the same, the strange inexorable way of the gods in dealing with the lives of men.

Indeed in most countries, art, as we know it, seems to have had its origin in religion, and in those problems and mysteries that surround the idea of death, the possible existence of divine powers, and the conception of a future life. Plato took for granted that the gods were the poets' concern, and banned Homer for vulgarising the great myths of the past, till they became nothing more than frivolous and futile stories. But religion, however primitive, must always be to a certain extent, a reconciling influence. It is easy to see that a belief in the omnipotence of Universal Love must lead to a sense of human fellowship and unity. But it is not also true that, in earlier days of the world's history, a common sense of suffering from the malice of indifferent and capricious gods, may have drawn human beings together, as, indeed, a common grievance always tends to do. From the belief that all men are the victims of cruel gods sprang that strange tolerance and pity which at its strongest made possible works of art like 'The Trojan Women.' In this play, with absolute impartiality, a Greek tragedian mourns the sorrows of the defeated enemies of his country.

It would be hard to exaggerate the influence of religious ideas on art. For the imagination of Egyptians and Greeks alike seem to have been obsessed by the mysteries of the unseen world, and the relations, sympathetic or unsympathetic, between gods and men.

Art and worship are as closely related as art and love. Thus, though we may find some military Pharaoh among Egyptian statues, and an occasional representation of a disc thrower, or Crestes and Electra, among the Greeks, the number of secular images is small compared to the mass of representations of Isis and Osiris, or Apollo, Athene and Aphrodite. Greek tragedy had its humble beginning in a cloric dance round the altar of Dionysus. Nearly all the great architecture of the world has been inspired by the desire to build Temples for worship. Modern painting is the direct descendant of the Madonna and Crucifixions of the Middle Ages, modern drama the child of the Miracle play. Music has never wandered far from its origin though it may be a far cry from the Pipes of Pan and the Lyre of Apollo, to a mass by Beethoven or Bach, it is no greater than the gulf that separates the host of cruel anthropomorphic gods of the ancient poets and sculptors, from our more spiritual conception of the One, absolute and eternal, who is Love, Radiance and peace are the marks of great art through the ages, whether it is the perfection of Shelley's Skylark or Keats' Odes or the gracious atmosphere that surrounds the Madonna of Leonardo da Vinci, or the beauty of the Apollo of Pheidias that was found many hundreds of years after the sculptor's death, submerged under the Tiber. Thus sometimes it seems that peace is the great secret of art, and that by destroying peace in the human mind, war is aiming the most deadly blow at the constructive or creative power in man.

It is a sin against art to destroy the monuments of the past. But it is surely a far greater sin to weaken and destroy human imagination, and render null and void the beauty that is yet unborn.

Many people were disappointed that the war produced no great poetry. But why should anyone expect war to produce great poetry? Why should the forces of destruction and ugliness produce a triumph of constructed beauty? War can produce a war memorial, like the sculpture on the arch on Constitution Hill, or the Royal Artillery Memorial. But all really beautiful things are the children of peace and love.

PART III

Irish nationalism before independence

Gore-Booth was immersed in anti-conscription and pacifist campaigns in Britain and she overlooked the escalating political instability in her own country. This final section includes Gore-Booth's writings in relation to Irish nationalism. Although not generally remembered as an Irish nationalist, the writings in this section reveal Gore-Booth as dedicated to the cause of Irish independence. This devotion was often expressed in her poetry, evident in the first two entries in this section. However, her main political writings on this topic do not begin in earnest until after the Easter Rising of 1916. The Rising was to have a deep impact on Gore-Booth's personal and political life.

The onset of the First World War was undoubtedly the catalyst for the Easter Rising. The Irish Parliamentary Party had gained real ground at Westminster prior to the outbreak of war and the issue of Home Rule for Ireland had then been a foremost concern for many British and Irish political activists. The Irish Parliamentary Party, led by John Redmond, returned a triumphant result in the general election of January 1910 and the party held the balance of power in a hung parliament. The Liberal Party, with a very minor majority of only two seats, approached Redmond for his support. Asquith, as leader of the Liberals, guaranteed his continued support for Home Rule in exchange for Redmond's backing. The Irish Parliamentary Party and the Liberals entered into an agreement and formed the next government. The Irish Parliamentary Party was placed in the same position at the December 1910 general election, solidifying their power in the House of Commons. After the December election the House of Lords lost their power of absolute rejection over bills, giving Home Rule a chance to be passed through the House of Commons.

Asquith duly introduced a third Irish Home Rule Bill on 11 April 1912. The bill was successful but its introduction was held off until 1914. Home Rule for Ireland gained royal assent on 18 September 1914, passing into law. By then Britain had declared war on Germany and its allies, and, due to the outbreak of hostilities, implementation of the bill was postponed until peace was restored. Convinced that the British government would fully introduce Home Rule after the war was over, Redmond pledged that members of the Irish Volunteers would join the British army and support the imperial war effort. Redmond may not have fully appreciated the ramifications of his pledge due to an emerging popular belief that the war would be over by Christmas. Stuart Hallifax notes that the 'early illusions of a brief, glorious war [was] created by politicians, newspapers and generals, driving men to join up quickly rather than miss the "fun"'.[1]

1 Stuart Hallifax, '"Over by Christmas": British Popular Opinion and the Short War in 1914', *First World War Studies*, 1(2) (Oct. 2010), 103.

The Irish Volunteers were a parliamentary organisation established in November 1913 to ensure the effective introduction of Home Rule, by military force if necessary. Not surprisingly, Redmond's pledge split the organisation. Within the first year of war more than 80,000 Irishmen enlisted in the British army, many of these came from the ranks of the Irish Volunteers. A minority force remained loyal to the leader of the Irish Volunteers, Eoin MacNeill, and to the director of organisation, Patrick Pearse. The failure to implement the Home Rule Bill coupled with the recruitment of Irish men into the British army antagonised the remaining devoted nationalist group. A rebellion against British rule in Ireland was becoming inevitable.

The intensity of nationalist feelings was realised on Easter Monday 24 April 1916 when Pearse took up position outside the General Post Office in the centre of Dublin city and proclaimed a Republic of Ireland. A provisional government of Ireland was established and the symbol of this new State, the Irish tricolour flag, was raised. So began an armed rebellion against British forces, now referred to as the Easter Rising. The Irish proclamation was signed by members of the provisional government of Ireland, Thomas Clarke, Sean MacDiarmada, Patrick Pearse, James Connolly, Thomas MacDonagh, Eamonn Ceannt and Joseph Plunkett. The strategy of the two main forces, the Irish Volunteers and the Irish Citizen Army, was to seize control of key areas across Dublin.[2] Once key sites were secured the nationalists would hold out until Irish Volunteers across the country rose in support. Due to confusion over order and countermanded order a mass uprising of Volunteers throughout the country never occurred and the nationalists were forced to surrender six days later.

Countess Markievicz was by then a central player in the Irish nationalist movement and she took up arms as second in command to Commandant Michael Mallin. A battalion of Irish Citizen Army troops, led by Markievicz and Mallin, held St Stephen's Green, a 20-acre public park on the south side of Dublin city. When they were overpowered by British snipers the troops relocated to the enclosed premises of the College of Surgeons nearby. A force of over 16,000 British soldiers, supported by a naval patrol vessel, the *Helga*, easily overpowered the small and poorly armed force of Irish nationalists. Markievicz was arrested after the surrender and sentenced to death for her part in the Rising; this would later be commuted to life in prison.

In the aftermath, British authorities responded severely. Dublin was placed under martial law with General John Maxwell appointed as Commander-in-chief. Maxwell organised closed court-martial trials, which, unlike civil trials,

2 The Irish Citizen Army was formed in 1913 in response to the violent clashes between locked-out workers and the Dublin Metropolitan Police during the bitter labour dispute referred to as the Dublin Lockout. For further information, see Francis Devine (ed.), *A Capital in Conflict: Dublin City and the 1913 Lockout* (Dublin: Four Courts Press, 2013).

did not include a jury or allow legal counsel. The sentence for many of the organisers of the rebellion was death. On hearing of her sister's death sentence Gore-Booth made her way to Dublin, arriving on the morning that her injured friend, the trade union organiser James Connolly, had been strapped to a chair and shot by a firing squad in Kilmainham jail. Sentencing was swift and less than two weeks after the Rising had ended, fifteen men, including the seven signatories of the proclamation, had been executed. The harshness of the punishments generated public outrage in Ireland and in America. The fact that lines of communication were damaged during the rebellion, coupled with strict codes of wartime censorship, meant that information regarding those executed often only made it outside of Ireland after the men were dead.

On her return to London in May 1916, Gore-Booth delivered one of the first Irish eyewitness accounts of the aftershock in Dublin to a London Society. Her speech was later published as a 'Holograph Account of a visit to Dublin in the Aftermath of the Easter Rising', by Esther Roper. It is a fascinating and unique portrayal which was most certainly an attempt to educate English people about the reality of British rule in Ireland. Gore-Booth's writings in this section are in stark contrast to her earlier pacifist articles in Part II of this volume which oppose violent warfare of any kind. Throughout all of the writings in Part III Gore-Booth is careful not to denigrate the Easter Rising but instead she focuses on the atrocities perpetrated by British authorities. A recurring focus is on the 1916 executions including an emotional account entitled the 'Sinn Féin Rebellion', published in the *Socialist Review*. This periodical was committed to expressing pacifist ideals and it is therefore notable that Gore-Booth's article, in which she refuses to vilify an armed rebellion, was published in this journal.

Key characters emerge in Gore-Booth's writings in Part III including Francis Sheehy-Skeffington and Roger Casement. Sheehy-Skeffington was a writer, a pacifist and a suffrage campaigner. He worked closely with his wife Hanna who, along with Margaret Cousins, established the Irish Women's Franchise League in 1908. Francis founded and edited the official newspaper of the organisation, the *Irish Citizen*.[3] The death of Sheehy-Skeffington greatly affected Gore-Booth and she used the account of his murder to highlight the atrocities perpetrated by the British forces in Dublin. Sheehy-Skeffington was a committed pacifist and did not take up arms in the military uprising. He attempted to keep public order in Dublin city.

On 25 April, in the midst of heavy fighting, Sheehy-Skeffington held a meeting at which an interim Citizens' Defence Force was established to

3 See: Sonja Tiernan, '"Challenging the Headship of Man": Militant Suffragism and the *Irish Citizen* Magazine', in Mark O'Brien and Felix M. Larkin (eds), *Periodicals and Journalism in Twentieth-Century Ireland* (Dublin: Four Courts Press, 2014).

protect Dublin civilians during the rebellion. On his way home that evening he was arrested without charge and taken to Portobello barracks in Rathmines. During the night Sheehy-Skeffington was taken out, with his hands bound, to accompany British soldiers on raids of the city. He was returned to the barracks the next morning where the captain of the guard, J. C. Bowen-Colthurst, ordered that Sheehy-Skeffington and two other unarmed civilian men be brought into the yard of the barracks.[4] On Colthurst's order all three men were shot dead by a firing squad of seven men. In an attempt to justify the murder of Sheehy-Skeefington, Colthurst ordered that his house be ransacked in search of incriminating evidence. In this way Hanna Sheehy-Skeffington and her young son were subjected to further humiliation and fear. Gore-Booth provides an emotional account of this episode in her 'holograph account'.

Colthurst was later tried by court-martial, found guilty of murder and declared insane. He was detained at Broadmoor Asylum but only served eighteen months before being released on a full pension. Gore-Booth wrote articles and poetry condemning the murder of Sheehy-Skeffington and regarding the treatment of his widow, Hanna Sheehy-Skeffington.

Roger Casement also features predominantly in this section. Casement was arrested before the Rising and was the only leader to undergo a public trial in the aftermath of the rebellion. Casement's background and the circumstances of his arrest ensured that his trial was high profile. He was captured off the coast of County Kerry, where he landed from a German U-boat. The submarine was meant to rendezvous with the *Aud*, a German ship with a large cargo of rifles and ammunition, sent to arm the Irish Volunteers. After a failed attempt to contact the Volunteers on land, the crew were forced to scuttle the *Aud*. Casement was exhausted and ill when he reached land and was quickly arrested by British soldiers. He was brought to Dublin and from there he was sent to England and imprisoned in the Tower of London. He was treated differently from the other leaders of the Rising as he had previously been employed by the British Foreign Service and had received a knighthood for his humanitarian work in the Congo. As a former and respected official of the British government, Casement's involvement with the Easter Rising and his association with German military forces caused a political scandal in England. Casement was sentenced to death at a trial for high treason in the Old Bailey.

Gore-Booth instigated a high-profile campaign for Casement's reprieve. Her campaign concerned high-ranking politicians and law enforcers who became anxious that through her efforts Casement might actually escape execution. On examination of British Home Office papers, prime ministers'

4 The other men were Thomas Dickson, editor of a loyalist paper the *Eye-Opener*, and Patrick McIntyre, editor of the anti-Larkin paper the *Searchlight*.

correspondence and newspaper articles, included in Part III, it is apparent that Gore-Booth's campaign forced the British authorities to launch an investigation, days before Casement was due to be executed. It is also apparent that through her actions Gore-Booth inadvertently led British authorities to step up their smear campaign of Casement, through which they distributed extracts from his so-called Black Diaries detailing his homosexual activities.[5] Gore-Booth's final publication about Casement was published in the *Catholic Bulletin* in 1918 during a time of strict press censorship. Her article openly condemns Casement's execution but escaped the rigours of wartime censorship possibly due to the religious nature of the publication.[6]

In the aftermath of the Easter Rising a renewed nationalist ideal was sweeping through the country. Clair Wills notes that 'Irish public opinion was not so much reversed as crystallised by the combination of the executions and better information about the events in Dublin.'[7] Indeed the executed leaders quickly became martyrs to the Irish cause, while in the wake of the fighting, instances of brutality by British soldiers were uncovered. The bodies of a number of unarmed civilians were discovered buried in cellars and yards of Dublin houses in the North King Street area, allegedly killed by South Staffordshire Regiment soldiers. An inquest was held on 16 May at which the city coroner, Dr Louis A. Byrne, considered the cases of Patrick Bealin with mention of James Healy. The bodies of the two men were found in shallow graves in the cellar of a licensed premises at 177 North King Street. Bealin was a foreman at the public house and Healy worked as a clerk at Jameson's whiskey distillery; they were unarmed and had no part in the rebellion. After hearing witness statements and military accounts the jury reached a verdict:

> We find that the said Patrick Bealin died from shock and haemorrhage, resulting from bullet wounds inflicted by a soldier, or soldiers, in whose custody he was, an unarmed and unoffending prisoner. We consider that the explanation given by the military authorities is very unsatisfactory, and we believe that if the military authorities had any inclination they could produce the officer in charge.[8]

Questions regarding these atrocities were put to Asquith in the House of Commons over the following months of 1916. Although the Prime Minister agreed that the incident should be investigated, he refused to conduct a public inquiry. A private inquiry was launched and the results were kept from the

5 Jeffrey Dudgeon, *Roger Casement: The Black Diaries, with a Study of His Background, Sexuality and Irish Political Life* (Belfast: Belfast Press, 2002).

6 Brian Murphy, 'J. J. O'Kelly, *The Catholic Bulletin* and Contemporary Irish Cultural Historians', *Archivium Hibernicum*, 44 (1989), 71–88.

7 Clair Wills, *Dublin 1916: The Siege of the GPO* (London: Profile Books, 2009), p. 103.

8 *Sinn Féin Rebellion Handbook* (Dublin: Irish Times, 1917), p. 30.

Figure 9 Illustrated birthday card by Gore-Booth to her sister Constance Markievicz on the occasion of her birthday, 4 February 1917, in prison

public under advice from Home Office official, Sir Edward Troup, for fear of 'hostile propaganda'.[9]

By the end of 1916 hundreds of Irish people remained in prison across Britain, many without sentencing. Asquith's leadership faced challenges from political opponents and from within the Liberal Party. His ability to appease

9 Richard Norton-Taylor, 'Documents on suppression of Easter Rising reveal cover-up over the killing of innocent bystanders', *Guardian* (11 January 2001).

Figure 10 Countess Markievicz arrives at Liberty Hall, with Eva Gore-Booth, June 1917

the political situation in Ireland and to govern his country through the Great War was questioned. In December 1916 Asquith was forced to resign. The Secretary of State for War, David Lloyd George, was nominated as Prime Minister. Lloyd George almost instantly granted an amnesty, releasing Irish prisoners held at Frongoch Internment Camp, Reading Gaol and two women held at Aylesbury. Countess Markievicz remained imprisoned and Gore-Booth visited her sister regularly, acquiring a concern for prisoner welfare. Gore-Booth wrote to her sister often but unfortunately the vast majority of those letters have never been recovered. Part III includes poetry written to Markievicz, and Figure 9 shows an illustrated birthday card by Gore-Booth sent to her sister in prison on 4 February 1917.

In order to finally decide on the issue of Home Rule, Lloyd George called for an Irish Convention to be formed which would decide on the appropriate action to be taken. For such a Convention to work successfully a general amnesty was called releasing those still imprisoned in connection with the Easter Rising. Under these terms Markievicz was released from Aylesbury prison in June 1917. She spent a number of days with Gore-Booth and Roper at their flat in London before returning to Ireland. Gore-Booth accompanied her sister to Dublin where they were met with a heroic welcome as thousands of people lined the street to welcome Markievicz home. Such public demonstrations highlighted the growing support for the Irish nationalist movement. Figure 10 shows Markievicz surrounded by the welcoming crowd, with Gore-Booth pictured to left of the image, in front of Markievicz.

The Irish Convention first assembled in Dublin in July 1917. After eight months of deliberations the members of the Convention reached a conclusion.

Figure 11 Arthur Griffith and Éamon de Valera leaving the Mansion House after the anti-conscription conference, 1918

On 8 April 1918 the chairman, Horace Plunkett, published his final report to Lloyd George which recommended 'the establishment of a Parliament for the whole of Ireland with an Executive responsible to it, and with full powers over all internal legislation, administration and direct taxation'.[10] The Convention findings clearly pointed out the implications of the 'Irish question' during a time of hostilities. Point 29 stated, 'as regards the question of conscription, we are ready to take it for granted that no attempt would be made to apply it to Ireland without the consent of the Irish Parliament. Any attempt to impose conscription upon a nation without its sanction is utterly impolitic and unjust, and is bound to end in disaster.'[11]

Ignoring the forthright references to conscription, the British government agreed to enact the Home Rule Bill under condition that conscription would be extended to Ireland. Eight days after the Irish Convention report was published, on 16 April 1918, the extension of the Military Service Bill enforcing conscription in Ireland was announced. This new legislation would ensure that all Irishmen between the ages of 18 and 50 would be called to join the British army. Members of the Irish Parliamentary Party walked out of Westminster in protest. MPs John Dillon and Joseph Devlin returned to Ireland to organise against conscription. A meeting was held in the Lord Mayor of Dublin's residence at the Mansion House. The Mayor, Lawrence O'Neill, hosted the meeting which saw the formation of the Irish Anti-Conscription Committee. Figure 11 shows Arthur Griffith, founder of the nationalist party Sinn Féin with the then president of the party, Éamon de Valera, leaving the conference.

The committee developed an anti-conscription pledge which Catholic bishops agreed would be taken at the door of every church around the country before mass on Sunday 21 April (see Figure 12). Political instability in Ireland again intensified as anti-conscription activities increased, including a general workers' strike on 23 April. Gore-Booth rallied to the support of the Irish anti-conscription movement. For her part in the propaganda campaign Gore-Booth wrote to British newspapers. 'The ruin preparing in Ireland' was published in the *Manchester Guardian.* Gore-Booth's campaign against the introduction of conscription in Ireland differs immensely from her previous campaigns in England. Her work there was based on ideals of pacifism and the promotion of choice for the individual. In her campaign against conscription in Ireland, Gore-Booth never mentions pacifist ideals but focuses instead on the fact that the introduction of conscription is yet another forced oppression of Irish people by British forces. Despite efforts, forced conscription was never introduced in Ireland.

10 *Report of the Proceedings of the Irish Convention* (Dublin: His Majesty's Stationery Office, 1918), p. 6.

11 *Ibid.*, p. 40.

Figure 12 Signing the anti-conscription pledge, 1918

In her final years Gore-Booth became an outspoken campaigner against the death penalty. She was particularly concerned by the Restoration of Order to Ireland Act, introduced in 1920. The act effectively replaced trial by jury for alleged Irish Republican Army cases. Those suspected of republican activity were tried and sentenced by a military court-martial. Kevin Barry, a 19-year-old medical student from Dublin, was the first person to be sentenced and executed under this system. He had been convicted of killing three British soldiers. He was hanged in Mountjoy Prison on 1 November 1920. By December 1920 martial law was proclaimed in Counties Kerry, Limerick, Cork and Tipperary. This was extended to cover Waterford and Clare in January 1921. Martial law dictated that all weapons and ammunition in these counties must be surrendered to the authorities. Anyone found in possession of arms would be arrested, tried by court-martial and could face a death sentence. Throughout 1921 the number of executions of Irishmen rose at an alarming rate. In response, Gore-Booth and Roper became secretaries of the Committee for the Abolition of the Death Penalty, a branch of the League of Peace and Freedom. During the final eighteen months of her life, Gore-Booth devoted herself almost entirely to writing about religious topics and delivering talks to theosophical societies.

'The Land to a Landlord'

The One and the Many, 1904

You hug to your soul a handful of dust,
And you think 'the round world your sacred trust—
But the sun shines, and the wind blows,
And nobody cares and nobody knows.

O the braken waves and the foxgloves flame,
And none of them ever has heard your name—
Near and dear is the curlew's cry,
You are merely a stranger passing by.

Sheer up through the shadows the mountain towers
And dreams wander free in this world of ours,—
Though you may 'turn the grass to gold,
The twilight has left you out in the cold.

Though you are king of the rose and the wheat,
Not for you, not for you is the bog-myrtle sweet,
Though you are lord of the long grass,
The hemlock bows not her head as you pass.

The poppies would flutter amongst the corn
Even if you had never been born,
With your will or without your will
The ragweed can wander over the hill.

Down there in the bog where the plovers call
You are but an outcast after all,
Over your head the sky gleams blue—
Not a cloud or a star belongs to you.

'An Irish Marching Song'

Donegal News, 9 January 1909[12]

Fear not to fall for the land ye love,
Irish earth beneath you, Irish sky above,
Bear the standard onward down the sacred glen,
All the saints in Ireland once were Irish men.
O'er the Wicklow Mountains, through the plains of Meath,
Irish skies above you, Irish earth beneath!

12 Originally published in *Bean na h-Éireann* (*Irishwoman*), a nationalist woman's magazine.

Past the faery hillside where the ragweed gleams –
Tread the grass down gently over buried Dreams,
Where the heroes linger tranced underground,
Through the pale green twilight of the faery Mound,
On the spell-bound spirits of the faithful few
See the tears of Ireland fall like magic dew.
They shall strait from slumber, those we mourned as dead,
They have heard our footsteps marching overhead,
Rending dreams and darkness at the trumpet call,
By the tears of Ireland freed from faery thrall,
Spirits of dead heroes, they are with us now!
Pale the starlight flashes on each starlit brow,
Twilight voices calling over land and sea,
'Ireland, holy Ireland, we are true to thee!'
Those who long before us for their country died,
Kings and queens and heroes marching at our side,
Keep the watch-fires burning on the haunted hill,
Those who fought for Ireland fight for Ireland still.
Thousands march beside us through the land we love,
Irish earth beneath them, Irish skies above.
Over dead and dying, on the battle rolls,
All the winds of Ireland keen for Irish souls.

Holograph account of a visit to Dublin in the aftermath of the Easter Rising

Speech delivered to a London society, 1916[13]

As the Leinster steamed into Dublin Bay on that May morning of 1916 the world seemed transfigured with beauty and delight. There was nothing to remind one of that blind will of domination, violence and greed that has for centuries made of these blue waters a highway of destruction. White sea-gulls flashed against a blue sky and the mountains had about them the radiance and peace of the early morning hours. The sea shifted and glittered and dreamed. It was hardly possible to believe that any man could look upon the vessel's shining track merely as the road to Empire and domination. Yet, as the siren suddenly shrieked out its harsh warning, the sight of a great mass of khaki-clad soldiers crowding round the gangway shook the glamour of the scene and brought queer memories of past generations.

13 Later published by Esther Roper in *Prison Letters of Countess Markievicz* (1934; London: Virago, 1987), pp. 42–53.

Soldiers of all times, of the same nationality and on the same quest. Soldiers in the queer bulky armour of the Middle Ages, soldiers in the gay colours of the Elizabethans, soldiers in Cromwell's drabs, soldiers in the stiff reds of the last century, and now soldiers in khaki. Soldiers with bows and arrows, soldiers with spears, soldiers with swords and muskets and all manner of old-fashioned weapons, soldiers with quaint and unwieldy cannon, and soldiers with rifles and revolvers and machine-guns. Soon there would be soldiers with tanks and aeroplanes. An endless procession of soldiers, with every kind of weapon, always on the same errand, always going, as they are going now, to conquer and hold down Ireland.

And Ireland the Unconquerable suffering them helplessly, watching them land in their thousands, with that same old self-conscious gesture of hers, half passionate, half-cynical, partly tragic and wholly contemptuous. Like the human soul smiling through an agony of weakness at the secret of her enigmatic strength.

It was easy to pass unnoticed through the rather sheepish crowd on the pier, who were doing their best to look Prussian and efficient. The soldiers were not at all aggressive. It was hard to believe they were engaged in crushing a Rebellion and holding down an oppressed nation. By the most vivid stretch of the imagination, you could not credit them with any sinister designs.

Dull and lethargic they seemed for the most part, sometimes they were quite amiably frivolous. One wondered if Cromwell's soldiers were like that. 'Stay where you are, for God's sake!' I heard a laughing soldier say in mock-tragic accents to a group of civilians who were in too great a hurry to land. 'If I let you go over there, I shall be court-martialled and shot at dawn!'

Ten minutes after that the world turned black, as I read the words that shrieked in huge letters from every hoarding in the town: 'Execution of James Connolly.' 'James Connolly shot this morning.'

In days past I had known James Connolly, most kindly and humane of men. A man who had that quality, rare indeed among politicians, that however absorbed he might be in fighting for a cause, he did not forget to answer the appeal of individual suffering.

Afterwards, the story went round that one of those told off to shoot him was a miner, one who had personal cause of gratitude to him.[14] But he did not know who it was he was going to shoot. Anyway, he stood there with the rest, submissively waiting for the word of command. So would any other soldier,

14 James Connolly was a committed socialist and trade unionist; his many campaigns helped workers in America, Britain and Ireland. One of the greatest influences on Connolly was Keir Hardie, originally a miner's leader in Ayrshire. Fergus A. D'Arcy. 'Connolly, James', James McGuire and James Quinn (eds), *Dictionary of Irish Biography* (Cambridge: Cambridge University Press, 2009).

the very man who joked about executions would have done it. Without anger or hate or any conscious cruelty, but simply because he was told to. So insidious a thing is that vile creeping obedience that deprives man of his sense of right and wrong, his very soul and will and mind.

Realisation of the happenings of the past weeks rushed us in a flood as we drove through the smoking ruins of O'Connell Street.

The driver seemed rather nervy, surly and suspicious, most unlike the usual talkative Dublin driver. He confined himself to a long grumble about being starved with his family during the Rebellion, not being allowed out of the house for three days. It had been impossible for him to get food for himself and his children.

Driving past Stephen's Green, he began to tell us some rather fictitious details about dead bodies of men and women being carried away at night and buried secretly.

And my thoughts rushed back to that dreadful Sunday in London when I had read an account in Lloyd's Weekly News a circumstantial account of the finding of my sister's dead body in Stephen's Green, and of the terrible days that followed, when I had almost wished the discredited story had been true, so much worse does it seem to the human mind to be executed coldly and deliberately at a certain hour by the clock than to be killed in the hurry and excitement of battle. Perhaps this is because such a death is so wholly unnatural.

In every form of natural life, destruction comes silently and unexpectedly or, at the worst, wrapped in a haze of uncertain hours and vague moments. The foreknowledge of the exact minute of death is a form of mental torture entirely invented by human beings, in the fiendish ingenuity of vengeance sanctified by pious traditions. The world, as God made it, may be cruel in many things, but it is not cruel enough for that supreme and unnatural outrage.

This slow and excruciating and delicately applied brain torment has been brought to a terrible pitch of perfection by a generation that prides itself on the abolition of the rack, and the rougher methods of their ancestors, too blunted themselves to realise the more refined and exquisite possibilities of brain and nerve torture.

But the worst had not happened. My sister, condemned to death for her part in the Rebellion, had been reprieved.

And now I was on my way to visit her in prison.

After visiting the kind friend who had by some means procured the permit, the three of us started for Mountjoy.

The Dublin streets were terrible. They had a sort of muddled desperate look, rather like but infinitely more tragic than the look one used to see in London on an air-raid night, just after the warning was given. As if everybody, even the very houses, were crouching down, hiding from something.

Oddly enough, we chanced on the same car that had driven us from the station earlier that day. But the car driver was transfigured when he heard the address to which we were going.

All his surliness and suspicion vanished in a moment, and as we got down at the gate of Mountjoy, he turned on us with a beaming smile. 'It's little I thought this morning when I drove you from the boat, it was to the prison I'd be taking you!'

From his manner you would have thought (as doubtless he did) that the dingy prison gate was the entrance to some very select Paradise, sacred to the greater Saints and the more exalted Archangels.

Prisons are all the same, built after the same dreary pattern. Very imposing and grand on the outside, they gradually get squalider and squalider the farther you get into them. We were let in through a little postern door in the main gate by a long-suffering porter who spends the livelong day opening and locking the gate. He does not guard the prisoners, but he is like a sentinel in a besieged city, opening the door for a moment to let in a cart of supplies and shutting it again hastily in the face of the enemy. For to all that live in that gloomy place, out free and kindly human life is the enemy to be shut out at all costs – except the prisoners, and sometimes one thinks that the only people in a prison whose point of view has not become wholly perverted and insane are the prisoners. For they have no 'duty' to prevent their being kind and loving to their neighbours.

The Mountjoy porter looked at our permits, and presently the big iron gate was unlocked and we crossed the yard into that inner building which is the prison itself. As I walked through the long corridor, my mind was obsessed by one horrible thought: 'They have shot all her friends; James Connolly and Eamonn Ceannt only that day: did she know? Should I have to tell her?' Afterwards I knew that this was a quite unnecessary anxiety. She knew everything. The shots that killed Padraig Pearse and the others she had listened to morning after morning in her cell at Kilmainham.

Suddenly there was her face behind a sort of cage: it was cut into sections by the cross-bars. But one could half see, half guess how calm and smiling she was.

She talked very fast, and was full of all sorts of commissions she wanted carried out, asked a great many questions and seemed only really puzzled by one thing: 'Why on earth did they shoot Skeffy?' she said.[15] 'After all, he wasn't in it. He didn't even believe in fighting. What did it mean?'

At the time I could not answer her: afterwards I found out. Nobody who has gone through the ordinary prison visit can realise how unsatisfactory it is, nor what a strain it is, to fling one's intimate conversation across a passage with

15 Francis Sheehy-Skeffington.

a wardress in it, to a head appearing at a window opposite. And then to know that these few minutes must last one for months, and that one has probably forgotten something important.

There was much to hear: her adventures in the Rebellion, details of her court-martial, her anxiety for the wife of a dead colleague who was ill, in hiding and without money.[16] Many and very insufficient directions as to how to find her. About her own treatment the prisoner had not much to say. She was a 'convict' and a 'lifer' and that was all about it. And anyway, it was splendidly worth-while.

For one glorious week, Ireland had been free ... and then back she went to stories of that wonderful time, of the night-scouting and the trench in Stephen's Green and the machine-gun on the Shelbourne and how they were forced to retreat into the College of Surgeons. And how they could have held out for days, and the shock and grief of the order to surrender on that Sunday morning when I had run up and down London trying to find out if she was really dead. And she told of the executed colleague who had marched with her down Thomas Street where Emmet had been hung a hundred years ago, for the same cause, by the same power. They had discussed together what seemed to them the only doubtful point in the immediate future: whether they would be shot or hung.

This rebel had a very strange story. He had been in the past for many years a private in the British Army. In India long ago he had met another Irish soldier, who told him when next they met he would not be fighting for England.[17]

In South Africa, years after, he came on him again, a prisoner condemned to death for fighting with the Boers against England.

This man made such an impression on the other Irish soldier, awakening in him a sense of shame to be found on the side of Empire and the conquistadores and oppressors of Ireland, that he got away from the Army as quickly as possible and joined the growing rebel army in Ireland. Now he, too, had been shot.

At the end of twenty hurried minutes of rapid talk we said goodbye for the next four months, and the oddly becapped head disappeared from the window, vanishing into what unimaginable scenes of dullness, dinginess and squalor.

The next morning we set out early to try and find my sister's friend and spent many weary hours walking through endless poverty-stricken streets, questioning naturally suspicious and incredulous people, and causing many

16 After Commandant Michael Mallin was executed his pregnant wife, Agnes, went into hiding with her three sons and a daughter. On Markievicz's instructions, Gore-Booth discovered Agnes, provided her with financial aid and introduced her to a local Inchicore priest, Father Ryan, who protected the Mallin family.

17 Mallin enlisted with the Royal Scots Fusiliers in 1889 and served until 1902.

a fit of nerves no doubt, to those who were afraid of being suspected of rebel tendencies, and who now obviously thought we were Government spies. In the course of our wanderings we passed one of the great fortress-like barracks that seem to over-awe Dublin. Round the gates a miserable crowd collected, of patient white-faced men and women, standing under the great gray wall in a sort of hopeless gray dejection. We were told that they had been there for days. They were the relatives and friends of prisoners, waiting to try and get some news of them. And the story goes that four soldiers having been killed in the fighting, the young officers in the barracks had sworn to have forty rebel lives in exchange.

No one will ever know what went on in those barracks behind those towering walls.

An old woman came towards us in the road, crying and begging for news of her son who had been deported to England. She was sure they would force him into the Army. 'He won't don the khaki. He won't don the khaki,' she reiterated drearily. Perhaps it was some vague tradition of what had happened after the last rebellion that made her so certain of what would happen to him. 'A year ago,' she wailed, 'his work was taken from him because he would not don the khaki, and he'll not don the khaki if they shoot him for it.'

Poor soul, I hope her son came back safe and sound and without any khaki. At the time it seemed impossible to persuade her that there was the slightest hope that he would not be shot.

In the end we found a little chapel full of people, where a priest was saying Mass. After the service was over, we went to the vestry and appealed to him for help. Though not a Sinn Feiner, he was a very sympathetic man, and he had been outraged and horrified at the treatment of the Irish prisoners behind that terrible wall, starved, deprived of water and every necessity of life, left to lie for days crowded together, 500 lying on the floor in unspeakably insanitary conditions, some of them wounded, one of these with only his boots for his pillow. So that many of the men were hardly conscious when they were court-martialled. The priest told us of the people waiting there outside day after day, begging for news and of the utter callousness of the authorities. His voice was choking with grief and indignation. He had been a doctor in his youth. It was the horrible inhumanity of the whole thing that he minded. One poor girl was in prison for waving to my sister as she passed marching among the other prisoners on her way to the barracks. Yes, he could find the woman we wanted: he knew some of her relations. It would be quite easy.

At lunch at our hotel we listened with some interest to a conversation between a soldier and a local Unionist. They were shouting to one another from different tables. 'I must say,' said the Unionist, 'your people were pretty free with your bullets. A friend of mine, a strong Orangeman, had stayed in his house for three days as directed, and at the end of the third day he opened the front door to get a little air and the soldier in the street shot him dead.'

'Stupid sort of thing to do, to put your head out at a time like that,' said the soldier, shrugging his shoulders.

Truly, life is cheap in these days and death needs little formal apology or introduction. Fresh from that Flanders shambles the soldiers forget that many civilians have kept a pre-war standard of value, for their own lives at all events.

At the same time, talking to Mrs. Sheehy-Skeffington that afternoon, one realised there was much more in the story of her husband's murder than mere military carelessness and indifference. Both she and her husband were strong pacifists and they possessed no weapons, but the windows of the room in which she sat were still broken by the volley fired into it by the soldiers when there was no one in the house but herself and her little boy of seven. Since then the story of her husband's murder has been told, but at that time the horror was still fresh. She showed us the poor little parcel returned from the barracks, containing a watch, a tie and a collar, worthless things that bore pathetic witness to the almost insane truth, – that those who did not scruple to steal human lives were yet most honourable and honest in their dealings with property – to them a much more important matter.

Hearing Mrs. Skeffington talk, one realised that though her husband never had a weapon in his hand, militarism was wise in its generation, and in Sheehy-Skeffington militarism had struck down its worst enemy – unarmed yet insurgent Idealism. It was not for nothing that the half-mad officer who carried out the murder was promoted a week afterwards.

The authorities knew their business well.

All his life Skeffington had never 'ceased from mental fight' against all forms of tyranny, oppression and cruelty. He was a born rebel, a questioner of ancient traditions, a shaker of ancient tyranny. He refused to go out against authority, but because he did not acquiesce in any violence between human beings.

In a social state founded entirely on blind obedience to certain traditions and ideas, mental freedom means disaster, and the man who knows no obedience is the enemy.

If the unthinkable had happened and Skeffington had been in the British Army, he would not have shot James Connolly or Padraig Pearse. Not only would he have died protesting against these terrible crimes, but he would have tried to rouse the conscience of every soldier he came near. Individual conscience in the Army means mutiny. It is the deadly and most fatal enemy of militarism.

Skeffington, on fire with hatred of violence and cruelty, attending forty recruiting meetings, speaking in the street against war, defending the cause of

Labour, denouncing all oppression in the name of Liberty, Mercy and Kindness, was a greater danger to the authorities than many a more violent revolutionist.[18] For revolutions and counter-revolutions are familiar in this weary world, but his voice was the voice of a new era, a terrible possibility, that nightmare of individual evolution and militant goodwill that shakes the dreams of militarism with a strange threat.

Truly, it was easy enough to understand 'why they shot Skeffy,' though the only crime they could accuse him of was an effort to persuade a hooligan crowd not to loot shops.

Militarism has a true instinct and a short way with its enemies. But perhaps the future is with Skeffington.

Dublin was thrilling with horror that afternoon at the revelation of the murders in King Street.[19] A deputation had gone to the Prime Minister to place the facts before him, and to insist on an investigation into how many inoffensive citizens had been dragged down into the cellars and brained with the butt-ends of the rifles of perhaps drunken soldiers. People smiled. They might indeed pretend to insist, but everyone really knew that such investigations are never made.

Meanwhile Dublin was a city of mourning and death.

Roger Casement had been taken from Arbour Hill Barracks to the Tower. There was a feeling of strain and embarrassment everywhere. People broke down and wept for very little, even in the streets. Dazed and miserable, with the sound of the bombs still in their ears, they were beginning to collect in groups and tell one another stories of individual sufferings, injustices and atrocities.

It was not till later that they began to hold up their heads in pride, thinking of the strange heroisms of the dead, and rejoicing in the fact that once again in her long struggle for liberty Ireland had shown the world that she did not acquiesce in her age-long slavery, any more than she had done in the days of Elizabeth, Oliver Cromwell, William Pitt, George III, or any of her old conquerors and tyrants. That was the Irish point of view. The English one was different.

On the way back to London about a week later, travelling up from Holyhead, was a woman in the carriage with us who talked about the Rebellion.

18 Sheehy-Skeffington organised numerous anti-recruitment meetings, mainly at Beresford Place in Dublin. He was arrested on 23 May 1915 under the Defence of the Realm Act, as his speech that day was deemed 'to prejudice recruiting'. National Archives, Kew, Colonial Office Record Series vol. 1, Dublin Castle Special Branch Files, CO 904/215/408, report on anti-militarist meeting held at Beresford Place by Patrick J. McCarthy Constable 36G, 23 May 1915.

19 The North King Street massacre discussed above in the introduction to this Part.

'Dreadful people the Irish,' she was saying, 'so cowardly too, and ungrateful, to stab us in the back like that, after all we've done for them!'

Between these points of view no reconciliation seems possible. Except perhaps in the future: that universal reconciliation of humanity in goodwill, which was the creed of that troublesome idealist, Francis Sheehy-Skeffington.

'Easter Week'

Broken Glory, 1918

Grief for the noble dead
Of one who did not share their strife,
And mourned that any blood was shed,
Yet felt the broken glory of their state,
Their strange heroic questioning of Fate
Ribbon with gold the rags of this our life.

'Francis Sheehy-Skeffington, Dublin, 26 April 1916'

Broken Glory, 1918

No green and poisonous laurel wreath shall shade
His brow, who dealt no death in any strife
Crown him with olive who was not afraid
To join the desolate unarmed ranks of life.

Who did not fear to die, yet feared to slay,
A leader in the war that shall end war,
Unarmed he stood in ruthless Empire's way,
Unarmed he stands on Acheron's lost shore.

Yet not alone, nor all unrecognized,
For at his side does that scorned Dreamer stand,
Who in the Olive Garden agonized,
Whose Kingdom yet shall come in every land,

When driven men, who fight and hate and kill
To order, shall let all their weapons fall,
And know that kindly freedom of the will
That holds no other human will in thrall.

'To Constance in Prison'

Broken Glory, 1918

Outcast from joy and beauty, child of broken hopes forlorn,
Lost to the magic mountains and parted from all flowers,
Robbed of the harvest moon that shines on far-off fields of corn,
Bereft of raindrops on green leaves, bright wrecks of fallen showers.

Nay, not outcast, whilst through your soul a sudden rapture thrills,
And all your dreams are shaken by the salt Atlantic wind,
The gods descend at twilight from the magic-hearted hills,
And there are woods and primroses in the country of your mind.

Yours is that inner Ireland beyond green fields and brown,
Where waves break dawn-enchanted on the haunted Rosses shore,
And clouds above Ben Bulben fling their coloured shadows down,[20]
Whilst little rivers shine and sink in wet sands at Crushmor.

'Christmas Eve in Prison'

Broken Glory, 1918

Do not be lonely, dear, nor grieve
This Christmas Eve.
Is it so vain a thing
That your heart's harper, Dark Roseen,
A wandering singer, yet a queen,
Crownèd with all her seventeen stars,
Outside your prison bars
Stands carolling?

Letter to C. P. Scott, editor of the *Manchester Guardian*, on behalf of Sir Roger Casement[21]

July 4th
Dear Mr. Scott,
Miss Bannister who is Roger Casement's only near relative in England asked me to forward you the enclosed appeal. She is trying to get influential people to write to Mr. Asquith and the Home Secretary to urge them to reprieve her

20 Ben Bulben is a rock formation near Gore-Booth's ancestral home of Lissadell House. It is the site of many Irish legends.
21 Parliamentary Archives, Lloyd George Papers, LG/D/18/15/14.

adopted brother. There are a great many grounds for clemency, his past record of work for humanity in the Putumayo business, his personal character that all sides allow there were no sordid motives for his crime, but that if he is hung it will be for ignorance not for wickedness, as he did what he himself considered supremely right however mistaken he may have been.[22] If patriotism among Englishmen for England is a virtue it is surely a terrible severity to hang an Irishman for patriotism to Ireland against England.

It has been said that his action caused the deaths of many people, but I do not think this correct. He may have shared the illusion with many, but anyone reading even a little school magazine like Pearse's at St Edna's must realise that if Casement had never existed the rebellion would have been exactly the same.[23]

Apart from this personal point of view there is the political side. Anyone who knows the exasperation it caused in Ireland by the 15 executions of men who have now become national heroes even to the mildest nationalists will realise what the effect of this last horror is likely to be. Then the evidence seems quite trustworthy of the seething indignation in America and the fact that the stories of the Dublin executions is rapidly turning American sympathy against England. I have before me a resolution passed at a mass meeting at Boston, it's too long to quote but it is unmeasured in its condemnation of the barbarous and brutal crimes committed in Ireland 'the murders perpetrated in the streets etc etc.'[24] And one hears of such resolutions being passed everywhere. I am not saying that statesmen should give in to public opinion but surely when the public opinion of a great continent is on the side of mercy, statesmen might be wise to consider whether they are not injuring this country's good name by doing an action that rightly or wrongly will be considered an act of useless cruelty by a huge number of the inhabitants of a neutral country. And here

22 Casement worked for the British consular services and was ordered to investigate reports of atrocities at rubber plantations in numerous African regions, including the Congo. Michael Laffan notes how Casement 'encountered plentiful evidence that the collection of rubber was associated with forced labour, extortionate taxes, mutilation, murder and depopulation'. 'Casement, Sir Roger David', McGuire and Quinn (eds), *Dictionary of Irish Biography*. Casement's reports were published, exposing horrific practices: Roger Casement, 'Correspondence Respecting the Treatment of British Colonial Subjects and Native Indians Employed in the Collection of Rubber in the Putumayo District', *House of Commons Sessional Papers*, 14 February 1912 to 7 March 1913, vol. 68.

23 Patrick Pearse established a bilingual school for boys on the south side of Dublin. The school, St Enda's, published its own newsletter, *An Macaomh* (*The Youth*.)

24 At this time there was an estimated 20 million people in America of Irish descent. The meeting to which Gore-Booth refers is possibly the national convention of the Ancient Order of Hibernians in Boston, representing 250,000 Irish people, which officially protested the hanging of Sir Roger Casement.

in England surely many people must feel that so many innocent people like Sheehy-Skeffington were shot in Dublin, it would be an act of grace to give us one life of a rebel in return. When all is said, many calm minded people feel sadly that England erred on the side of severity, would it not be a great hope for the future to err a little on the side of clemency, instead of incurring the present bitter feeling in Ireland by another slow deliberate and most heart rendering execution?

Please forgive me for bothering you again. I can hardly bear to talk to Miss Bannister. I remember what I went through when I thought they would shoot my sister. I know she is in the same agony for its all so cruel and so terrible I can't help writing to beg you to use you great influence with the Government people to get a reprieve.

With many apologies
Yours V Sincerely,
Eva Gore Booth.

The case of Roger Casement[25]

[This Document is the Property of His Britannic Majesty's Government]

Printed for the use of the Cabinet. July 1916.

CONFIDENTIAL

I CIRCULATE for the information of my colleagues the following Home Office memorandum with regard to the letter addressed to Sir Edward Grey by Miss Eva Gore-Booth, a sister of the Countess Markevitz [*sic*].

H. S.[26]
July 21, 1916.

Similar letters have been addressed by Miss Eva Gore-Booth to the Prime Minister, Lord Bryce, Lord Emmott, and the Home Secretary, in which the same point is made that Casement came to Ireland on a desperate, self-sacrificing errand to stop the Sinn Fein rising. If this were the fact, why was the 'Aud,' with 20,000 rifles, machine guns, and ammunition, in close attendance upon him? What use was to be made of the code dropped by Casement containing such expressions as 'We have our positions at …' 'Railway communications have been stopped,' 'Our men are at …' 'Further ammunition is needed,' 'Further rifles are needed,' 'How many rifles will you send us?' 'How much ammunition will you send us?' 'Will send plan about landing

25 The following papers were held in a file marked 'Confidential Report,' in the Lloyd George Papers at the Parliamentary Archives, E/9/4/12.

26 The Home Secretary, Herbert Samuel.

of …' &c.? Why – did Casement bring a large green flag with him?

It is impossible to say exactly what was passing in his mind and what he thought from time to time of the prospects of his adventure. He refused to go into the witness-box and be cross-examined on these points, but by his own admissions at New Scotland Yard, which were made after he had been cautioned, and so might fairly have been used in cross-examination, it is clear that he had from time to time urged the Germans to send a much larger force of men and more guns and ammunition with him to Ireland, and that they refused. There was the difficulty of transport and discharge of large cargoes of arms. He says that he then insisted on going alone without his Irish Brigade.

It is probably true, that Casement knew when he landed, or shortly afterwards, that the 'game was up,' but it is impossible to believe, that he came to Ireland for the purpose of stopping the rising. He looked on the rising as hopeless when the plans in connection with his landing and reception and the landing and distribution of the 'Aud's' cargo had miscarried; but, if all had gone well, there can be little doubt that Casement would have taken an active part in the rising, notwithstanding that he had sense enough to know that, while it might serve the Germans' purpose to some extent, it must inevitably end in dismal failure.

The idea of saying that he had come with the intention and for the purpose of stopping the rising appears to have occurred to Casement only after his capture. It is at any rate entirely inconsistent with the proved facts.

I append an extract of Casement's examination at New Scotland Yard.

E.B.[27]

Extracts from Casement's Examination at New Scotland Yard.

Q. Do you know how many men she had?

A. No.

Q. Do you know she had a cargo of pit-props?

A. No. I knew nothing about her cargo, except that she had rifles, machine-guns, &c. I wanted more, many more rifles, cartridges, &c., and I was told that was all could be sent.

Q. The numbers do not affect anybody. Will you give them?

A. Does it matter since the ship's gone? I am very sorry for the people. There were 20,000 rifles.

Q. Machine-guns?

A. Not a large number. Quite insufficient to have any effect.

Q. Do you not know the charterer?

A. No. The proposal came upon me as a thunderclap. I came out of bed without the doctor's advice and came from Munich, and they put it to me that

27 Legal adviser to the Home Office, Ernley Blackwell.

I should go. Of course there could be no question. It arose in this way – my friends wished us to stay in Germany, and when I came to that part of the letter written by a friend of mine in which he was asking for this help, the official letter said of course Sir Roger Casement should stay in Germany. I said under no circumstances could I stay. If there is going to be fighting in Ireland I must go: and the officer in charge of the business, a high official, said you cannot stay. Mr. Monteith begged me to go, and I said you have nothing to do with it.[28] Then we discussed merely details as to whether a large armament could not be sent, and these military officials said 'No,' it is impossible to send more at that time at any rate, and certain essential parts of what my friends were asking for were not being sent.

Q. Hand grenades, I suppose?

A. No. Only human beings. If you are desirous of knowing, I said I have been here for a year and a-half and begged you again and again to send rifles to Ireland, and you refused always. Now you spring it at my head at the eleventh hour, when I have long given it up, of hoping to arm my countrymen. At last you have come with this offer of belated help, and it synchronises with what I can only regard as a hopeless rising in Ireland, where my countrymen will be shot down. Obviously I think it is cowardly, dastardly, and I go alone. They wanted me to take all my Irish boys. Those young men.

Q. About fifty?

A. More than fifty. We had a terrible fight, and I won the day. I said I won't do it. I shall not have it said that I handed these men over to the hangman.

Q. What was their reason for sending you without many arms?

A. Legitimate; for the first place it would have to be a very big ship; and they knew there would be difficulties in landing and that a larger consignment could not be got out in good time. It would be a very hurried discharge ...

Sir R. C.: On the 16th March I came from Munich from the hospital. On the 7th March Monteith came to me from Berlin telling me that they proposed to land arms in Ireland, and I wrote him that if arms are to be sent first make sure that you can establish communication with the people in Ireland, otherwise it is murderous. I propose to go to Ireland myself and take one or two men myself, and send one man back. I then wrote a telegram from the hospital urging the necessity of sending a submarine with me, as I am the only person who can speak authoritatively. I never dreamed of the rising, then. The rising would take place on the 23rd April, whether arms came or not. They wanted artillery, &c., and they told us that this could not be given us, and they would not give us any officers. They said they would give

28 Robert Monteith, a member of the Irish Volunteers sent to Berlin to help form an Irish brigade with Casement. Monteith travelled on board the submarine with Casement; he escaped capture by British soldiers.

us so many rifles and machine guns, and you can take your Irish Brigade. I said 'No; that will be murder.' I said I would go myself. They said, you must take some[one] used to machine guns, as it is a military necessity. We had a long conversation, and I said I leave it to you with your military knowledge. I said that the danger would not lie from the shore but from the sea, and our machine guns will not be any good against a warship. If my friends can organise a rising on the 23rd April I'll go myself and I landed in Ireland and knew the thing to be hopeless. The General Staff told me that the Irish Brigade were not under my orders. I said, you can make them go if you like, but you will see that they won't go, and, in the end, they gave in. If you want this thing to succeed and think that gunners are vitally necessary, I do not think they are necessary. They said, not at all. It will be a success and you will be able to dictate terms to the British Government.

Mr. Basil Thomson states that neither he nor anyone present on any occasion made use of such an expression as, 'It is a festering sore, it is much better that it should come to a head.'[29]

I CIRCULATE, for the information of my colleagues, a letter addressed to Sir Edward Grey by Miss Eva Gore Booth, a sister of the Countess de Markevitz. [*sic*]

Foreign Office, July 19, 1916.

Dear Sir, 33, Fitzroy Square, London, July 17, 1916.

I am taking the great liberty of sending you the enclosed papers and begging you to read them. It seems quite clear from the priest's evidence that Casement really came to Ireland in a frantic attempt to dissuade the Sinn Fein leaders from what he considered the fatal mistake of the rising. It seems to me an intolerably ghastly idea that he should be hung as a result of this self-sacrificing and devoted effort, facing, as he did, almost certain death for the sake of preventing bloodshed and misery in Ireland. It would be impossible to exaggerate the feeling in Ireland on this matter, and the hopeless despair and bitterness with which the prospect of another execution is regarded – what they consider the deliberate and cold-blooded execution of a man who was not even in the rising, but whose generous and romantic personality has made him a favourite national hero. And this feeling is not confined to Sinn Feiners, but is shared by many who, like myself, are not Sinn Feiners, but long for peace in Ireland. May I beg you to use your power on the side of mercy. An act of grace now would do more to conciliate the ordinary Irish people than any concessions to political leaders, however valuable these may be.

29 Basil Thomson, head of the Criminal Investigation Department at Scotland Yard.

Please forgive my troubling you with this letter. I do not think this evidence has yet been made known.

Yours faithfully, Eva Gore Booth.

P.S. – Although I am not in the Sinn Fein movement, I do think I understand something of their point of view through my sister, Constance de Markevitz. [*sic*] E. G. B.

On the 6th April Casement was in a nursing home in Germany, when he heard through a spy's report that there was going to be a rising in Ireland.[30] He went straight to Berlin, where with great difficulty he got a submarine to take him to Ireland. The submarine broke down off Heligoland, and he had to wait for some days to get another. His object in going was to stop the rising, which he considered a fatal mistake. The captain of the second submarine did not know Ireland, and landed him on a part of the coast where he knew nobody. Nobody, of course, expected him. He hid himself while Bailey and Monteith went to Tralee to get a motor-car.[31] They found a shop with Sinn Fein colours, went in, and arranged for a car. One went in the car, the other cycled; but they were followed by police, and never found Casement, who was meanwhile arrested. Meanwhile another car, nothing to do with Casement, met with an accident and two men were drowned. When Casement, in the train, heard someone mention this he thought it must be Bailey and Monteith, and broke down.

Casement begged to be allowed to communicate with the leaders to try and stop the rising, but he was not allowed. On Easter Sunday, at Scotland Yard, he implored again to be allowed to communicate or send a message. But they refused, saying, 'it is a festering sore; it is much better it should come to a head.' It is quite clear from this that if Casement had not been so frightfully anxious to stop the rising he would not have been caught and be in danger of being hanged. This was not told at the trial, because Casement would not allow it.[32] He said the Irish people would think he was going back on them, and trying to save his neck by telling the world he did not approve of the rising. Anybody knowing his character would understand this, and the almost fantastic sense of pride and honour that he has.

30 Along with her letter of appeal, Gore-Booth enclosed this article from the *Dublin Evening Mail* with an account of Casement's arrest.

31 Daniel Bailey, a sergeant in the Irish Brigade. He travelled with Monteith and Casement on board the submarine.

32 Casement's trial lasted for four days at the Old Bailey; the jury found him guilty on 29 June 1916. Gore-Booth's letter was sent after his trial and before his appeal was launched. Casement's appeal failed on 24 July and he was hanged for treason on 3 August 1916.

These are the absolute facts. Whatever people think of the Sinn Feiners, they must know that they are courageous to a fault, and incapable of trying to – save their own lives by shuffling.

'After that,' Father Ryan continued, 'I was sent for and allowed to speak privately with the prisoner. He told me his name, and after some conversation of a purely spiritual nature, he said, "I want you to tell the volunteers in the town and elsewhere to keep perfectly quiet. Tell them I am a prisoner and that the rebellion will be a dismal hopeless failure, as the help they expect will not arrive." The chaplain reminded the prisoner that he had come as a chaplain at his request and not a political ambassador. "Do what I ask you," pleaded Sir Roger, "and you will bring God's blessing on the country and on everyone concerned." (Father Ryan promised to think it over.) I came to the conclusion that it would be the best thing not alone for the police, but for the volunteers and the country, that I should convey the message to the volunteers, and thereby be the means through which bloodshed and suffering might he avoided. I saw the leader of the volunteers in Tralee, and gave him the message. He assured me that he would do his best to keep the volunteers quiet, and they did keep quiet. I also told the head constable of the steps I had taken, and be agreed with me that it was perhaps the wisest course to follow.'

Dublin Evening Mail, Saturday, May 20, 1916.

Dear Mr. Gavan Duffy, Roscrea, County Tipperary, July 12, 1916

Sir Roger Casement saw me in Tralee on the 21st April, and told me he had come to Ireland to stop the rebellion then impending. He asked me to conceal his identity as well as his object in coming until he should have left Tralee, lest any attempt should be made to rescue him. On the other hand he was very anxious that I should spread the news broadcast after he had left.

Sincerely yours,

F. M. Ryan, O.P.

P.S. – My address for three weeks after next Saturday will be, 'The Presbytery, Buncrana, Co. Donegal.'

F. M. R.

Roger Casement: plea for further appeal

Manchester Guardian, 29 July 1916

Sir,

Dr. Herford in his plea for a reprieve for Roger Casement puts forward a sympathetic view of the peculiar circumstances of Irish nationality. May I as an

Irish woman appealing to the broad-mindedness of English people ask them to pause in their indignation against those who have rebelled against their rule and consider what they have known for years of the tragic romance of rebellion and heroic death that has such a hold on Irish imaginations?

Irish national aspirations expressed in the most uncompromising and 'treasonous' language have been applauded over and over again in English theatres. The appeal of Kathleen ni Houlihan, the desolate spirit of Ireland, crying out to her children for love and loyalty has wrung many a cheer from an English audience. Have none of those enthusiastic people any pity or understanding for those whose hearts and minds have been bewitched by that cry and have left happy homes and prosperous careers to follow the dream image of Ireland that has suddenly emerged out of the mists of their half-forgotten childhood to walk once more the actual world?

In Yeats' play 'Kathleen ni Houlihan,' this spirit in the disguise of a lonely old woman goes from cabin to cabin calling to dreamer and peasant to give up all that makes life worth living, nay even life itself, in her service.

> It is a hard service they take that help me. Many that have been free to walk the hills and the bogs and the rushes will be sent to walk hard streets in far countries; many a child will be born, and there will be no father at its christening to give it a name. They that have red cheeks will have pale cheeks, and for all that they will think themselves well paid.

You may think such ideas criminal madness; but the fact remains that those who hold them exist in great numbers. Severity will not intimidate these people. For however wrong-headed they may be according to common-sense standards, there is not one of them who knows what fear means. Over and over again in Irish history severity has been tried, with the result of that long list of national saints and martyrs that are household words in every cabin in Ireland. It is the memory of the fate of such men as Casement that will bring nought for hundreds of years the well-meaning efforts of politicians to bridge the gulf between England and Ireland with conciliatory measures of political organisation. It is easy enough for the Government to hang Casement. In England hanging is a 'degrading punishment.' But in Ireland to be hung by the English Government is a crown of glory, and his memory will be enshrined and worshipped for ever in the hearts of his fellow-countrymen.

Yours, &c.,
Eva Gore-Booth.
London, July 28.

'Roger Casement'

Broken Glory, 1918

I dream of one who is dead,
As the forms of green trees float and fall in the water,
The dreams float and fall in my mind.

I dream of him wandering in a far land,
I dream of him bringing hope to the hopeless,
I dream of him bringing light to the blind.

I dream of him hearing the voice,
The bitter cry of Kathleen ni Houlighaun
On the salt Atlantic wind.

I dream of the hatred of men,
Their lies against him who knew nothing of lying,
Nor was there fear in his mind.

I dream of our hopes and fears,
The long bitter struggle of the broken-hearted,
With hearts that were poisoned and hard.

I dream of the peace of his soul,
And the early morning hush on the grave of a hero
In the desolate prison yard.[33]

I dream of the death that he died,
For the sake of God and Kathleen ni Houlighaun,[34]
Yea, for Love and the Voice on the Wind.

I dream of one who is dead.
Above dreams that float and fall in the water
A new star shines in my mind.

33 Casement was executed on 3 August 1916 at Pentonville prison. Gore-Booth petitioned the Home Office to release Casement's body to be buried in Ireland, but the Home Office refused. Casement was buried in an unmarked grave on the prison grounds. His body was finally repatriated in 1965. He received a State funeral and is now buried in the republican plot at Glasnevin Cemetery in Dublin.

34 Fr McCarroll, a Catholic priest, walked Casement to the scaffold. The last words the priest spoke to him were: 'now Roger for God and Kathleen Ní Houlihan'.

The Sinn Féin rebellion

Socialist Review, August–September 1916

When the news of the Irish Rising trod hard on the heels of the startling story of Casement's dramatic landing in a collapsible boat on the Irish coast, people in this country took for granted that the two events were connected. It was easily assumed that Casement's sudden appearance was part of a mysterious concerted plan, and that he had come to take part in the Rising. It now, however, appears that the real meaning of that strange adventure was a frantic effort on Casement's part to reach Ireland in time to stop the Rising.[35] It is claimed for him that in a spirit of reckless self-sacrifice he left a position of safety to face almost certain death in a heroic attempt to save his country from the disaster he foresaw.

No light was thrown on Casement's real object at his trial, and when the story came out of his interview with Father Ryan, most people were baffled and perplexed by the whole business. It seemed so impossible to believe in an attitude of mind that would enable a man to go through that terrible ordeal without mentioning a fact which, whatever the 'blame' of his conduct in Germany may have been, was bound to tell in his favour and save him, maybe from a dreadful fate. Such, at least, is the plea urged in his behalf by his friends, and backed by substantial evidence.* But it found little acceptance in England. People on this side of the Chanel could not believe that an Irishman would rather be hung than state publicly that he had tried to stop the Sinn Fein rising, and so seem to blame his fellow-countrymen in their failure and defeat. And inability to understand this fact is significant of one of those mental barriers which make it so difficult for English rulers and officials to adjust their strict notions of the divinity of law and order to what is to them the old idiosyncrasies of the Irish temperament.

In England the State has gradually taken to itself a sort of sanctity in the eyes of the majority. Loyalty is the highest virtue, rebellion is the 'sin of witchcraft' (whatever that somewhat anachronistic sounding crime may be). Authority is enthroned in the souls and minds of men. Indeed the divine pretensions of the Roman Emperors could have brought them no fairer harvest of submission. In Ireland the position is reversed. The Republican Proclamation points out how 'six times in 300 years the Irish nation have asserted their right to national freedom and sovereignty in armed rebellions.' The element of foreign

35 This article was reprinted by Esther Roper, *Prison Letters of Countess Markievicz*. A footnote by Roper states 'It must be clearly stated that Roger Casement was not against the Rising, only, knowing what he did, he feared that at the moment failure was inevitable. He was not able to get reliable information as to Irish events and hopes of success, and so came, at risk of his life, to warn his country people of the situation.'

ascendancy has prevented the State from assuming a semi-sacred character. Tradition has grown up slowly from generation to generation in the Irish mind and the idea of rebellion has gradually assumed the sanctity that among English people is associated with the organized authority of the State. So that in Ireland the great rebels are all national heroes and martyrs, and their names are household words, revered and honoured as in England the names of kings and queens are revered and honoured – with this difference, that in Ireland the halo of tragedy is round the heads of all the heroes, and nobody speaks lightly of those who have won great honour through extremes of suffering and self-sacrifice. Loyalty as conceived by masses of Irish people is not, as it is in England, a faithful adherence to the successful and governing classes, but a passionate clinging to an often lost cause, and to the memory of dead and defeated heroes. In a past number of St. Enda's Magazine Pearse has given expression to this strange, troubled patriotism so common in Ireland:

> It has been sung of the Gael that his fighting is always merry and his feasting is always sad. Here at St. Enda's we have tried to keep before us the image of Fionn during his battles – careless and laughing, with that gesture of the head, that gallant, smiling gesture, which has been an eternal gesture in Irish history; it was most memorably made by Emmet when he mounted the scaffold in Thomas Street, smiling, he who had left so much; and more recently by those three who died at Manchester. When people say that Ireland will be happy when her mills throb and her harbours swarm with shipping, they are talking as foolishly as if one were to say of a lost saint or of an unhappy lover, 'that man will be happy again when he has a comfortable income.' I know that Ireland will not be happy again until she recollects that old, proud gesture of hers, that laughing gesture of a young man that is going into battle or climbing a gibbet.

To understand this paragraph is to understand one side, at all events, of the Sinn Fein rising. The stories of irrepressible gaiety that have filtered through from Dublin, the pleasant tea-party in the midst of machine-guns in Stephen's Green, 'the Countess in male attire, smiling and garrulous, discussing the situation with her English prisoner, and ordering the bill to be sent to the Irish Republic'; the man in the Post office who played 'The Wearing of the Green' and 'Who Fears to Speak of '98?' on the bagpipes all through that terrific bombardment that reduced O'Connell Street to a heap of smoking ruins; the man who put up a recruiting notice (on what had once been a wall at the corner) bearing the inscription: 'Men of Ireland, join the British Army and save your towns and fields from the fate of the towns and fields of Belgium', and last, but not least, that sardonic Jacobin who cut out the heads of two high personages from the picture in the College of Surgeons and wrote underneath in large letters, 'Deleted by the Censor.' Pearse's gesture of a young man mounting the scaffold seems to find its echo in the story of the mock execution of the girl scout of fifteen whom all torture of that ghastly scene could not move to betray her comrades. 'You're a brave girl and you deserve the Victoria Cross,' said one of the soldiers at last, struck by the courage with which a child could face unflinchingly the prospect of immediate death. 'You can keep your Victoria Cross,' she said, surely with that very gesture of Pearse's, the gay gesture of defiance in the face of defeat and tragedy which to his mind was the eternal heritage and ideal of the Gael.

Pearse's own death was in the great tradition. Those unfaltering eyes of his that he begged might be unbandaged that he might have his last look at Ireland seem to have unnerved the soldiers. Twice the order was given to fire, with no result.

Connolly, dying in frightful agony, carried out on a stretcher and propped up to be shot, could yet pray for the soldiers who formed the firing party. 'Never let what you are doing to-day disturb you,' said MacBride to the officer, who, it was said, showed some emotion. 'I have been looking down rifle barrels all my life, and I'm not afraid now.' MacDonagh thanked the court-martial who had just condemned him to death. He said: 'It would not be seemly to go to my own doom without trying to express, however inadequately, my sense of the high honour I enjoy in being one of those predestined to die in this generation for the cause of Irish freedom.' From the English point of view, these men were doubtless rebels and deserved their fate. But surely many thoughtful Englishmen must feel dubious of the wisdom of shooting a man who dies thanking you for the high honour you have done him in allowing him so glorious a death.

It seems a tragedy indeed that a rising which on its intellectual side was a mixture of Dumas, Mazzini, and that eternal saga of gentle fighting and courteous dying that haunt some of the finest minds in Ireland, should end in those incendiary bombs and executions that are the usual vindications of military power, and which translate their victims into the realm of romance and glory forever.

And yet there is another side to the whole question which, though perhaps more prosaic, is even more tragic still. Behind the dreams of the Sinn Feiners and the generous idealism of Casement, and the world-wide Republican dream of Connolly, there was a substratum of that kind of solid facts that are always the groundwork of revolution. Writing in the *Daily News*, 12th June, Clara Moser (Hon. Sec. of the Housing Sub-Committee of the Dublin Watch Committee) discusses the rebuilding of the Sackville Street area. She points out that one important aspect of the case has been overlooked. 'It is usual,' she says, 'to find the most filthy areas behind and often surrounded by the best class of property. According to the report of the Departmental Committee appointed by the Local Government Board to inquire into housing conditions in Dublin, there were in 1914, 37,552 persons occupying houses which were fast approaching the state of being unfit for human habitation, and 22,701 persons occupying houses unfit for human habitation and incapable of being made so. So long as these conditions are allowed to exist... there will be bred in the minds of the inhabitants that form of discontent which ends in desperation, and which must always be expected to break out in ruinous violence.' Can anyone who followed the course of the Transport Workers' strike and the ruthless way it was crushed by the starvation of three-quarters of the population, wonder that such desperation should have found an outlet in rebellion? It is impossible here to do more than touch on the economic state of Ireland, but if it was more realised in England people would arrive at a better understanding of Irish discontent with the present organization of government. We hear with enthusiasm of the noble work of the English doctors and nurses who have gone out to Serbia to fight the epidemic of typhus. Typhus is endemic in South Connemara. In one recent outbreak the local doctor, who had applied to Dublin in vain for help, had to do every bit of nursing and doctoring himself, even down to putting the dead into their coffins. We do not hear of units, fitted up at great cost by English philanthropic societies, going over to Ireland to combat this pestilence, nor to wage war on the terrible condition of dirt and poverty, of which it is the result. Though England may often seem to be the Good Samaritan of Europe, by some malign fate and in spite of the good intentions of many individuals, her rule in Ireland seems to be followed too often by the old round of misery, poverty, destitution, dirt, disease, starvation, strikes, despair, rebellion, execution, and everlasting bitterness.

As far as Nationalist aspirations are concerned, they may once have found expression in the national representation at Westminster, but when Mr. Redmond started the recruiting campaign for the British Army (that campaign that was to prove that all Ireland was united in loyalty) great numbers of hitherto mild malcontents went over to the extremists who, of course, regarded such an action as treachery to Irish ideals and traditions. It is difficult for English people to realise the anger roused by this campaign amongst masses of the Irish people, brought up in that fierce tradition of secret hostility that has, alas! been handed down through the centuries. It is perhaps necessary to live in Ireland to understand the root fact known to every person there, Unionist or Nationalist, Sinn Feiner or Orangeman, that Ireland is not a county of England, but an island surrounded by sea, with a separate and, indeed, a terrible history of its own, often unaffected by events of national importance to English people, and torn and rent by internal happenings that are wholly unknown or quite irrelevant to the mass of English people, rumours of which indeed often barely penetrate into the minds of those who sit in high places and rule both countries. A sort of perverted malice seems to have taken charge of the relations between the two.

The Sinn Fein rebellion was a blow to all who hoped for a gradual lessening of hostility. But the severity with which the rebellion was crushed was, many of us believe, a far worse blow. England had her opportunity, an opportunity of treating the Irish Rising as De Wet's Rising (1914) was treated in South Africa.[36] The rising was crushed, her enemies were at her feet. What a glorious opportunity for killing with clemency the old tradition of hatred and the memory of the atrocities of '98 that have festered so long in the imagination of the Irish people. By some malign fate, as ever, England showed her hardest side in her dealings with Ireland. Those irresponsible and extraneous shootings and horrors which seem to be inseparable from the advance of a conquering army in a hostile country were not enough. Fourteen deliberate executions of men widely known and admired were carried out under heart-rending circumstances. And thus Ireland's old tradition of defiance and hatred gets new lease of life, and her ideal gesture remains through the ages 'the laughing gesture of a young man going into battle or climbing a gibbet.' The cry of Kathleen ni Hoolihan is ever in her people's ears:

> 'He died for love of me; many a man has died for love of me.'

And,

> I will go cry with the women,
> For yellow-haired Donough is dead,
> With a hempen rope for a neck-cloth,
> And a white cloth on his head.

And again,

> They shall be remembered for ever,
> They shall be alive for ever,
> They shall be speaking for ever,
> The people shall hear them for ever.[37]

Indeed, it is only in the sense of physical frustration and failure that the way of severity has been able to crush the Sinn Fein rebellion. For there is no solution of the Irish question possible that is not founded on goodwill between the two nations.

* It is stated that on 6 April Casement was in a Nursing Home in Germany, when he heard through a spy's report that there was going to be a rising in Ireland. He went straight to Berlin, where with great difficulty he got a submarine to take him to Ireland. The submarine

36 The onset of the First World War ensured that South Africa, as a British dominion, was led into the hostilities. In the wake of the Boer War this caused political instability and a South African rebellion erupted. When the rebellion was quashed, the leaders were sentenced to a term in prison and fined; they were released two years later.

37 *Kathleen ni Hoolihan*, by W. B. Yeats.

broke down off Heligoland and he had to wait some days to get another. His object in going was to stop the rising. The captain of the second submarine did not know Ireland, and landed him on a part of the coast where he was subsequently arrested, as recorded at his trial. Casement begged to be allowed to communicate with the leaders to try to stop the rising but this was not allowed. He succeeded, however, in confiding a message through Father F. M. Ryan, OP, who testified as follows in a letter to Mr Gavan Duffy, the solicitor for the defence:

> Roscrea, Co. Tipperary,
> July 12, 1916.
> Dear Mr. Gavan Duffy, – Sir Roger Casement saw me in Tralee on April 21, and told me he had come to Ireland to stop the rebellion then impending.
>
> He asked me to conceal his identity, as well as his object in coming, until he should have left Tralee, lest any attempt should be made to rescue him. On the other hand, he was very anxious that I should spread the news broadcast after he had left. Sincerely yours (Signed) F. M. Ryan, O.P.

For God and Kathleen Ni Houlihan

Catholic Bulletin, 1918

The two years now closing have been to many years of death and exaction. Tragedy after tragedy has overwhelmed our world with pity and terror. But to Irish people especially that pity and terror has come mixed with a strange exaltation. And to the little band, of lovers and friends who watched in breathless suspense and agonised hope that supreme and long drawn out agony that dragged slowly on through three terrible months to its inevitable end, there were sudden flashes of intense realisation, moments when the heart's tragic defeat was merged in the mysterious victory of the soul. In some silent compelling way, sorrow itself-seemed to be drawn up at times into that calm atmosphere of beauty and peace that wrapped, round in a strange smiling security the untroubled spirit of Roger Casement, as he moved serenely through tempests of reviling and torture and the scorn of men, without fear and without hatred. 'He sent grateful messages to all who prayed for him and loved him—that I was to tell all that he died for Ireland, and that he wished them to know that he had no bitterness in his heart for anyone ... He was wonderful, the peace, the tranquillity, the courage with which he faced death and talked of it ... My heart is divided between joy and sorrow.' Such was the witness of one who was with him a day or two before the end. But the simple and spiritual beauty of his nature expresses itself most clearly, perhaps, in the letter to a friend, an old Irish peasant woman, dated July 14th; a letter so poignant in its pathos, so selfless in its detachment, that the darkness of certain death that hangs over its simple and gay friendliness, seems only like one of those cloud shadows, that at twilight so often deepen the beauty of the sunlit hills of Ireland, with the sudden wistfulness of an unseen and secret presence.

'My dear Brigid, – I am writing to you through a friend, asking her to send this letter on to you, as she will be able to find out where you are. Your letter came to me yesterday, here in this prison cell, and it was like a glimpse of the garden, with the wallflowers and the Japanese cherry, to get your message.

First, I want to tell you that your Crucifix, the medals and the scapular came to me three weeks ago, but the letter only yesterday. They are always with me, and please God will be as long as I am here.

Remember me to so many, and thank those friends who pray for me— and don't pay any attention to the lies. They are compliments really, and we need not mind compliments, you and I, Biddy dear.

Do you remember the Cradle Song, I liked so much? Get Cathal to sing it for me, and give him my love and thanks from my heart, also to Colm, if he is near you, and Dinny and Seaghan Dhu, whenever they come back to you and the old room again. I dreamt last night 1 was lying before the fire in it, and the boys were there telling stories, and you standing at the door with the pipes ... I have thought of you often, and of the garden, and of the last time I saw you, and the message I gave you. Do you remember? I know you carried it out, dear Brigid, because I heard you did. And so farewell— and may God's blessing rest on you and yours and be with you in your work - and may the heartfelt thanks of one in much sorrow and affliction of soul be part of your reward for your affection. - Always your friend, Roger Casement.'

The *Manchester Guardian*, describing the passing of the death sentence on Roger Casement, comments thus on the prisoner's attitude: 'Sir Roger Casement heard these words and smiled wanly, looking down, one thought, as if to reassure his friends who were near the dock. Then erect and quite self-possessed he turned and disappeared behind the green curtain. He had kept his dignity, his almost incredible detachment, to the last.'

That 'incredible detachment' was a constant source of wonder and inspiration to his friends. History holds up for our admiration the figure of Sir Thomas More apologising to his executioners for having to ask them to help him to climb the scaffold, and adding with smiling politeness, that 'for his coming down he would shift for himself.' That story might have been written of Roger Casement at any moment during those long months through which he faced a certain and horrible death, with something more than courage, a supreme gentle courtesy so selfless that it had forgotten the very meaning of fear. 'I was going to read it out in Court,' he said in one of his last letters of a certain document, but he explained that the print was very small, 'and besides I felt sorry for the jury. They had had enough, and their kindly faces deserved a change of scene from that dreadful Court.' It is not often that a prisoner just about to be condemned to death concerns himself about the discomfort and boredom of the jury, and one cannot help wondering what rare secret of character was hidden behind those simple words. There are many degrees of selfishness in human beings and there are many unselfish people. But the certainty of a lonely and horrible death would find out the weak point in most of us, and it would seem natural and pardonable in most people, if, at the supreme and tragic moment of their destiny, their minds were concentrated on their own agony, to the exclusion of other people's petty discomforts. But Roger Casement was not like most people. There was something in him that made it impossible for him to be self-absorbed, however strange and desperate his circumstances might be. Perhaps the keynote of his nature might be found in that sentence with which he explained his loyalty to Ireland, and the reason he felt no loyalty to the Empire that governs her by force. 'Loyalty,' he said, 'is a sentiment, not a law. It rests on love, not on restraint.' The same might be said of the shining qualities in his own character. They were not founded on mere laws or external restraints, but on a great universal love of human beings, and goodwill to all men. It was his nature to consider and feel for other people's difficulties, sufferings and hopes with no careful and forced unselfishness, but with an enthusiastic and eager affection, that no private suffering of his own could dull, and that made him lose entirely the limited personal point of view common to most people. It would be easy in defence of this view to quote the known facts of his noble and self-sacrificing cause. To say that he threw away health and ordinary human happiness through years of hard and terrible work, in unhealthy climates, trying to bring to light atrocities and cruelties in Putumayo and the Congo, and saving thousands of innocent victims from outrage, mutilation and death. Indeed, it might be said of him that the desolate and oppressed never appealed to him in vain. The loyalty that is founded on love had a very different effect on his life to that of the more common form of loyalty founded on mutual hate, self-interest and fear. Instead of making him bitter against others, it deepened his sympathies with all oppressed nations, and made him, besides being the champion of Ireland, a fighter in the cause of enslaved nationalities and individuals all over the world. And let no one imagine that his international activities and sympathies did not react for good on the cause of his own country, by accentuating her position in the eyes of the world, as all his work tended to do, as one of the oppressed small nationalities of Europe, a comrade of Poland, Finland and the rest, in her struggle for freedom, and not merely as a rather rebellious and troublesome province in a corner of the British Empire.

Roger Casement was one of the world's great champions of the weak against the strong, of goodwill and freedom against militarism and empire, of life against death, and thus he takes his place with the seers and prophets of all ages. But if Roger Casement was in a sense international and had room in his heart for all the oppressed and defeated, yet, to him had come more specially the call of Kathleen Ni Houlihan in her great need. And it was for the sake of her he loved with all the passion of his idealistic and romantic nature, that he left his safe asylum, and in full knowledge of what must be the result of his action, made his way to Ireland to be ready with help and advice in the hour of danger and difficulty. 'We salute you as we would salute Wolfe Tone,' wrote 'three obscure citizens of Ireland' to the condemned prisoner of Pentonville, in one of those many touching tributes of love, admiration and gratitude from his own people, that were indeed his due, who had given up, for their sake, everything that most men hold precious. For truly never was there a man who more deliberately threw away his own life and liberty in a cause that was dearer to him than life or liberty. 'I am going with a halter round my neck,' he told a friend before he left Germany. And from that day onward, I do not think he ever faltered in the certainty that he was one of those who are (as Thomas MacDonagh put it in his speech before the court-martial) 'predestined to die in this generation for the cause of Irish freedom.' He was never of those whose courage has to lie bolstered up with illusions.

'To-morrow,' he wrote, 'I go to the Appeal Court to hear my counsel against the Indictment. And I shall return here. That is the one thing I am sure of. However interesting from the point of view of treason law in this country, I anticipate no other interest than that of listening to the arguments for and against and coming to the place I started from in the morning. If I had Solon for an advocate the result, I fancy, would be the same.'

Up to the last his sympathy for suffering in all countries never failed. On July the 16th he wrote: 'I am glad, indeed, to hear the news from Putumayo and the fathers there. The Franciscans were loved in Peru from of old. It is a good thing to think of them there now in that dreary region, and I am glad for their sake. Once I grieved at it, and thought I was sending them, or asking for them to be sent out to bitter trial and disappointment, but it is not so, and they will see the fruit of their privations and of their self-sacrifice in the lives they save, and in the increase of life and happiness around them, to replace the old dreadful and mortal misery.'

But in those last weeks of cruel loneliness it was to Ireland that his heart turned: 'To-day,' he wrote, 'my mind is far away down by O'Sullivan Beare Land and over there where I shall never be again, not even in dreams, by Clare and Aran and Garumna. I wonder how it will all be a hundred years hence, and whether any of the old speech and thought that sprang from it, and prayers that grew from it will survive. Goodbye, my dear friend, and I hope all your young ones will grow up in that Gospel and no other and that it may be well with them hereafter ... I shall not forget you wherever memory goes with me.'

The growth of Roger Casement's religious convictions in the isolation of prison life could be surprising to no one who understood the character and ideals that had been his through years of active work. If it be fact, as he said, that true religion rests on love, it is easy to see how the long years of selfless devotion and affectionate friendships had brought him into harmony with the unseen purposes of the universe, and very near to the Divine meaning of human life. 'I can only accept in my soul from love,' he said, and indeed to one who had such a great heart and such a universal love for the brother whom he had seen, it could have been no great step to that other mysterious love. In religious matters, as in all things, he was very honest with himself, would not let himself be hurried by emotion into taking any step without the consent of his mind as well as his heart.

'And then,' he wrote, 'I don't want to jump or rush—or do anything hastily— just because time is short. It must be my deliberate act, unwavering and confirmed by all my intelligence. And alas! to-day it is not so. It is still, I find, only my heart that prompts, from love, from affection for others, from association of ideas and ideals and not yet my full intellect. For if it were thus the doubts could not beset me as vigorously as they do. I are not on a rock but on a bed of thorns ... You must continue to help me as you have done in the way you want, and in the way you say so many more are doing.'

His was no facile deathbed conversion, prompted by fear or sentiment, but a gradual adjustment of the whole mind and soul into relation with the unseen, an adjustment that began with pain and struggle and uncertainty, and ended in the peace of a personality in harmony with itself and with God, exalted above fear, trouble or bitterness.

We cannot know much of the working of his inner mind during the long and lonely hours of his imprisonment, nor of those mental processes that led up with growing and gathering conviction to the unfaltering certainty of that confession of faith which was perhaps the last voluntary action of his life. But we can find traces in his last message to his friends of that religious exultation and other-world peace that was a marvel to those who were privileged to see him. 'Give my love to all my friends, and to all who have worked for me. My last message to everyone is Sursum Corda, and for the rest, my goodwill to those who have taken my life, equally to all those who tried to save it. All are my brethren now.'[38]

Roger Casement was ready and willing to die, as he said, for the cause of Irish freedom. And, indeed, it might be said of him, that while many have died for their countries and for great causes in all ages, no man has ever, in the annals of history, done more than he did, by the manner of his dying, to exalt and glorify the country of his love 'He died,' said one who was with him at the last, with all the faith of an Irish peasant woman ... He marched to the scaffold

38 *Sursum corda* is a Latin phrase meaning 'lift up your hearts'.

with the dignity of a prince and towered straight as an arrow over all of us on the scaffold. He feared not death and prayed with me to the last. I have no doubt that he has gone to Heaven.'

Eva Gore-Booth

The ruin preparing in Ireland

Manchester Guardian, 26 April 1918

Sir,

I have before me an account from an Irish correspondent of the present state of feeling in Dublin, in which special attention is drawn to the union of all classes in determined resistance to conscription, a resistance to the death which is being undertaken in a spirit of passionate revolt and religious faith which may turn Ireland into a nation of rebels and martyrs, but never into an army of conscripts. My correspondent is reminded, by the silent tension and the pause before the struggle, of the Pause in Holland before the Duke of Alva came. And, truly, a small incident such as the grim message sent by the Bishop of Killaloe to the Royal Irish Constabulary at Roscrea will serve to indicate the tension of feeling. 'Make your peace with God,' said the Bishop, 'make it quickly; which side you take is a matter for your own conscience.'

The struggle between the English authorities and the Irish nation is no new thing in Ireland. What is remarkable in this crisis is the way in which many who might be expected to side with the authorities have thrown in their lot with the nation in what is considered by many her death struggle. Thus the Irish Privy Council has protested against conscription; so have the Catholic K.C.'s whose names include the Dublin stipendiary magistrate (just retired), the Second Serjeant at Law and Prosecutors for Dublin, for Belfast City and for Cork City (this man is also chairman of the General Munitions Tribunal for Ireland), the Crown Prosecutors for co. Kilkenny and standing counsel for the Post office, the Crown Prosecutor for co. Louth and prosecuting counsel for the Post Office, the Crown prosecutors for co. Leitrim, co. Kerry, co. Meath. It is understood that two of these gentlemen have refused the Solicitor Generalship. Chief Baron Palles (Unionist) has just given several thousand pounds to the Archbishop's Defence Fund Against Conscription.

The attitude of the general public, as manifested in the extraordinary and most impressive services and pledge-takings on Sunday and the one day's strike on Tuesday, is well known. They are determined to resist provocation and stick to passive resistance as long as possible, but it is an understatement to say that three-quarters of the male population will not allow themselves to be taken alive. Provocation has already begun. A small meeting at Carrigaholt was interrupted by the soldiers. They were sitting talking in a little room. The chairman asked for two minutes more. Instead the soldiers were ordered to clear the room, and as the people walked quietly out they were prodded in the back with bayonets. Four men were wounded, one of whom died.[39] The soldiers stated that the people pressed on the bayonets, but a man cannot put his back against a vertical bayonet if he is standing on the floor. The jury brought a verdict of wilful murder.

The women workers are pledging themselves not to take the place of a man who is conscripted. The following are the words of a woman landowner who works her own farm: - 'I am a farmer, I have farmed land all my life. Your Government has demanded compulsory tillage and compulsory military service. That means that women must till the land. We will not do it. If my brother is taken he will not be taken alive, and I shall be left with farm and stock. I will do this. Neither crops nor cattle shall go to you. I will kill the stock; I will destroy the crop if I have to dig it up by the roots with my hands and then I will take my rifle. I have used a rifle all my life, and I will take it and go out and fight and die.'

Ireland is indeed, the first time for many a year, united as a nation; the very policemen go about with no-conscription badges, and Messrs. Dillon, De Valera, Healy, and O'Brien take council with the Lord mayor of Dublin, the transport workers, the trade unions, the proletariat, and the Catholic hierarchy. But the bitter regret on the lips of Irish trade unionists is that the English Labour party appears to be deserting them in their hour of need.

The usual preparations which are made for the military conquest of a country are going on apace. Before it is too late will not any far-sighted statesman intervene to prevent the creation of a second Belgium.

Yours & co.,
Eva Gore-Booth

39 An account of this case was recorded from a censored press article in the following way: 'Thomas Russell, dead from a soldier's bayonet thrust, given in his back as he was leaving the Carrigaholt reading room. The place had been ordered cleared because he was teaching a class of the Irish language that Sunday afternoon ... and no effort was made to have Sergeant Duff and his three privates produce the guilty man. Four of Russell's pupils were also wounded by the soldiers' bayonets.' Katherine Hughes, *English Atrocities in Ireland: A Compilation of Facts from Court and Press Records* (New York: Friends of Irish Freedom, 1920), p. 11.

Sinn Fein prisoners

Manchester Guardian, 26 November 1918

Sir,

As I am being constantly asked if my sister, Countess Markievicz, has been released, may I say that both she and Mrs. Clarke are still in Holloway Prison, in spite of the facts that Mrs. Clarke's health is in a very precarious state and that my sister has been nominated as Parliamentary candidate for St. Patrick's division, Dublin.[40]

Yours, &c.,
Eva Gore-Booth.
33, Fitzroy Square, London, W.

An Irish prisoner

Manchester Guardian, 29 April 1920

Sir,

As an instance of the sort of thing that is happening in Ireland may I draw your attention to the injustice of the treatment of Mr. Barton, M.P. for county Wicklow? In 1915 Mr. Barton, believing England's claim to stand for justice, joined the army and served as an officer till 1917, when he was allowed to leave on account of the claims of his own estate in Wicklow and his agricultural work in helping the development of the surrounding country and assisting the farmers in many ways.[41]

Meanwhile his official work in Dublin after the rebellion had brought him into touch with the Sinn Fein prisoners on one side and on the other side with the methods by which Ireland is at present ruled, and his sympathies became deeply aroused in the struggle for freedom. In 1919, he was arrested, but after a short time in prison before being charged or tried he made a dramatic escape

40 Kathleen Clarke, wife of the executed Rising leader Tom Clarke, had established the Irish National Aid and Volunteer Dependants' Fund in order to grant financial assistance to the families of those killed or imprisoned as a result of the rebellion. In April 1918, after the conscription crisis erupted in Ireland, British Intelligence claimed to have uncovered a Sinn Féin plot with Germany and they arrested seventy-three members of the organisation. Markievicz and Clarke were imprisoned in Holloway jail. After becoming ill, Clarke was eventually released in February 1919, into the care of Gore-Booth.

41 Robert Barton was born into a wealthy Anglo-Irish landowning family in Wicklow. He sympathised with the cause of Irish independence and went on to become the First Minister for Agriculture at the first meeting of the Dáil.

over the wall of Mountjoy.[42] He was arrested again in February 1920, and charged with having made a seditious speech in the spring of 1919, and tried by court-martial. It was alleged that he had said in the course of this speech that 'if Fleming [a Sinn Feiner] died in prison Lord French would be held responsible.' As is the custom amongst Sinn Feiners, he did not recognise the court, and did not defend himself. On the unsifted evidence of three policemen he was sent to Portland Prison as a convict for three years.[43]

He is now serving this savage sentence for the sake of an alleged speech made over a year ago, in which he had the temerity to hold the Viceroy responsible for the action of the Irish Executive in imprisoning Fleming. As Fleming is still alive (April, 1920) there can be no question whether Lord French is responsible or not for his death. Surely those English people who realise what the conditions of a convict prison are like would hardly wish, for their own sakes, to see such a sentence carried out on a man for expressing a violent opinion on the hypothetical case of a friend dying from the effects of imprisonment, an event likely enough to rouse strong feeling in anyone.

Yours, &c.,
Eva Gore-Booth.

Irish peace and executions

Manchester Guardian, 1 July 1921

Sir,

May we draw attention to the fact that Patrick Casey has been condemned to death in Limerick, and that the sentence may be carried out any minute? The crime of which he was accused was that of being in possession of arms and 13 rounds of automatic pistol ammunition.[44]

The evidence seems strangely inconclusive to anyone accustomed to the procedure of civil courts. In any case, to carry out a death sentence now for such as technical offence as the possession (not the use of) a weapon is to render futile any effort to bring about a state of feeling in which a peaceable

42 With the help of Richard Mulcahy, Barton escaped from Mountjoy. He went over the prison wall using a rope ladder on 16 March 1919. Pauric J. Dempsey and Shaun Boylan, 'Barton, Robert Childers', McGuire and Quinn (eds), *Dictionary of Irish Biography*.

43 Many efforts were made to have Barton released. He was finally freed in July 1921 in order to help with truce negotiations.

44 Patrick Casey was arrested at Milford in Cork for possession of a gun and ammunition. He was charged at New Barracks in Limerick and sentenced to death by firing squad. Casey's sentence was eventually commuted to fifteen years' penal servitude with no explanation. Seán Enright, *The Trial of Civilians by Military Courts: Ireland 1921* (Dublin: Irish Academic Press, 2012), pp. 206–7.

settlement is possible. Surely if the military machine goes on acting without regard to any change in the moral atmosphere it is the duty of the civil Government of this country to interfere before it is too late. If there is to be any chance of peace with Ireland all executions must stop.

Yours, &c.
Clare Annesley.[45]
Eva Gore-Booth.

The victim's friends[46]

Service, April 1923

I want to say a word about a class of sufferers who, I think have not been much mentioned tonight, and with whom and whose sufferings I have had a good deal of peculiar experience. That is the sufferings of the friends and relatives, perfectly innocent people, of those who are condemned to death. Well, my experience was in 1916, at the time of the Irish rebellion, when I was in close touch with the friends and the near relatives of many of those who were executed. My own sister was condemned to death and reprieved, and there were three of my friends of whom two were shot and another was hung after three months of the treatment described so graphically by our speakers tonight. All I can say is that never as long as I live do I wish to go through what I went through myself, and what I saw other people go through during those months. I know many people will never recover at all. One woman I knew, a well-known woman, a literary woman, and the shock was so great that she fell ill and died, and every friend knew that she died from the result of it.[47] Those who have not been through it, do not know what the tension is, the going to and fro, the appeal. 'Is there any hope?' and the sort of certainty underneath of the deep and terrible cruelty of the law by which nobody has any hope. I think that is proved, and in this case it was not nearly so bad as in ordinary cases, because you must remember that these people, who were taken to death, thought they were right. They thought they were fighting for a noble cause

45 Lady Clare Annesley, the daughter of 5th Earl Annesley, was a close friend of Gore-Booth's and an outspoken pacifist.

46 Speech delivered to a special meeting to consider the abolition of capital punishment, held in London in March 1923. Members of the Committee for the Abolition of the Death Penalty and members of the Labour Party attended. *Service* published the proceedings of the meeting in the April issue of the journal which was entirely devoted to the cause for the abolition of the death penalty. At their annual conference in June of that year, the Labour Party passed a resolution seeking to abolish capital punishment.

47 Dora Sigerson Shorter. Gore-Booth wrote a poem in her memory claiming that Shorter died of a broken heart due to the events of the Easter Rising.

and dying as martyrs, who would be loved and honoured by their friends and countrymen for ever. But in these other cases, a man has not got any great idea behind him: it is all disgrace, horror, tragedy. He is thrown in on himself, has no occupation: he is thinking, thinking, thinking. I do not think you can imagine a more diabolical torture, if you can think it out. We have done away with the rack and bodily torture, but I am perfectly certain mental torture is just as painful. I do not think anyone has the right to inflict that on another. I think we all ought to realise the extreme of pain that society is inflicting, and because of that we must stop it, not in two, three, four or five years. While we are talking about it, more people are going through this dreadful agony, and their relations and friends are also going through the extremes of agony. We ought not to allow it and we must not leave any stone unturned until we have done away with it. There can be nothing right in a country where such a thing is possible.

Francis Sheehy-Skeffington

Previously unpublished essay given to Hanna Sheehy-Skeffington[48]

When Mrs. Sheehy-Skeffington made public her terribly lucid and accurate account of Francis Sheehy-Skeffington's murder in the midst of an almost single handed attempt to prevent looting and rioting during the wild scenes of the Irish Rebellion, it was perhaps the first among the terrible incidents of those days to give a slight shock to that profound sense of triumphant self-satisfaction, that is apt to lull the conscience of the victor in any conflict, however unequal. As Mrs. Sheehy-Skeffington pursued her relentless and irresistible way, disentangling the motives and circumstances of the murder, and bringing it home to the responsible authorities, little cold doubts must, for the first time, have crept into the mind of many a patriotic Englishman concerning the nature of what they had hitherto accepted as the wholly just and necessary severity by which the desperate struggle of insurgent nationality had been so quickly crushed.

It was the strange destiny of Sheehy-Skeffington the pacifist and idealist, to die amid scenes of the violence that he abhorred, and that he had always refused to take part in. But such an end was not wholly out of keeping with the stormy career of one who was first and foremost a rebel against all injustice and oppression. Sheehy-Skeffington himself must surely have rejoiced had he known that his death would be not only a continuation of his life's work, but one of the most effective blows ever struck at the militarism he so hated. For he was no passive accepter of things as they are. He was a fighting pacifist, and

48 National Library of Ireland, Sheehy-Skeffington Papers, ms 22,654.

might have said with Blake, 'I will not cease from mental fight, nor shall the sword fall from my hand, till I have built Jerusalem.'

Though the Jerusalem of his dreams was in a greener, and perhaps sadder land, than that which held Blake's vision.

He was an out and out rebel against all forms of oppression cruelty or servitude, mental or physical. His rebellion never took the form of physical force, only because physical force was one of the world's great tyrannies that he would have given his life to destroy. In his well-known letter to Thomas MacDonagh, he says, 'I advocate no mere lazy acquiescence in injustice, I am and always will be, a fighter. But I want to see the age-long fight against injustice clothe itself in new forms suited to a new age, I want to see the manhood of Ireland no longer hypnotised by the glory of arms, no longer blind to the horror of organised murder.' And again, 'Can you not conceive an organisation, a body of men and women banded together to secure and maintain the rights and liberties of the people of Ireland, a body animated with a high purpose, united by a bond of comradeship, trained and disciplined in the ways of self-sacrifice and true patriotism, and equipped with the weapons of intellect and of will that are irresistible? An organisation of people prepared to dare all things for their object, prepared to suffer and to die rather than to abandon one of their principles but an organisation that will not lay down as its fundamental principle. We will prepare to kill our fellowmen.'

His ideal of a free Ireland was as vital and commanding as MacDonagh's own, but in Sheehy-Skeffington's case it was united to other no less commanding ideals. Internationalism, peace, the equality of the sexes, the emancipation of Labour, were some of the causes to which he devoted his life's energies. There is much in his public life that reminds one of the poet Shelley. There is the same almost quixotic generosity, the same hatred of oppression and cruelty, the same absolute disregard of personal aims or even comfort, the same reckless directness of spirit, the same noble idealism and disregard of all conventional and artificial dignities. James Stephens in his 'Insurrection' gives a very vivid sketch of his character, 'He was the most absurdly courageous man I have met with or heard of. He has been in every trouble that has touched Ireland these ten years back, and he has always been on the generous side, therefore and naturally, on the side that was unpopular and weak. It would seem indeed, that a cause had only to be weak to gain his sympathy, and his sympathy never stayed at home. There are so many good people who 'sympathise' with this or that cause, and having given that measure of their emotion, they give no more of it or anything else. But he rushed instantly to the street, a large stone, the lift of a footpath, the base of a statue, any place and every place was for him a pulpit; and, in the teeth of whatever oppression, of disaster, or power, he said his say. There are multitudes of men in Dublin of all classes and creeds who can boast that they kicked Sheehy-Skeffington, or that they struck him on the head with walking sticks or umbrellas, or that they smashed their fists into his face, and jumped on him when he fell. It is by no means an exaggeration to say that these things were done to him and if it is true that he bore ill-will to no man, and that he accepted blows, and indignities and ridicule with the pathetic candour of a child who is disguised as a man and whose disguise cannot come off. His tongue, his body, all that he had and hoped for were at the immediate service of whoever was bewildered or oppressed. He has been shot. Other men have been shot but they faced the guns knowing that they faced justice however stern and oppressive; and what they engaged to confront was before them. He had no such thought to soothe from his mind anger and un-forgiveness. He, who was a pacifist was compelled to revolt to his last breath, and on the instruments of his end he must have looked as on murderers. I am sure that to the end he railed against oppression and that he fell marvelling that the world can truly be as it is. With his death then he passed away a brave man and a clean soul.'

Sheehy-Skeffington's career differed widely from that of most politicians in that to him it was never an end in itself, but always a long consistent struggle to further certain ideas, ideas that were far more important to him than any personal success.

Like James Connolly he was an enthusiast on the subject of the freedom of women, it is characteristic of him that his first public act, after a brilliant College career was to resign his post as Registrar of University College on the question of the position of women in the new University.[49] Throughout his whole life, he never allowed the women's question to be pushed aside by the pressure of other interests. In the midst of the excitement and the bitterness of the great transport workers strike and all the work it involved, he was able to hold out-of-door meetings for the locked out workers and to appeal to them to remember in the midst of their own struggle that there were workers even worse paid than they were, and in a more difficult industrial position, and to enlist their sympathies in the women's struggle against oppression. Up to the time of his premature death, he and his wife were two of the leading spirits in the Irish Women's Suffrage agitation and they were engaged in a constant struggle to press the claims of women to equality to all fields of life and labour.

When at College he was a worker in the cause of International Peace. His love of Ireland led him into early association with the Irish Party. Michael

49 Sheehy-Skeffington was nominated as the first lay registrar of the recently formed University College Dublin (UCD) in 1902. In 1904 he resigned from the University because of the 'college's reluctance to admit women on equal terms with men'. Patrick Maume, 'Skeffington, Francis Sheehy-Skeffington', McGuire and Quinn (eds), *Dictionary of Irish Biography*.

Davitt, whose biography he afterwards wrote, was the hero of his childhood. He helped at College to found the Young Ireland branch of the United Irish League, and it was only in later years that his sympathies were gradually alienated from that official party whose political action he learnt to distrust. He worked hard in the cause of Labour, helping to found the Independent Labour Party of Ireland in 1908. Later he threw himself wholeheartedly into the Irish Transport Workers struggle for better wages, and was one of the Citizens Peace Committee that worked for arbitration and good terms for the locked out workers at the end of that cruel industrial war. His journalistic career was the reflection of his many public enthusiasms and activities. He hoped at one time to edit the *Nationalist* and at another he was associated with Frederick Ryan in the editorship of the *Democrat*. In 1913 he took over from James Connolly the editorship of the *Irish Citizen*, a weekly Suffragist organ which he edited till his death. He also issued for some time, singlehanded a weekly commentary on Irish affairs called 'Dialogues of the Day.' He also wrote for the *Review of Reviews* and was the Irish correspondent of several newspapers, notably the *Manchester Guardian* & the *London Herald*, the *American Call* and *L'Humanité*, the organ of the great French Socialist whose death at the outbreak of war was oddly enough compassed by the same military fanaticism responsible for Skeffington's assassination.

Sheehy-Skeffington's strong and effective campaign against Conscription, bringing him as it did twice within the reach of the Law, would easily account for his unpopularity in official circles. He advocated no violence but only a determined passive resistance in the interests of liberty and peace. On these lines in 1914 he addressed about 40 weekly meetings, appealing to Irish men to take no part in what he considered 'the horror of organised murder.' When the rebellion broke out his principles prevented him taking any militant part in it, but his eager and energetic nature would not allow him to remain passive or to keep away from the danger zone. When Captain Pinfield (an English Officer) was said to be bleeding to death in the street he went out, at the risk of his life, under cross-firing to try to assist him. He interested himself in an effort that was being made to prevent looting and rioting by the hooligan elements in the population, after the police had been withdrawn from the streets.

The tragic story of his assassination has been told by Mrs. Sheehy-Skeffington. 'Returning to his home on Tuesday April 25 between 7 and 8 o'clock (his description had already been circulated at the city bridges) he was arrested at Portobello Bridge, and conveyed to Portobello Barracks.' Though no charge was entered against him orders were issued from headquarters that he was to be "detained" and he was kept a prisoner in a separate locked cell. At midnight he was forcibly removed by Captain Bowen-Colthurst of the Royal Irish Rifles and taken, a hostage, with his hands bound behind his back as far as Portobello

Bridge with his captors. On the way he beheld the murder of the boy Coade, left weltering in his blood, his jaw bashed in by the butt end of a rifle.[50] At the bridge he was left in [the] charge of Lieutenant Leslie Wilson with orders that he was to be shot if there were any surprises, or any attack on the raiding party which went to raid and bomb Alderman Kelly's premises a little further down. Escorted back with the raiding party and other prisoners, he was locked up for the night, handcuffed. He asked in vain that word should be sent to his wife who lived within ten minutes distance of the Barracks. At ten next morning Captain Bowen-Colthurst again removed him from the guard, and had him shot without warning and without any form of trial in the yard adjoining the cell. Noticing a movement in his body the officer had a second volley fired at the wounded man as he lay on the ground. That night his body, sewn in a sack, was buried in the barracks. On the following Sunday bricklayers were brought to remove from the walls all traces of the crime.

Such was the death of Sheehy-Skeffington. The history of the man, afterwards declared insane, who was directly responsible for his murder is instructive. On Friday the 28th in company with the Colonel and a company of soldiers he raided his victim's house, fired a volley into the window and kept the seven years old boy and his mother under arrest while he searched and sacked the house.

On May 6th more than a week after his crime, he was promoted, and on May 9th sent with a detachment to Newry. The officer, Sir Francis Vane by whose efforts he was at length arrested has since been relegated to unemployment and deprived of his command. Captain Bowen Colthurst was eventually declared insane by the court-martial.

What seems to distinguish Sheehy-Skeffington's career from that of many others who have given their lives to great causes was his unshakeable practical faith in some fundamental rightness in human nature. James Stephens has told, in graphic language that when he was oppressed by any intolerable wrong or cruelty, he would rush out into the street and appeal to people for help in rebuilding the world nearer to his heart's desire, and that he resented no rebuff or personal affront and never lost his faith in the hidden treasure of generosity and goodwill buried somewhere under the fortress of selfishness and callousness that seems so often to block all approaches to the human mind. To say this of him is to say that he had in him a spark of that divine insight, that is unfaltering and unshakeable not because it cherishes illusions and dreams but because it feels itself in some strange way to be in touch with the ultimate truth of things.

Eva Gore-Booth.

50 J. J. Coade, an unarmed 17-year-old boy, returning home from mass, was hit with the butt of a gun and shot by Captain Bowen-Colthurst. Coade died of his wounds.

'After the Storm'

The House of Three Windows

Suddenly everywhere
Clouds and waves are one,
The storm has cleared the air,
The sea holds the sun
And the blue sky –
There is no under, no above,
All is light, all is love –
Is it like this when you die?

Figure 13 Eva Gore-Booth

Selected works about Eva Gore-Booth

Aldrich, Robert, *Gay Lives*, London: Thames & Hudson, 2012.

Barone, Rosangela, *The Oak Tree and the Olive Tree: The True Dream of Eva Gore-Booth*, Italy: Edizioni Dal Sud, 1991.

Clarke, Frances, 'Booth, Eva Selina Gore', in James McGuire, James Quinn (eds), *Dictionary of Irish Biography*, Cambridge: Cambridge University Press, 2009.

Condren, Mary, 'Eva Gore-Booth from a *Psychological and Poetic Approach to Christ in the Fourth Gospel*, in Angela Bourke, Siobhan Kilfeather, Maria Luddy *et al.* (eds), *Field Day Anthology Vol. IV Women's Writing and Traditions*, Cork: Cork University Press, 2002, pp. 659–63.

Crawford, Elizabeth, 'Eva Gore-Booth', in *The Women's Suffrage Movement: A Reference Guide 1866–1928*, London: Routledge, 1999, pp. 249–51.

Donoghue, Emma, 'How Could I Fear and Hold Thee by the Hand? The Poetry of Eva Gore-Booth', in Eibhear Walsh (ed.), *Sex, Nation, and Dissent in Irish Writing*, Cork: Cork University Press, 1997, pp. 16–42.

Doyle, Maria-Elena, 'A Spindle for the Battle: Feminism, Myth, and the Woman-Nation in Irish Revival Drama', *Theatre Journal*, 51(1) (1999), 33–46.

Foley, Declan with Janis Londraville, 'The Quiet Revolutionary', in *John Quinn: Selected Irish Writers from His Library*, West Cornwall: Locust Hill Press, 2001, pp. 149–65.

Fox, R. M, *Rebel Irishwomen*, 1935: Dublin: Progress House, 1967.

Hawley, John. C, 'Eva Gore-Booth', in William. B. Thesing (ed.), *Dictionary of Literary Biography, Volume Two Hundred Forty: Late Nineteenth and Early Twentieth Century British Women Poets*, Detroit: Gale Group, 2001, pp. 69–78.

Herbert, Michael, 'Eva Gore-Booth', *North West Labour History Journal*, 1 (2003), 22–8.

James, Dermot, *The Gore-Booths of Lissadell*, Dublin: Woodfield Press, 2004.

Leeney, Cathy, 'The Spaces Outside: Images of Women in Plays by Eva Gore-Booth and Dorothy Macardle', in Melissa Sihra (ed.), *Women in Irish Drama: A Century of Authorship and Representation*, Basingstoke: Palgrave Macmillan, 2007, pp. 55–68.

Leeney, Cathy, *Irish Women Playwrights, 1900–1939: Gender and Violence on Stage*, London: Peter Lang, 2010.

Lewis, Gifford, *Eva Gore-Booth and Esther Roper: A Biography*, London: Pandora, 1988.

Lewis, Gifford, 'Eva Gore-Booth', *Oxford Dictionary of National Biography Online*, Oxford: Oxford University Press, 2004.

Ní Dhuibhne, Eilís, *Voices on the Wind: Women Poets of the Celtic Twilight*, Dublin: New Island, 1995.

Roper, Esther, *Eva Gore-Booth: An Address Given at the Unveiling of a Window Placed in Her Memory in the Round House*, Manchester: Manchester University Settlement Papers No. 1, 1928.

Tiernan, Sonja, '"Engagements Dissolved:" Eva Gore-Booth, *Urania* and the Radical Challenge to Marriage', in Mary McAuliffe and Sonja Tiernan (eds), *Tribades, Tommies and Transgressives: Histories of Sexualities Volume I*, Newcastle: Cambridge Scholars Publishing, 2008, pp. 128–44.

Tiernan, Sonja, '"No Measures of Emancipation or Equality Will Suffice:" Eva Gore-Booth's Radical Feminism in the journal *Urania*', in Sarah O'Connor and Christopher C. Shepard (eds), *Women, Social and Cultural Change in Twentieth Century Ireland*, Newcastle: Cambridge Scholars Publishing, 2008, pp. 166–82.

Tiernan, Sonja, 'Sligo Co-operative Movements (1895–1905): The Birth of an Irish Political Activist', in Shane Alcobia-Murphy, Lindsay Milligan and Dan Wall (eds), *Founder to Shore: Cross-currents in Irish and Scottish Studies*, Aberdeen: AHRC Centre for Irish and Scottish Studies, 2010, pp. 189–96.

Tiernan, Sonja, 'Tabloid Sensationalism or Revolutionary Feminism? The First-Wave Feminist Movement in an Irish Women's Periodical', *Irish Communications Review*, 12 (2010), 74–87.

Tiernan, Sonja, 'Challenging Presumptions of Heterosexuality: Eva Gore-Booth a Biographical Case Study', *Historical Reflections/Réflexions Historiques*, 37(2) (2011), 58–71.

Tiernan, Sonja, 'Eva Gore-Booth: The Women's Suffrage Movement among Trade Unionists', in Tiffany K. Wayne (ed.), *Feminist Writings from Ancient Times to the Modern World: A Global Sourcebook and History*, Westport, CT: Greenwood, 2011, vol. II, pp. 404–7.

Tiernan, Sonja, *Eva Gore-Booth: An Image of Such Politics*, Manchester: Manchester University Press, 2012.

Welch, Robert, 'Eva Gore-Booth', *The Concise Oxford Companion to Irish Literature*, Oxford: Clarendon Press, 1996.

Selected works by Eva Gore-Booth

Poetry, prose and plays chronologically

Poems, London: Longmans Green & Co., 1898.
The One and the Many, London: Longmans Green & Co., 1904.
New Songs: A Lyric Selection Made by AE from Poems by Eva Gore-Booth and Others, Dublin: O'Donoghue & Co., 1904.
Unseen Kings, London: Longmans Green & Co., 1904.
The Three Resurrections and the Triumph of Maeve, London: Longmans Green & Co., 1905.
The Sorrowful Princess, London: Longmans Green & Co., 1907.
The Egyptian Pillar, Tower Press Booklets, series 2, no. 3, Dublin: Maunsel, 1907.
The Agate Lamp, London: Longmans Green & Co., 1912.
The Perilous Light, London: Erskine MacDonald, 1915.
The Death of Fionavar from the Triumph of Maeve, London: Erskine Macdonald, 1916.
Broken Glory, Dublin: Maunsel, 1918.
The Sword of Justice, London: Longmans Green & Co., 1918.
A Psychological and Poetic Approach to the Study of Christ in the Fourth Gospel, London: Longmans Green & Co., 1923.
The Shepherd of Eternity, London: Longmans Green & Co., 1925.
The House of Three Windows, London: Longmans Green & Co., 1926.
The Inner Kingdom, London: Longmans Green & Co., 1926.
The World's Pilgrim, London: Longmans Green & Co., 1927.
Poems of Eva Gore-Booth: Complete Edition, Esther Roper (ed.), London: Longmans Green & Co., 1929.
The Buried Life of Deirdre, London: Longmans Green & Co., 1930.
The Plays of Eva Gore-Booth, Frederick S. Lapisardi (ed.), San Francisco, CA: Mellen Research University Press, 1991.
Fiametta: A Previously Unpublished Play by Eva Gore-Booth, Sonja Tiernan (ed.), New York: Edwin Mellen Press, 2010.

Pamphlets and booklets

Women Workers and Parliamentary Representation, Manchester: Lancashire and Cheshire Women Textile and Other Workers' Representation Committee, *c.*1905.
Women's Wages and the Franchise and Certain Legislative Proposals, Manchester, 1906.
Women's Right to Work, Manchester: William Morris Press, 1906.
Is the Case Urgent? Manchester: National Industrial and Professional Women's Suffrage Society, *c.*1910.
Whence Come Wars? London: Women's Printing Society, 1914.
Religious Aspects of Non-Resistance, Bishopsgate: Headley Brothers Printers, 1915.
The Tribunal, London: National Labour Press, *c.*1916.
Rhythms of Art, League of Peace and Freedom Pamphlet, London: Pelican Press, 1917.

Journal articles, chapters in edited collections

'Fair Pay for Women', *Women's Tribune*, 1906.
'Women and Politics: A Reply', *Nineteenth Century*, March 1907, 472–6.
'Women's Suffrage and the French Revolution', *Academy*, 14 September 1907, 909.
'Women's Suffrage and the French Revolution', *Academy*, 28 September 1907, 957.
'The Women's Suffrage Movement among Trade Unionists', in Brougham Villiers (ed.), *The Case for Women's Suffrage*, London: T. Fisher Unwin, 1907, 50–65.
'Women and the Suffrage: A Reply to Lady Lovat and Mrs. Humphry Ward', *Nineteenth Century and After*, September 1908, 495–506.
'An Equitable Adjustment', *Common Cause*, 30 September 1909, 432.
'Running a Suffrage Candidate', *Common Cause*, 25 November 1909, 432.
'Women and the Nation: The Workers III – "No Trades for Women"', *Englishwoman*, 5(2) (1909), 507–17.
'Women's Wages and the Law of Supply and Demand', *Nineteenth Century and After*, August 1914, 384–93.
'Women and Trade Unionism', *Nation*, 31 July 1915, 573.
'The Sinn Fein Rebellion', *Socialist Review*, August–September 1916, 226–33.
'For God and Kathleen Ni Houlihan', *Catholic Bulletin*, 1918.

Index

Page numbers in *italic* refer to illustrations